Preaching as a Social Act

PREACHING
AS A SOCIAL ACT
THEOLOGY & PRACTICE

Arthur Van Seters
EDITOR

Abingdon Press

Nashville

PREACHING AS A SOCIAL ACT
THEOLOGY AND PRACTICE

This book is printed on acid-free paper.

Library of Congress Cataloging-in-Publication Data

Preaching as a social act: theology & practice/Arthur Van Seters, editor.
    p.   cm.
ISBN 0-687-33827-1 (alk. paper)
   1. Preaching. I. Van Seters, Arthur, 1934-
BV4211.2.P734   1988   87-24162
251—dc19   CIP

MANUFACTURED BY THE PARTHENON PRESS AT
NASHVILLE, TENNESSEE, UNITED STATES OF AMERICA

to Rowena
whose shared life
has been both a window and a doorway
—through the first
I have viewed the world more fully
—through the second
others have entered our world more completely

Contents

Contributors

Arthur Van Seters, editor
Principal and associate professor of biblical interpretation and preaching at the Vancouver School of Theology, Vancouver, British Columbia; 1986 president of the Academy of Homiletics; and author of several papers for the Academy on social dimensions of preaching.

Justo L. González
Writer and author of a number of books including *A History of Christian Thought* (3 vols.) and *The Story of Christianity* (2 vols.); formerly taught at the Evangelical Seminary of Puerto Rico and Candler School of Theology; currently visiting professor of theology at the Interdenominational Theological Center, Atlanta, Georgia.

Catherine Gunsalus González
Professor of church history, Columbia Theological Seminary, Decatur, Georgia; author of numerous articles and, with her husband, the book *Liberation Preaching*.

Don M. Wardlaw
Professor of preaching and worship, McCormick Theological Seminary, Chicago, Illinois; a past president of the Academy of Homiletics; and editor of *Preaching Biblically, Creating Sermons in the Shape of Scripture*.

Edwina Hunter
Associate professor of preaching, Pacific School of Religion, Berkeley, California; national president of the Ministers' Council, American Baptist Churches/U.S.A.; and researcher in the area of intercultural preaching.

Walter Brueggemann
Professor of Old Testament, Columbia Theological Seminary, Decatur, Georgia; in constant demand as a lecturer; and author of many works including *The Land, The Prophetic Imagination,* and *The Creative Word.*

Ronald J. Allen
Professor of New Testament and preaching, Christian Theological Seminary, Indianapolis, Indiana; and author of *Our Eyes Can Be Opened: Preaching the Miracle Stories of the Synoptic Gospels Today* and *Contemporary Biblical Interpretation for Preaching.*

Thomas H. Troeger
Associate professor of preaching and parish, Colgate Rochester Divinity School; 1987 president of the Academy of Homiletics; poet and author of *Creating Fresh Images for Preaching* and (with Carol Doran) *New Hymns for the Lectionary.*

Acknowledgments

An editor is a receiver and I have been the recipient of much. From the Academy of Homiletics, and especially its research group on the Social Dimensions of Preaching, I have benefited from encouragement and stimulation. I am profoundly grateful for the amiable participation of the contributors to this volume. They have been diligent and patient throughout our work together. Their colleagueship and that of Gregory Baum, Terry Anderson, and Neil MacKenzie have been personally challenging and satisfying to me in many ways. Jane Knight and Ann Bemrose have caringly typed the manuscript, sometimes revising strange (and not so strange) computer disks! Major editorial assistance from beginning to end has been bountifully given with extraordinary attention to detail and kindly persistence by my colleague Elizabeth Hart, librarian at the Vancouver School of Theology. I am indebted to the School itself for a six-month sabbatical to work on this project, including financial support, and to the Association of Theological Schools in the United States and Canada for its generous Award for Theological Scholarship and Research. Abingdon Press and its former senior editor, Carey Gifford, have been strongly supportive of the project. Finally, I want to pay tribute to my wife, Rowena, who has probably taught me more about my own preaching than any other single person. She has sustained me in this undertaking in more ways than she knows.

A.V.S.

Introduction:
Widening Our Vision

Arthur Van Seters. Preaching has extraordinary resilience. At the end of the sixties some were proclaiming the "empty pulpit"; others were experimenting with dialogues or novel forms or "doing sermons."[1] In a culture of television, multiscreens, and laser beams what would become of the pulpit? But now preaching is definitely "in." Publishing houses are producing record numbers of books on preaching and continuing education preaching courses are among the most popular. In addition, through the seventies and continuing in the eighties, TV evangelists have reached vast audiences across North America and beyond.[2]

All of this is true; yet in common parlance "to preach at someone," "to give someone a sermon," or "to sound preachy" are decidedly pejorative expressions. How has preaching overcome this negative stereotype? Does the popularity of the pulpit reflect a new "awakening" to the gospel? Are people in our society looking for the reassertion of authority from the pulpit? Or are preachers just tired of traditional assertive discourse and becoming fascinated with newer indicative, narrative, and imaginative ways of speaking? In this connection, how does the media "preaching" of advertisers, commentators, and wide-screen-message films affect sermon listeners in the pews? When these and similar questions are answered, will we also know how our culture is influencing preaching and what effect preaching is having or may have on our culture? This last double question has vexed me (and certainly many others) over the last decade,³ and has been sharpened by two particular incidents. Some years ago as a visitor for ten consecutive weeks in a large urban church, I heard consistently lucid, graphic preaching. Biblical texts were explained and concretely connected with the daily lives of the members of the congregation. I found myself drawn into the sermons, but gradually I began to feel uneasy. Something was overriding the "hearing of the Word." Every biblical text seemed to yield a strangely similar message and that message appeared to be shaped not so much by the text as by a certain "sensible" interpretation of culture. At this point I found myself reflecting on the meaning of the Scripture passages as they had been read earlier in the service and invariably that meaning clashed with what emerged in the sermon.

For example, a sermon on the so-called parable of the talents (Matt. 25:14-30) became an occasion for urging attention to God's challenge that we risk. In our society, the preacher said, this meant being competitive with our money—not in a cutthroat way, of course, but as a struggle to develop our God-given capacities. The resultant conflicts from competition were like athletic rivalries; they pushed participants toward higher achievement. They even established a certain bond, or at least respect, between competitors. In the parable, the one-talent servant wouldn't compete and was rejected.

The sermon contained more, related to personal and spiritual development, and was better stated, but I remember being bluntly offended by the one talent being taken from the poorest servant and given to the richest one who already had ten talents. How was this heard by this affluent congregation in a world where the gap between rich and poor seemed to be increasing rather than diminishing?

A second incident happened in Central America. I remember listening to a sermon discussion on the same text by a group of peasants on the outskirts of San Jose, Costa Rica. They heard the gospel in this passage challenging the poor not to be overwhelmed by a sense of powerlessness and fear. The Rule of God was a metaphor that stood against the reigning metaphors of societies organized by monetary arrangements. The parable for them was a heuristic device (not their language!) to awaken a new consciousness among those alienated because their labor was so devalued that they easily gave up. Before God their small efforts, especially when they linked themselves together, could be just as effective as the efforts of those who seemed more powerful. This, they felt, was a parable for the poor, not for the rich. The third servant's passivity was an affront to wake them up.

These experiences set me pondering and my mind went back to the parabolic preaching of Jesus that made the presence of God vivid to his followers.[4] The effect on their lives was profoundly vitalizing and the beginning of a movement that ultimately, in Augustine, gave a new framework for understanding reality when classical culture was in decay.[5] All of this started an avalanche of questions.

- How did Jesus' preaching of God's rule relate to the society of first-century Palestine?
- How did Augustine interpret that for the crumbling Roman Empire of the fourth century?
- How do we North Americans "hear" this gospel today in our post-industrial world?
- How does the social position of interpreters and listeners affect the concrete interpretation of the Word of God?
- How can preachers discern whether their message is shaped by a theology rooted in Scripture or by a current, commonsense view of reality today, and when are these in conflict?
- How can we as preachers or as pew-sitters become aware of how the dominant perception of the world has affected our own views of ourselves and of our society?
- How do we preach from texts that seem to move against the perspective of the congregation as members of society?
- How can the sermon elucidate the gospel already operative in the actions of the people of God but in ways they have not yet noticed?

These are social questions crying for answers. They are also theologically important.

Social Dimensions of Preaching

Paying attention to the societal dimension of preaching is not new. As Daniel Patte points out, the Apostle Paul was doing this when he applied the gospel in new situations as he introduced it to the wider Mediterranean world. In each case he expressed his preaching "in terms of these new situations," as did the Reformers after him. We too, he adds, need to emphasize those aspects of Paul's teaching appropriate in our "cultural, social, religious and ecclesial setting."[6] Down through the centuries, including our own, preachers have spoken not only to the personal and spiritual needs of congregational members in their social context but also to the spiritual and human needs of these contexts as corporate entities. Furthermore, they have done so reflecting the ethos of their respective cultural situations.

This book is built on this tradition. It focuses on how preaching is shaped by, but also gives shape to, its societal reality. Sometimes it names the obvious. For example, when Fred Craddock distinguishes between listeners as audience and listeners as congregation,[7] that is a social dimension of preaching. A group of people are being viewed as a gathering of strangers in the first, and a community of people who know one another and the preacher in the second. Beyond this kind of naming, the following chapters make deliberate and systematic use of the social sciences to explore various dimensions of the social nature of preaching. In doing this there is no intention to devalue the personal, spiritual, liturgical, and other aspects of preaching. Indeed, this is not a sociology of preaching,[8] but an exploration of how theology and the concrete realities of society are linked in the act of preaching.

The writers of the following chapters make some use of the social sciences to analyze how preaching is related to its societal context. Because of this, some may regard this as a book on "prophetic preaching" designed for "social activists."[9] This is not that kind of book. It is true that several contributors do call attention to the negative impact of individualism in our culture, and some chapters distinguish between preaching that affirms and preaching that calls for transformation. There is an explicit discussion of "prophetic preaching" in the Afterword, but, to repeat, this volume concerns the pervasiveness of social dimensions implicit or explicit in all preaching. Every sermon is uttered by *socialized* beings to a *social* entity in a specific, *social* context and always at a *social* moment. The sacred texts that ground preaching come to expression in the *culture* of a community (whether ancient Israel or the early church). The language of the sermon is socially shaped whether it is traditional or contemporary or a mixture of both. All of this is true regardless of our social awareness, position, or viewpoint. All preaching then is a social act.

A number of factors draw our attention to this development. Among the more important are the following:

1. In the twentieth century we have developed extensive transportation and communication networks so that it is commonplace to speak of our world as a global village—a community where people know one another. Since we are affected by the realities we know, we now feel more and more connected. This is due also to forums such as the United Nations and especially to the post–World War II development of a global economic system.[10]

2. The social movements of the sixties and seventies have radically altered our consciousness of racism and sexism. We have also become more aware of discrimination with reference to such things as class, age, disability, and left-handedness. These have been interwoven with other movements such as the anti-Vietnam protest in the civil rights preaching of Martin Luther King, Jr.[11]

3. The social sciences, long relegated to a secondary position behind science and philosophy (and still secondary in the opinion of some), have risen in prominence and influence in the last several decades. As theologian Gregory Baum has stated with reference to sociology, for example:

Sociology has acquired an extraordinary cultural presence. At the university the language of sociology occupies a predominant place. It is present in the exercise of the human sciences

and in the making of university policy. For better or for worse,
it has replaced the universality of philosophical discourse.
Sociology has penetrated the marketplace and the realm of
political debate.[12]

Baum adds that the study of sociology has also been
experienced by many as "a liberating intellectual activity"
enabling "people of different social, cultural and religious
backgrounds to come together in a common perception of
the social reality."[13] Since the discipline of sociology originally
emerged in the midst of the radical changes in Britain and
Europe brought on by the French and Industrial Revolu-
tions, it is not surprising that, with the escalating tensions of
our world in this part of the twentieth century, the turn
toward this kind of analysis should gain in influence.[14]

But a word of caution is in order here. Linking an analysis
of society with the phenomenon of radical change has tended
to depreciate the importance of tradition. Edward Shils has
argued that the Enlightenment ethos surrounding the
French Revolution pitted scientific procedures (and their
accompanying rationality) against traditional knowledge and
beliefs. The development of social science as a discipline was
shaped by this ethos. We need, therefore, to critique this
analytic tradition and recover "the traditionality of knowledge"—knowledge has a history; it goes back in time.[15]
Analysis is a process of taking things and ideas apart to
examine them. Tradition emphasizes the handing on of what
connects things, people, and ideas. The *social* urgency of this
shift away from tradition has been made painfully obvious,
for example, in the tragic history of North American land
claim "settlements" with Native Peoples, because their
"traditional" way of life has repeatedly been regarded as
backward compared with modern systems of economic
development.[16]

4. Increasingly, analysis of society has been deliberately
applied to the study of theology (and occasionally theology to
the study of society). The historical critical analysis of
Scripture has been expanded to include this new dimension,
and books and articles have poured forth like a torrent.[17] In
the area of theology per se various kinds of liberation,

political, and contextual theologies have appeared in bewildering array.[18] David Tracy and Max Stackhouse, among others, have called for a public theology[19] and Dennis McCann and Charles Strain have issued "an invitation: practical theology as public discourse."[20] Preaching as an integrating theological discipline cannot remain aloof. Its time has come.

The Theological Urgency in This Societal Dimension

But preaching is first and foremost a theological act; it is a proclamation of the Word of God. Whatever movements bring to our consciousness the ability to see various social dimensions in the activity of preaching, a commitment to pursue this investigation gains its urgency in theology itself. It is not enough to argue this by the inference that because we influence, and are influenced by, society, society must come into the direct purview of preaching. While it is both true and obvious that people are social beings, there has been a perpetuation of an unfortunate polarity. Individuals have been treated as if they could be separated from their corporate reality. With this separation the world becomes merely a backdrop to God's personal encounter with individuals as though the entire world is profane, no longer part of God's creation.

Is this why some conservative, fundamentalistic preaching which, although enormously popular at present, "makes little attempt to analyze the world" in terms of its social structures? In considering this phenomenon, Robert Bellah asserts that this kind of preaching rightly recognizes that religious experience and belief are powerful. Both intense group life and the demand for personal sacrifice in these church communities are profoundly important; but their stance encourages a withdrawal into privatism, lacks a sense of the common good, and fails to recognize the importance of tradition and history.[21] Theologically, this means circumscribing God within a private sphere, viewing the church as a closed community, and putting a quest for certitude in place of authentic faith.[22]

Those who see religion in this privatistic way, naturally,

view preaching as suspect or on tenuous ground when it
speaks not only of personal conversion, faith development,
and spiritual nurture, but also of political realities, economic
arrangements, care of creation, and the like. But such
discomfort represents a theological shift that has capitulated
to cultural changes in our modern world. The classical view
(both Protestant and Catholic) held that theology was "the
queen of the sciences," that all knowledge was directed
toward knowing God. Theology dealt with ultimate questions
and all of life. All thought and all that happens on this earth
were finally related to God and redeemed by Christ, but with
the emergence of the industrial world, mechanistic compart-
mentalization separated interconnected parts of society and
set religion in a corner. This meant that in some sectors
theology was viewed as a matter of private opinion and
personal insight or intuition.[23] Since this ethos still pervades
much of our Western culture, it is not surprising that pulpit
discussion of the public or social sphere should be felt to be
inappropriate.

The church, which is the immediate context of preaching,
is a distinctively religious and spiritual community. To use
David Tracy's language, the church is "a strictly theological
reality, a grace from God," a community that stands "under
the eschatological proviso of the judgment of God."[24] The
church must indeed see itself as a people *of God*. But, as such,
it is also a *people,* a collectivity. In that it is a voluntary and
public association of people, it is a particular "sociological
reality."[25]

Preaching to the church is a form of public discourse in
which God is recognized as being related to human beings not
just individually but in the full context of their existence. The
Word of God addresses us in our personal lives and also as
members of the larger social world of which we are a part. We
may speak of God as personal, but do we also acknowledge
God as "fully social and radically present in the world?"[26] This
would be more likely if, with Tracy, the "world" is understood
"as a properly theological reality."[27] To push this further, the
gospel calls us to turn away from sin in all its manifestations—personal, of course, but also social and structural—
and also demands responsible stewardship against the raping

of our natural environment. Faithfulness to the gospel requires that preaching awaken the people of God (and through them the society in which they live) to all of these dimensions. Theology provides an imperative, therefore, to expose hidden political meanings and then to evaluate them in terms of gospel values. "Theology must assume responsibility for its socio-political impact."[28] Preaching, as the vehicle of theological proclamation, is urged by theology to be, among other things, a social act.

The Present Work

For my own part, this volume is rooted in the parish ministry, teaching, and a sabbatical visit to Central America. For ten years preaching was a central part of my pastoral ministry. It was a decade in which I sought, perhaps unsystematically, to involve the congregation in reciprocal processes of hearing the Word of God. For the last fifteen years I have been engaged in the teaching of biblical studies and of preaching with particular emphasis on social hermeneutics. In 1981 my sabbatical included visits to Costa Rica and Nicaragua. During that time all the socializing layers that had buried my lower-class immigrant childhood were stripped away. The God whose love I felt in my family's faith was a God far beyond middle-class values. In the faces of my Latin American brothers and sisters, I felt God's love making living connections that gave new meaning to what I understood to be social. These are some of the formative influences that caused me to initiate the development of this project.

This book is primarily a corporate effort, not only in its production, but also in its conception. It owes its encouragement to the Academy of Homiletics and especially a Research Group within the Academy on "The Social Dimensions of Preaching." The papers and discussions in this group over several years have pursued various aspects of preaching's societal shape and influence. About two years ago I drafted an initial proposal and sent it to fifteen people, mostly in the Academy, but also to a teacher of the Sociology of Religion.

The response led me to rewrite the proposal from start to finish.

Those of us involved in the writing of these pages are mostly teachers of preaching, but we represent a variety of theological disciplines and write in different styles. None of us is a social science specialist. What we have written about the *social* dimensions of preaching arises from our experience, our reflection on society, and some familiarity with selected social science literature. The following chapters should be read as the contribution of theologians in the broad sense of the term. It is to be hoped that this may also stimulate dialogue between theology and the social sciences.

The larger context of preaching can be seen through, and as an extension of, the immediate sacramental context of the congregation. Catherine G. and Justo L. González show how we are sacramentally linked across political and social boundaries spatially, and across the generations and centuries temporally. To preach to the community of the baptized is to speak to those who are born again to see the world from a new, theological perspective. This preaching cannot ignore social factors from the wider context: status, stratification, diversity, attitudes toward change, and the influence of quasi-religious elements in our cultural ethos.

"Faith Church" is a community that is discovering how to discern its social world while interacting with its pastor in the formation of the sermon week by week. Don Wardlaw creates this imaginary congregation to concretize his analysis of the congregation as a social reality. He also shows how this community interacts with ancient Israel and the early church as the first recipients of Scripture. In the preaching moment, the social world of the past and the social world of the present come together in the proclamation of the Word of God.

In the biographies of two contemporary preachers whose preaching takes personal and societal transformation with equal seriousness, Edwina Hunter discerns formative factors underlying their perspectives and their passion. For them these factors interweave the social and the spiritual as seen in their experiences of their community of faith, their call to preach, and their spiritual and social formation. Later in the chapter, Edwina, as a former pastor and now a teacher of preaching, reflects on her own socialization and spiritual journey.

The Bible, so central to preaching, was formed in a particular culture, is now interpreted by social beings, and is received by a social community. Walter Brueggemann writes that in every stage of interpretation the textual process is both an act of faith and an act of "vested interests." Sociology can help us uncover these vested interests, and, in the process of proclamation, preachers can become clearer about how particular passages in particular situations call for transformation, or maintain equilibrium. The gospel provides criteria to make this discernment.

The language of preaching is the focus of the last two chapters. Language both reflects our social context and creates new images to expand our perception of our world. Ron Allen examines specific ways in which we use language, and how the genre of the text shapes its thrust; he also offers concrete homiletical strategies. Tom Troeger focuses on the mythic worlds created by metaphor, which he terms "landscapes of the heart," and demonstrates how communal, poetic idiom can speak to an individualistic, technological culture.

Like our social world itself, the various social dimensions of preaching overlap and our perception of them varies. In the Afterword I point to connections and differences between the chapters. While the work as a whole was written from a deliberate, systematic design, it is far from comprehensive. Some suggestions, therefore, of areas for further exploration are indicated, and broader issues such as "prophetic preaching" are elaborated briefly. This analysis on analysis, then, moves toward some synthesis. In the end, of course, analysis, and even synthesis, is not enough. This is at root a spiritual struggle that includes silence, contemplation, and compassion—and after that, preaching.

The Appendix enables pastors, students, and teachers of preaching to probe dimensions of their own preaching and preaching situations by setting out groups of questions. These have been distilled from the chapters as a way of sharpening and applying the analysis of this book. The list may seem overwhelming when taken as a whole, but the busy pastor is encouraged to use it selectively and to engage the congregation in sermon dialogue through the use of these questions.

We read books in different ways. One hesitates to suggest how a book, especially one of multiple authorship, may best be read; nevertheless a few comments may be helpful.

First, there is a certain logic to the present order, a looking outward and then inward, a movement from context to person to biblical text and finally to linguistic expression. Is this suggestive of the process of sermon development? Some, of course, might begin with language, or with the text.

Second, those not as familiar with social science disciplines may want to begin by consulting chapter 4, the second section, "The Classic Tradition of Sociology." This section outlines the origins and leading schools of sociology.[29] Finally, each chapter includes a sermon preached on a specific occasion, and is then followed by reflection. Theory and description need to become preaching, but growth in preaching is assisted by reflecting on what one has preached. This is a model that readers may find useful. However, self-reflection is only one component in this process, and the present format in no way diminishes the importance of feedback or reflection from listeners individually or in groups. No sermon is ever finished. Like tensive or metaphorical language it keeps on evoking meaning, feeling, and action. The format of each chapter is intended to encourage growth and new awareness.

Notes

1. These include Clyde Reid, *The Empty Pulpit: A Study of Preaching as Communication* (New York: Harper & Row, 1967), and John Killinger, *Experimental Preaching* (Nashville: Abingdon Press, 1973).

2. Peter G. Horsfield believes that widespread interest in religious television crested in 1976 with the election of a Southern Baptist to the presidency of the United States and that this phenomenon has manifested "a marked imbalance in the presentation of American religious faith and culture," *Religious Television: The American Experience* (White Plains, N.Y.: Longman, 1984), xiii-xiv. For another perspective of the TV evangelists, see Perry C. Cotham, "The Electronic Church," in *The Bible and Popular Culture in America,* ed. Allene Stuart Phy (Philadelphia: Fortress Press, 1985), 104-36.

3. This book will not address all of the above questions but they are listed

because they are connected with the present theme: preaching as a social act.

4. The question of the social class or classes of first-century Christians has been the subject of considerable analysis and debate recently. See, for example, the articles by Robin Scroggs, John P. Brown, George V. Pixley, Elisabeth Schüssler Fiorenza, Luise Schottroff, John G. Gager, and Robert H. Smith, "Sociological Readings of the New Testament," in *The Bible and Liberation: Political and Social Hermeneutics*, ed. Norman K. Gottwald (Maryknoll, N.Y.: Orbis Books, 1983), 335-457.

5. Lesslie Newbigin, *The Other Side of 1984: Questions for the Churches* (Geneva: World Council of Churches, 1983), 23-27. Newbigin is drawing on Charles Norris Cochrane, *Christianity in Classical Culture* (1940) and Michael Polanyi, *Personal Knowledge* (1958).

6. Daniel Patte, *Preaching Paul* (Philadelphia: Fortress Press, 1984), 13. Actually, the prophets were doing this kind of reinterpretation before Paul and the storytellers before the prophets.

7. Fred B. Craddock, *Preaching* (Nashville: Abingdon Press, 1985), chapter 5. I am personally indebted to Craddock for suggesting to me the title of this book.

8. This is not to disparage sociological studies of preaching such as those found in a special issue of *Social Compass*, 27, 1980, 345-438, and in Osmund Schreuder, "The Silent Majority," in *Communication in the Church*, ed. Gregory Baum and Andrew M. Greeley (New York: Seabury Press, 1978), 11-19.

9. For noteworthy contributions to liberative preaching, see Justo L. González and Catherine Gunsalus González, *Liberation Preaching: The Pulpit and the Oppressed* (Nashville: Abingdon Press, 1980); Allan Boesak, *The Finger of God: Sermons on Faith and Socio-Political Responsibility* (Maryknoll, N.J.: Orbis Books, 1982), especially the introduction, 1-17; and Dieter T. Hessel, "Liberating Bible Study and Preaching," in *Social Ministry* (Philadelphia: Westminster Press, 1982), 93-108.

10. In this connection see David H. Blake and Robert S. Walters, *The Politics of Global Economic Relations*, 2nd ed. (Englewood Cliffs, N.J.: Prentice-Hall, 1983).

11. It is significant, in view of present U. S. policy on Central America, that King's "Beyond Vietnam" sermon delivered some twenty years ago was ·reprinted in *Sojourners*, January 1983, 10-16, with a moving commentary by Vincent Harding, "The Land Beyond," 18-22.

12. Gregory Baum, ed., *Sociology and Human Destiny: Essays on Sociology, Religion and Society* (New York: Seabury Press, 1980), ix. In the introduction, Baum raises critical questions about sociology as a discipline of critical and analytical thought. Indeed, the book is an examination of several influential North American sociologists (Talcott Parsons, Robert Bellah, Peter Berger, and George Herbert Mead) who are "widely used and appreciated at North American universities," xi.

13. Ibid., ix.

14. See Anthony Giddens, *Sociology: A Brief but Critical Introduction* (San Diego: Harcourt Brace Jovanovich, 1982), 4-15, and Peter L. Berger, *Invitation to Sociology: A Human Perspective* (New York: Doubleday & Co., 1963), 6, 42-48.

15. Edward Shils, *Tradition* (Chicago: University of Chicago Press, 1981), 4-10, 21-23. Giddens has written his introduction to sociology with a "strongly historical stress." He adds, "Sociology and 'history' may be ordinarily taught as though they were distinct fields of study, but I think such

a view to be wholly mistaken," *Sociology,* vi. The importance of tradition will be apparent in several of the following chapters.

16. This illustrates what Shils calls "progressiveness" (*Tradition,* 1-4). For a penetrating analysis of a classic example, namely, "settlement" of land claims in Alaska, see Thomas R. Berger, *Village Journey: The Report of the Alaska Native Review Commission* (New York: Hill & Wang, 1985).

17. For examples see the articles in Gottwald, *The Bible and Liberation;* Norman Gottwald's extensive bibliography in *American Baptist Quarterly,* 2, 1983, 163-84, and the endnotes in John H. Elliott's review of Wayne A. Meeks' *The First Urban Christians,* in *Religious Studies Review,* 11, 1985, 320-35.

18. One thinks of the writing of Jürgen Moltmann, Johann Baptist Metz, Gustavo Gutierrez, Juan Luis Segundo, Rosemary Radford Reuther, James H. Cone, and Douglas John Hall, and general works such as Edward Farley, *Ecclesial Man* (Philadelphia: Fortress Press, 1975), and Roger Haight, *An Alternate Vision: An Interpretation of Liberation Theology* (Mahwah, N.J.: Paulist Press, 1985).

19. David Tracy, *The Analogical Imagination: Christian Theology and the Culture of Pluralism* (New York: Crossroad Publishing Co., 1981); Tracy's contribution to his joint work with John B. Cobb, Jr., *Talking About God: Doing Theology in the Context of Pluralism* (New York: Seabury Press, 1983); and Max L. Stackhouse, "An Ecumenist's Plea for a Public Theology," *This World,* 8, Spring/Summer 1984, 47-79.

20. Dennis P. McCann and Charles R. Strain, *Policy and Praxis: A Program for American Practical Theology* (Minneapolis: Winston Press, 1985), especially 208-22.

21. Robert N. Bellah, "The Role of Preaching in a Corrupt Republic," *Christianity and Crisis,* 38, 1978, 321-22. Earlier in this essay Bellah indicates the significant role religion played in the founding of the United States. It provided stability and encouraged social change. Indeed, he says, it is hard to think of any major reform movement "that did not come out of the Christian Church" (though "opposition to reform also came out of the church"), 318.

22. On this latter point Robert Towler, following William James, distinguishes five cognitive faith approaches: exemplarism, conversionism, theism, gnosticism, and traditionalism; he indicates how each opts for faith *or* certitude. Faith recognizes the inherently complex and problematic nature of events and experiences, while certitude seeks to escape doubt by ignoring the complex and problematic. *The Need for Certainty: A Sociological Study of Conventional Religion* (London: Routledge & Kegan Paul, 1984), 105-7.

23. Cf. Stackhouse, "An Ecumenist's Plea," 47-48. Stackhouse points out that there are two senses in which religion is indeed private. First, it is disestablished by the separation of church and state, and, second, belief and morality are unavoidably personal. But, he adds, this still leaves room for a "worldly theology" that can "set forth a metaphysical-moral vision that can judge, evaluate, guide and put in perspective" various social interests, 48-51.

24. Tracy, *Analogical Imagination,* 23.

25. Ibid., 21-28. For a discussion of the distinction between "church" and "sect" (in Weber's ideal types) see the Afterword.

26. Hessel, "Liberating Bible Study," 18.

27. Tracy, *Analogical Imagination,* 23.

28. Gregory Baum, "Three Theses on Contextual Theology," *The Ecumenist,* 24, 1986, 50. In this connection see also the volume of essays that connect spirituality and social compassion, edited by Tilden H. Edwards,

Living with Apocalypse: Spiritual Resources for Social Compassion (New York: Harper & Row, 1984).

29. For an introduction to sociology by a sociologist, see Giddens, *Sociology*. A succinct theological critique of the sociological approaches of Hans Mol (classical functionalism), Max Weber (pluralist/symbolic sociology), and Karl Marx (conflict sociology) can be found in Baum's "Three Theses on Contextual Theology." Michael Fleet has critiqued the work of both Talcott Parsons and Robert Bellah in terms of their respective social and political stances, "Religion and Politics: Talcott Parsons," *Ecumenist,* 18/1, 1979, 12-16; and "Bellah's Sociology," *Ecumenist,* 18/2, 1980, 27-32. See also note 12. It is essential that, as theologians and preachers, we read sociology critically and these works, largely from a liberation perspective, provide assistance.

1

The Larger Context

Justo L. González and Catherine G. González. Any sign is capable of different meanings according to the various contexts in which it is placed. A kiss, usually a sign of love, becomes a sign of betrayal in the story of Judas. Law and order, values which every normal human being cherishes, in certain contexts become code words for privilege and oppression. Likewise, the meaning of a sermon is greatly determined by the context in which it is preached.

Sacramental Context

More precisely, one should say that the meaning of a sermon is determined by the various contexts in which it is preached, for every act of preaching takes place in a series of contexts. Some of these multiple contexts are wider expressions of one another, as, for instance, the series of concentric circles that goes from the local community to the wider community, to the nation, and eventually to the entire globe. Others intersect one another at various levels such as social class, liturgical setting, economic conditions, personal struggles, racial prejudice, and denominational traditions. The result is that each act of preaching takes place within a unique constellation of contexts and that the more that constellation changes the more will the meaning of the sermon itself change, even if it is repeated verbatim.

In addition, the traditional context of preaching is the sacramental life of the church. From very early times, the church gathered both to hear the reading and exposition of Scripture, and to partake of the sacrament of Holy Communion. During the Middle Ages, preaching was relegated to such a point that eventually it became relatively rare, and the regular worship of the church was almost entirely reduced to Communion—the Mass. Seeking to correct this imbalance, the Protestant Reformers emphasized the importance of the exposition of Scripture, and insisted that Christian worship ought to consist of Word and sacrament. Eventually, the pendulum swung to the other extreme, and most Protestant churches have come to the point where preaching is the central act of worship, and Communion is rarely celebrated. As for baptism, it has often become a parenthesis in the service, after which we return to the "regular" acts of worship.

In spite of such extremes, the proper context of preaching is the sacramental life of the church. Preaching, as part of the worship of the church—in contrast to the preaching that takes place outside the church and is addressed mostly to nonbelievers—is addressed to the people of God. It is addressed to people who have been baptized and who seek to live their life out of that baptism. It is addressed to people who live through the nourishment of the Table. Therefore, even when there is no baptism and no Communion in a particular worship service, preaching takes place within the wider context of those two sacraments.

This is of crucial importance, for when we seek to place preaching within the context of the "wider community," meaning by that both the local community in which a congregation exists and the global community, part of what we seek is a *theological* understanding of that context. It is certainly true that in order to understand the nature of a community, we must look at the statistics that describe it. Such statistics are relevant and should not be avoided, for they provide data that would be difficult to gather from other sources. This is true of any given local community as well as of the global community that is always the context of preaching. But, for us Christians, the nature of a community, just as that of an individual's life and promise, is also a *theological* question. Therefore, when inquiring about the larger context in which preaching takes place—the human community at every level, from the neighborhood to the globe—it is helpful to begin by placing that inquiry within the sacramental context that is also the implicit or explicit context of every act of preaching in Christian worship.

As we look at the eucharist, the first thing that strikes us is that from very early times the sacrament of the Table was a sign of the unity of the church. Paul declares that "because there is one bread, we who are many are one body, for we all partake of the one bread" (I Cor. 10:17). This unity is also the theme of one of the earliest prayers to be said over the bread, which looks forward to the time when the church will be gathered from all over the earth, just as the wheat, which was once scattered over the hills, has become this one loaf (*Didache* 9.4). Soon it became customary, at least in the city of Rome, to take a fragment of bread from the celebration of Communion at the central gathering place (where the bishop presided over the service) and place it with the bread for Communion at the other worship services. Later, again as a sign of the unity of the church, the practice arose of keeping in each church a list of bishops of other churches and praying for them during Communion. The act of erasing the name of a bishop from such lists—the diptychs—was a sign of a breach in the unity of the church.

What all this means is that in the act of preaching, which takes place either directly or indirectly within the context of Communion, the entire body of Christ throughout the earth is part of the context. The church with which we worship is not only the congregation gathered at a particular place to hear a sermon; it is also the church universal, scattered throughout the earth. The context of a sermon is not only its immediate hearers, but also that church whose faith we share and with whom we worship. Concretely, this means that preaching should always take into account, not only the immediate context of the congregation, but also that wider context of the community of faith throughout the world. Preaching should certainly address the situation of the hearers. If it takes place, for instance, in a middle-class suburban congregation in the United States, it must deal with the issues and concerns of that congregation, but it must not do so at the expense of its catholic context. Preaching must be addressed to the needs of a parish; but it must not be parochial, for one of the needs of every parish is to be connected to the church universal. People in the above-mentioned suburban parish need to recognize that they are part of the same church that struggles for justice in South Africa and gathers for worship under a thatched roof in a village in India.

The catholicity of Communion, however, goes beyond geography. It certainly cuts across geographic and political borders, but it also cuts across the borders of time. When we celebrate Communion, we are joining the entire body of Christ, not only present, but also past and future. Christians in affluent countries in the twentieth century have grown used to such a fast pace of life and to such constant changes in the material environment that we tend to think that our problems are unique, that the past is worthless as a source of wisdom for modern times, and that our ancestors in the faith have little in common with us. And yet, Communion, as the context for preaching, reminds us that in those things that are most important, our being part of the body of Christ, we are one with our ancestors in the faith. Furthermore, this unity through the ages is part of what it means to be a faithful Christian today.

It is, however, the future-oriented dimension of Communion that most needs to be emphasized. The earliest Communion prayers that have survived have a clear eschatological dimension. Communion is not only the remembrance of the death of Jesus, it is also the remembrance of his resurrection and his coming again in glory. In other words, it is a reminder of the future order of peace and justice for which we wait. Therefore, Communion, with its eschatological announcement and pre-enactment, is a reminder to the church that we have a particular vantage point as we look at the entire context of our preaching and our life. The horrible statistics of famine and injustice are, as far as they go, a true description of our world. We must take them seriously and seek to do something about them. But the reason why we confidently undertake to undo injustice and promote peace is that we know that the world has a different future from the present reality; a different future which places reality under a new light.

This temporal catholicity of Communion and of the Christian faith is also the reason why the context of our preaching cannot be only the worldwide community of those who already believe. If such were the case, we would seek justice and peace only for those who are also believers in Jesus, but that is not the case. The eschatological expectation of the Christian church looks forward to a time when the meaning and significance of every human life will be revealed in Christ. Since this is our expectation, the context of our preaching and of our faith and living must go beyond the community—even the worldwide community—of those who presently believe and embrace all those who are invited to believe in Jesus Christ—the entire human race.

Finally, the catholicity of Communion also includes the whole of creation—even inanimate objects. Too often we make the mistake of forgetting that God is the Creator of the entire universe and that the entire universe is part of God's plan of redemption. Such a mistake contributes to our callousness toward the rest of creation, as if we could treat animals, fields, and forests in any way we please. After all, we tell ourselves, we are intelligent beings with a higher goal, spiritual beings with a particular kinship to God, and therefore the rest of creation must stand aside when it comes to our goals and interests, but Communion tells us otherwise. The sacraments are one of many signs God has given us that even in our most spiritual undertakings we are tied by an umbilical cord to the earth. Just as our physical bodies need the earth to be nourished, so does our spiritual life need the bread and wine of Communion—and the water of baptism—to be nourished. Therefore, the context of preaching is not only the human community, both local and global; it is also the entire community of God's creation. And just as in our preaching we must proclaim justice for the human community, so must we also seek justice for the entire community of creatures.

The sacrament of baptism is also part of the context of

preaching. In our regular worship services, we are normally speaking to those who are baptized, and part of the purpose of preaching is to unfold the meaning of our baptism. Baptism is the beginning of the Christian life, not simply as a ticket that allows us to enter into this fellowship, but rather as a birth that determines who we are for the rest of our lives. Just as our birth in a particular nation and setting is a constant factor throughout our lives, baptism is the point of departure, the definition of our selves, to which we must constantly return in order to understand who we are and who we are called to be in Christ.

Normally, it is within the community of the baptized that we are preaching. As such, we are, or at least we ought to be, a people with a different vision of reality. As people who are born again through water and the Spirit, we must see all of reality under a different light. Paul spoke of how his values had changed to such a point that what he had earlier sought and cherished he now considered of little worth (Phil. 3:7-8). The light of the gospel had given him a different vision of the world. What we seek to do through worship is, among other things, to renew and clarify the vision that derives from our new birth.

This is the wider context of our preaching. It is not simply the world around us. It is the world as seen and judged from the perspective of a people who have been set aside for a mission, born again into a new people. This is not otherworldliness. It is not a matter of believing that our real context is some other world. It is, rather, a matter of accepting and affirming this world as the proper context for our preaching and for our entire Christian lives, but at the same time seeing it under a different light or from a new perspective.

All of this sounds very abstract, but does have some concrete and radical applications. If we look, for instance, at the international economic order apart from our baptism and Christian faith, we could look at it simply as North Americans, and our main concern would then be how to preserve those elements in that world order that benefit our economy and how to change those that do not. On the matter of Japanese imports, for instance, our question could be posed in terms of what are the best policies to ensure that such imports do not undercut American industry and employment. But if we look at the same question from the perspective of those who have been baptized into Christ and who live out of the hope of a new order of peace and justice, our question would have to include concern for Japanese as well as for North American workers—and for Third-World countries whose citizens may suffer due to the policies of both Japan and the United States. If we take our baptism seriously, we have become sisters and brothers of all those all over the world who have been baptized, largely due to our past missionary efforts. And we have become potential brothers and sisters to the rest of humankind, whose human condition as well as faith is part of our present mission. Their well-being must be our concern just as much as that of our own families, and this places every issue in the contemporary world under a different light!

Social Factors in the Preaching Context

When we preach to a congregation in a particular community in this country, we are very much aware that members of our congregation are concerned, not only about the issues of the local community, or about those relatives who live with them, but also about loved ones who may be far away. Parents may be worried about a child in another city whose marriage is going through difficult times. Another member may be thinking about a parent in a distant city who needs special attention. Still another has not heard from a spouse in military service in Central America. All of this is part of the context of our preaching, and appropriately so. What we must do, however, is to make certain that part of the context is also our concern for our black sister in South Africa and for our struggling Asian brother.

In spite of all this, and of the catholicity of the church, there is no doubt that specific social, political, and economic contexts affect both the sermon itself and the manner in which it is heard. Given that fact, it is important for a preacher to learn to analyze how the context of an act of preaching affects what is said and what is understood. No word is ever spoken apart from a context. No word has meaning apart from a context. Therefore, in order to be faithful, the preached word must be faithful *in its context*. This means that it is of fundamental importance for preachers to learn to analyze the setting in which their preaching takes place. This is to be done, not simply in order to speak to that setting, which we have been told over and over, but also in order to make certain that our words, spoken and interpreted in that setting, are responsible.

Given that task, a useful approach is to list some of the specific elements in common preaching situations, to show how they affect the meaning of what is said, and to seek ways to correct the misinterpretations that such contexts may produce. By way of example, we shall briefly discuss four levels at which these dynamics take place.

1. *Social Status.* One of the most common blind spots for preachers who come from backgrounds that have traditionally implied power—for instance, male, white, North American, or any combination of these—is the degree to which who they are affects the way people hear them. Those who come from the opposite end of the scale of social acceptance are more readily aware of such matters, for they experience them daily. A black woman, for instance, is very much aware that she is given different degrees of credibility and authority in various groups. How she is heard depends on whether she is addressing black women, black men, white men, or white women. For her, this is such a daily experience that she does not have to be told that such relationships are part of the context of preaching. A white male pastor, on the other hand, can easily ignore such dynamics, although they are no less present when he preaches. The first and most immediate social context of preaching is thus the inevitable intrusion in the dynamics of preaching of the social relationships between preacher and hearers. To ignore this is to risk being misunderstood or speaking the "right" word to the wrong people.

The way to correct this should be quite obvious. We must analyze our own social standing before those to whom we speak. Are there social factors—race, culture, class, gender, education—that give us a certain status, positive or negative, vis-à-vis our congregation or part of it? How does that status impinge on what we are saying? How will we be heard by people who consider themselves our equals? How will we be heard by those who, for whatever reason, grant us special status? How will we be heard by those at the other extreme? Do we have these various situations among our listeners? If so, we must make certain that our words address each of them.

A second and more crucial way to respond to this first issue is to take steps to make certain that, to the highest possible degree, our words are spoken, not on our own authority but on that of Scripture. The more a sermon rests on the authority of Scripture, and the less on the status of the preacher, the better. Preachers who speak on their own authority are credible only to those who grant them superior status. In the modern world, where the status that is automatically granted to preachers is declining, it is particularly important that we do what preachers should do in any case: speak on the authority of Scripture, and not simply on our own.

2. *Catholicity of Focus.* Naturally, factors such as class, race, culture, and nationality also affect the dynamics of preaching. Unfortunately, many of our churches have allowed themselves to be stratified by class, so that various congregations are comprised of people of specific classes. This makes for a more comfortable social life within the congregation, but it does not make for clearer listening to the Word of God. We all need the various perspectives that the universal church can bring to our understanding of the Word. This is part of the meaning of catholicity: a vision of the word *cath'holon,* "according to the whole." A group of Christians with a particular social, political, and economic perspective, no matter how learned or earnest they are, can never listen to the entire message of Scripture with the same degree of freshness, or find in it the same level of challenge, as a more diverse group. Unfortunately, part of the given context of most of our preaching is the narrowness of our Christian communities, segregated as they are by class, race, and levels of education, and, in too many of our activities, also by age. Thus, the second contextual factor that must be taken

into account in most situations of preaching and Bible study is the lack of the variety of perspectives that should enrich the church catholic.

The obvious way to respond to this challenge is to do all we can to make certain that the church at each place is as much a representation of the church catholic as possible. This is particularly important for congregations composed mostly of those who are relatively powerful in a society—more specifically, in our society, of white affluent North Americans—and who therefore in their daily dealings are not forced to listen to or to learn from those who are less fortunate. A segregated suburban congregation is deprived of the richness of perspectives on the gospel that a more varied congregation enjoys or the richness forced upon an ethnic minority congregation that constantly hears the perspectives and interpretations of the dominant group.

Since, however, it is not possible for any congregation to embrace the rich variety of the church catholic, it is important for pastors to include that variety, both explicitly and implicitly, in their worship and preaching. Explicitly, one includes it by making reference to Christians living under other circumstances whenever possible. Implicitly, one includes it by making certain that nothing is said that one would not dare say before those other Christians who are not present. In a Thanksgiving service, for instance, we must be ready to repeat in the presence of our Native American sisters and brothers whatever is said about ownership of the land.

3. *Fear of Change.* Third, and to some degree a specific instance of the foregoing, we must be aware that for various reasons some people favor change, and others fear it. This goes beyond the natural fear of the unknown and has more to do with the social standing of various individuals and groups. Generally, those who are favored by the existing order wish to preserve it and resist any change that they cannot call "progress"—which means change in the same direction as before, more of the same, rather than something radically new. Those who suffer under the existing order sometimes fear that change will bring greater suffering and sometimes hope for a change that will somehow ameliorate their

situation. In between, a vast number are afraid of losing whatever control they have over their own lives, and therefore idealize the past, and fear that the present may be leading toward a chaotic future.

These various groups tend to view God in different ways. While for some, God is the sustainer of the order that exists, for others God is the great agent of change and the reason for hope in a new order. Most of our congregations, and a great deal of our theological tradition, lean against change. Therefore, Scripture tends to be interpreted in that direction. Generally, our churches are either in a situation of social stasis, or wish that such were their situation, and most of what we say is interpreted within that context.

Perhaps we ought to realize that neither change nor stasis is the basis on which we must judge what the will of God is. In Scripture, that will is shalom, love, peace, and justice. Therefore, in a situation where either change or the lack of it are considered values, we must insist on these biblical criteria. It is on this basis, and not on our likes and dislikes, that we must judge both every existing order and every change that interrupts it. Where there is no justice, change toward a more just situation is good; but change can also be evil when it curtails justice—as, for instance, when economic and political power is being concentrated in the hands of a smaller number of people.

4. *A Theological Heritage.* A final context that cannot be ignored is the theological upbringing that is a part of our heritage and of the heritage of most of the congregations in which preaching takes place. Under this heading, it is particularly important to underline two nefarious theological traditions that are part of the negative context that we must take into account.

The first such tradition is the false spiritualization of the gospel. From very early times, the church had to struggle against interpretations of the gospel that turned it into a religion of spiritual salvation. There were many such religions in the Mediterranean basin, and there were also many Christians who wished to reduce their faith to another such religion. Although the church officially rejected such notions, they have reappeared frequently. As a result, many of us were brought up thinking that, according to the Bible,

God is primarily concerned about "spiritual" things, that the gospel is good news only for the soul, and that themes such as social and economic justice are the concern only of a few portions of Scripture, such as Amos and James.

In some instances, a similar role is played by another theological tradition which teaches that whatever is must be God's will. If such is the case, what God expects from those who suffer injustice is not that they seek to change the existing order, but rather that they accept it with resignation. From this perspective, to "take up our cross" is not an active taking up of the challenge of the gospel, but rather the passive acceptance of whatever ills befall us. While such views are not prevalent in the dominant culture in the United States, they are widespread in oppressed communities both in this nation and abroad.

The change in this perception is probably the most revolutionary discovery of the new theology in Latin America. It is expressed, not only in theological treatises, but also in the worship of the people, such as in the following song from a Salvadoran peasant mass[1]:

Coro:
Nosotros pensamos
Que a la verdad
Vino su Palabra
Y nos hizo cambiar.

Chorus:
We truly believe that God's
Word has come to us and
made us change.

Me dijo mi abuelita,
"Si te quieres salvar
Las cruces de la vida
Tens que soportar."
Pero resignaciones
No es lo que quiere Dios
El quiere tus acciones
Como obras del amor. (Coro)

My grandmother told me
that if I wished to be saved I
would have to bear the
crosses of life.
But what God wants is not
resignation. God wants your
actions as works of love.
        (Chorus)

"Confórmense y trabajen,"
Nos ha dicho el patrón,
"Que sólo en la otra vida
Tendrán la salvación."
Pero Dios hoy no aguanta
Un nuevo Faraón
Y manda a todo el pueblo
A hacer su liberación. (Coro)

"Be content and work," the
boss has told us, "for only
in the next life will you be
saved." But God cannot
stomach a new Pharaoh, and
orders all the people to work
out liberation.
        (Chorus)

The traditions of spiritualizing the Word of God and of accepting whatever exists as God's will are part of the context of preaching. They are part of the *social* and *economic* context, for they do play a role in the social and economic ordering of society. Indeed, these are not simply theological notions; they are also ways in which we unwittingly justify our lack of concern for justice and for the physical needs of the poor and the oppressed. They are also one of the instruments whereby the poor and the oppressed have been traditionally kept from claiming their rights. No matter how much we believe we have left these things behind, they are part of the inevitable context of our preaching.

Let us then apply these principles to the analysis of a specific sermon.

Sermon: The Setting

The general content of this sermon was originally developed by the two of us as part of a Bible study on the whole Book of Jonah. It was given at a national gathering of Presbyterians strongly involved in social action. The form that is presented here is a sermon given by Justo at an Annual Conference[2] of The United Methodist Church, where he was specifically asked to address the issue of ethnic minorities in the church.

No Sign But the Sign of Jonah

JONAH 4 AND LUKE 11:30-32

Among my many fantasies, there is one in which I see myself preaching at the closing service of Annual Conference and choosing as my text Jonah 4: "God appointed a worm"[3] (verse 7).

I lack the necessary fortitude to do that, but still, I would like to draw your attention this morning to the Book of Jonah. This is probably one of the books most avoided by preachers. It is easy to see why this is so. Who has any desire to get embroiled in controversies about whether the book is historical data or literary fable, or about whether it was a whale or a fish that swallowed Jonah?

In passing, it may be interesting to note that this book has been controversial since ancient times, although for different reasons. Back in the fourth century A.D., Jerome decided to translate the Bible into the Latin that was in common usage in his time. This is what we now know as the Vulgate. When he came to the passage in the fourth chapter of Jonah in which we are told that God caused a plant to grow and shelter the prophet, he translated the name of the plant as an ivy. The traditional translation, however, said that it was a gourd. And we are told that when the bishop of a certain church in North Africa was reading Jerome's text, some protested that there was a mistake in the reading, for the plant was a gourd, not an ivy. The controversy became bitter. Letters flowed back and forth between North Africa, Rome, and Palestine, where Jerome was then residing. Soon there were two parties, the "gourdites" defending the old translation, and the "ivyites" defending Jerome's version. Jerome himself became exceedingly angry—which was not difficult for him to do—and declared that his opponents were drunkards and that the reason why they insisted on a gourd was that they wished to have a place to hide their liquor. Today, scholars tell us that the best translation is probably neither a gourd nor an ivy, but a castor bean!

It would be funny, were it not that it is so tragic. Because, you see, the point of the controversy is that they missed the point of the book.

The book is not about an ivy or a gourd or a castor bean. The book is about God's care for the Ninevites:

—the Ninevites, who were famous for their cruelty

—the Ninevites, who did not know God

—the Ninevites, who did not even know enough to be either liberal or fundamentalist

—the Ninevites, who had no idea whether Jonah had come by camel or by whale

—the Ninevites, whom one would expect to be the last people on earth to repent

—the Ninevites, who were the cruel enemies of Israel, and

whose destruction should have caused any good Israelite to gloat and rejoice.

But even more important, the Book of Jonah is not about a whale or a fish or a gourd or a worm. The Book of Jonah is about this strange God of salvation who appoints Jonah, and appoints a storm, and appoints a great fish, all so that Nineveh might not perish.

And it is about the prophet who knows full well the extent of God's mercy and grace, and does not like it. In effect he says, "Lord, I wish I could die. This is why when I was in my land I did not wish to come. For I know that you are a gracious God who repents from evil." Jonah did not refuse to go to Nineveh because he was afraid. He was no coward. Actually, when the storm threatened the ship it was he who suggested to the sailors that he be thrown overboard. Nor did he refuse to go to Nineveh because he did not like the usually unsuccessful role of a prophet or because he did not understand the purposes of God. On the contrary, he understood too well. He knew that God is a gracious God. He knew that God wanted to save Nineveh. He understood that God's mercy is such that he could well be successful and save Nineveh. He understood, and he didn't like it. Can you imagine what it would be like for Jonah to return home and have to tell his neighbors where he had been, and that he had actually saved their most dangerous enemy?

So, the Book of Jonah is about this strange God whose chosen ones may have to be tossed by wind and storm, robbed of all security, and even thrown to the depths of the ocean, all so that faraway Nineveh, enemy Nineveh, might be brought under the wings of God's gracious love.

Actually, this is how Jesus interprets the text. It is well-known that he declared that this "wicked generation . . . asks for a . . . sign, but none will be given it except the sign of Jonah" (Luke 11:29, NIV).

When we hear those words of Jesus, we immediately think of the three days in the belly of the whale, and of the parallelism with the time Jesus lay in the grave. And that is part of what the Gospel says about the sign of Jonah. At least, that is what the Gospel of Matthew says. But we forget that there is more than this to the sign of Jonah. Matthew and Luke both offer more clarification as to the meaning of this sign:

> For as Jonah became a sign to the [people] of Nineveh, so will the Son of man be to this generation. The queen of the South will arise at the judgment with the [people] of this generation and condemn them; for she came from the ends of the earth to hear the wisdom of Solomon, and behold, something greater than Solomon is here. The [people] of Nineveh will arise at the judgment with this generation and condemn it; for they repented at the preaching of Jonah, and behold, something greater than Jonah is here (Luke 11:30-32).[4]

The sign of Jonah is the Ninevites repenting and calling on the mercy of a God whom they do not know, while the prophet who does know God, bemoans that mercy.

The sign of Jonah is in the Queen of Sheba coming from the ends of the earth to hear the wisdom of Solomon when the king's sons refuse to follow that wisdom.

The sign of Jonah is in the harlots and the publicans going into the Kingdom ahead of the religious leaders of their time.

The sign of Jonah is in One who was rejected as a blasphemer by the religious leaders of his time and condemned to death as a criminal by the political leaders, rising up from the dead and sitting at the right hand of God, and being given a name that is above every other name, so that "at the name of Jesus every knee should bow, in heaven and on earth and under the earth" (Phil. 2:10), and even those of the religious and political leaders who condemned him. (In a way, this gives deeper meaning to the connection between the sign of Jonah and the three days in the belly of the whale, for the connection is not simply in the numerical parallelism of the number of days, but even more in that Jonah, after sinking to the depths of the ocean, rose again to call the mighty city of Nineveh to repentence.)

And, we might add, the sign of Jonah is in Cornelius, the military officer of the Empire that killed Jesus, becoming the occasion for Peter and the early church, like so many reluctant Jonahs, to discover the wideness of God's mercy.

And this sign of Jonah may well be in us, an unlikely crowd of different origins and races, in us, who were once "separated from Christ, alienated from the commonwealth of Israel, and strangers to the covenants of promise" (Eph. 2:12), in us being brought together under this one roof, into this one body, under this one promise of our salvation. Just as the sign of Jonah was in Jesus being raised from the dead, so is the sign of Jonah in our being born again through the waters of baptism, and through those waters rising to new life in Christ.

Today, people are again asking for signs. We want signs that the church is truly the church of God. So we look at our statistics: Is the church growing? Are our offerings increasing? Why is our membership declining? And we deceive ourselves into believing that the sign of Jonah is in our bright statistical spots, in our growing suburban churches, although we know full well that the reason why most of them are growing is simply that they are receiving members from other churches. Or we admire our own theological acuteness, or our plans for evangelism, or our organizational ability, or some thing or another at which we consider ourselves particularly adept.

But it may well be that no sign will be given to us but the sign of Jonah. It may well be that the sign of a church in which the Spirit of God is at work is precisely that the most unlikely folk are brought in, like the Ninevites at the time of Jonah or like the Queen of Sheba in the days of Solomon, or like the publicans and sinners in the time of Jesus. The sign of Jonah may well be that barriers of race and class that close and divide so many other communities are broken down in this community of the Spirit.

We may look for signs in our tall steeples, in our organizational charts, or in our quadrennial plans, but if the sign of Jonah is lacking every other sign is in vain.

This is what the Book of Jonah is all about. And, when seen from this perspective, it is a very important book for our total understanding of the biblical message.

But the book is not only about the Ninevites. It is also about Jonah. It is about a prophet who knows and understands about the grace of God, but wishes to limit that grace. It is about a prophet who rejoices in God's salvation, but who wishes to die when that salvation is offered to the wrong kind of people.

In this sense, there is a negative side to the sign of Jonah. Jonah is the prophet, a member of the household of God, who knows God's mercy but wishes to circumscribe it to include only those whom he likes. The same sign appears at the time of Jesus, in the Pharisees and the scribes who also know that mercy, but wish to control it and therefore reject Jesus and plot against him. The sign of Jonah has repeatedly appeared in the church with all its talk about love and openness, in contrast to its racism, classism, and private club mentality.

It may well be that on this point too we shall be given the sign of Jonah. The sign of Jonah may well be a call to obedience to a church that is full of evangelistic talk, but knows its complacency would be shattered if that talk ever resulted in action. It may be in a church that is willing to accept all kinds of people, as long as they play by the rules of the right kind of people.

If such is our church, when the sign of Jonah is made manifest in our midst we too will be angry, perhaps even to the point that we will wish to die. Perhaps members who feel about ethnic minorities the way Jonah felt about the Ninevites will leave the church or will withhold their funds. In any case, it will be a painful process, just as Jonah's process was painful. But, again, no sign will be given to us but the sign of Jonah.

You see, the message of the Book of Jonah—indeed, the message of the entire Scriptures—is about a God who has a strange set of priorities, a set of priorities that do not always agree with the priorities we as individuals or as The United Methodist Church set for ourselves. The entire Book of Jonah is about a God who appoints a prophet to go and save a people who do not even believe in God.

But, if you think that is strange, just look at the last verse of the book, and you will come to the conclusion that God's priorities are really mixed up: "Should not I pity Nineveh, that great city, in which there are more than a hundred and twenty thousand persons who do not know their right hand from their left, and also much cattle?"

Any of us could understand a God who would not wish to destroy a city that had become a center of civilization, whose king ruled over millions of people, whose architectural wonders would awe archaeologists for centuries to come, and whose roads spread in every direction.

But those are not the reasons why God wishes to spare Nineveh. The reasons are, quite simply, the one hundred and twenty thousand infants who are not yet old enough to know their right hand from their left, and the many animals in the city.

When this strange God of ours looks at Nineveh and decides to spare it, God is not looking at its king, but at its children; God is not looking at its armies, but at its animals.

Those who do not know this God of Jonah will most likely believe that the security of Nineveh lies in its armies, in its treasury, in its leadership, and in its king. But God tells Jonah otherwise. Nineveh has been spared because of its children and its animals.

The God who spared Nineveh, the God who in Jesus Christ told us that the last shall be first, has more respect for children than for armies, for animals than for buildings, for the poor whose lives are ruled by others than for those who boast of their power.

If this passage truly depicts the nature of God, it follows that each morning, when God decides to let this nation of ours stand one more day, God is not looking at the Pentagon, but at the Washington zoo; not at Wall Street, but at Harlem; not at the missile silos in the desert of the Southwest, but at those who pass by those silos as they seek in this country safe haven from oppressive regimes. And it follows also that each morning, when God decides to grant the Soviet Union one more day, God is not looking at the Kremlin or at the Russian missiles, but at the babushkas and their grandchildren.

And what is true of nations is also true of the church. The church does not stand or fall on what someone might do or not do at 475 Riverside Drive.[5] The church does not stand or fall on what the bishop and the cabinet might decide. The church does not stand or fall on the plans and pronouncements of General Conference. The church stands on the stone that the builders rejected, but has been made the cornerstone of the entire building—a sign of Jonah indeed! The chuch either stands on that foundation, or it falls.

If this is a building built on that Cornerstone who, being in the form of God, took the form of a slave, it follows that there must be a very special place in this building for those who come out of an experience of slavery.

If this is a building built on that Cornerstone who had nowhere to lay His head, it follows that this building must be first and foremost a home for the homeless and a sanctuary for the refugee.

If this is a building of the God of Jonah and the God of Jesus Christ, whose priorities, strange though they may seem to us, are crystal clear, it follows that there must be a special place in this building for those who bring to it the experience of a reservation, the experience of an internment camp, the experience of a ghetto, the experience of a barrio, the experience of being last, and forgotten, and persecuted.

No sign will be given to us, but the sign of Jonah, the sign of Jesus, that the blind see, that the poor have good news, that the unlikely are brought in. This we cannot change, for this is God's work. The question for us is, as this sign is given, what role will we play? What stance will we take? Will we, like Jonah, wish we could die, because we deplore God's mercy? Or will we remember that we also live by that mercy and join God's gracious work, and rejoice in it?

Reflection

Although this sermon was prepared and preached by one person, it draws on material that was developed by two. It bears the mark of organization by one mind, yet it contains that which originally occurred in dialogue.[6] The setting for the dialogue was a national gathering of Presbyterians with deep concerns for issues of social justice and ecology. The sermon itself was preached later at an Annual Conference of The United Methodist Church, to an audience with more varied interests. Neither setting was a local congregation, and the needs may well have been somewhat different from those found in a congregation. Yet many concerns obviously are common to both kinds of settings as well as to many in local congregations.

In both cases, there were in the audience people who were quite aware of the larger context in which the church lives its life. They were strongly committed to global issues of justice, to specific ministries with those at the margin of our own society, to peacemaking, and to environmental concerns. In fact, in both settings, there were probably more such people than are to be found in many local congregations. The sermon and the original Bible study needed to address them.

What are the particular needs of socially committed people

that the sermon must address? Such people are well aware of the context that surrounds the church, but are often alienated to some degree from the church, precisely because of its frequent apparent lack of awareness. Therefore, a sermon that addresses only those who need to become aware of the wider context often does not directly address the issues that are on the minds and hearts of these other hearers. In addition, there may well be a question as to whether the frustrations, the loneliness and the isolation that come from being concerned with long-range, difficult issues are really worth the struggle, since the problems seem insoluble. The call to be concerned—chiefly addressed to Christians who are not—does not deal with this reality either.

Yet in the setting in which the sermon was delivered, there may also have been a large proportion of those whose vision of the church reached hardly at all beyond the institution itself. In this respect, the sermon faced the same problem as would be found in most congregations, namely, that not all members are at the same stage in their Christian pilgrimage. Some need to be made aware of the wider social context and called to feel concern there. At the same time, others are strongly committed to the wider issues of peace, justice, and the environment. How does one preach in such a situation? This sermon has sought to do that in several ways.

First of all, there is the matter of the selection of the biblical text itself. So often, when the preacher wishes to make the congregation more aware of the wider social context, a biblical passage explicitly dealing with such concerns is chosen. The congregation then can relax, knowing what the preacher is planning to do, and wait until next Sunday, when the "real" concerns of the church come back into focus. What may be far more helpful is to preach from passages that are not so obvious and to show that such concerns are not an occasional tangent for both Bible and preacher, but are rather at the heart of almost all of the biblical message.

Here, a very familiar passage was chosen. In such a case, the preacher must take into account what assumptions about the meaning of the text the congregation already brings to the hearing. In the case of the Book of Jonah, many people assume the chief questions have to do with the controversies over the fish and the need to be obedient to God. Most commonly, people realize that there is a dimension of universality in the message of the book, but take for granted that such a dimension was significant for the people of Israel, who supposedly were more exclusive than we are. The verses on which the sermon focuses are usually glossed over. Focusing on them means that a new dimension can be seen. This requires a close reading of the text, over against what people remember from the story. It may mean printing the text and pointing out specific verses or quoting them with sufficient frequency that it becomes clear that these verses are present, that the ways in which the passage was remembered—the past interpretations brought to the present hearing—have overlooked these verses, that these are not the creation of the preacher but are the biblical text.

The task is to be biblical. It is to show that the concerns for global issues, for justice in the local community, and for the environment, are not recent issues, mere private matters that appeal to some Christians and are quite optional, but are part and parcel of the heart of the Bible itself. Our congregations are not biblically literate. Clear education must be done. To insist on looking at a text, to take seriously all the verses, to preach from that text in a clear and obvious fashion is to do such education. Optional use of pew Bibles is not enough. We must be more clearly biblical than the memories of the congregation, and perhaps even subtly raise the question of why the church had provided them with unbiblical traditions.

Using the lectionary as the basis for preaching does have the virtue of dealing with a wide variety of passages not chosen out of the pastor's list of favorites. In the present case, the lectionary was not used, originally because what was needed was a three-hour Bible study rather than a traditional sermon, and we wished to do a whole, brief book. In that original setting, we did hand out copies of the text and followed it along closely. In the sermon given here, the constant references to the text are clear.

Whatever text is chosen, the preacher must ask the question, even before developing the sermon, What understanding of this passage does the congregation bring to the hearing? Is it a familiar text? What will their reaction be to hearing it read as the Scripture lesson? The preacher's awareness of his or her own past attitudes may well be the starting point, and can be a way of identifying with the congregation. In the present instance, the sermon begins with a history of some of the controversies surrounding the book and places the issues about the fish in the long line of such questions. Obviously, as soon as the Book of Jonah is announced, the controversies will be in the minds of the congregation. They must be dealt with and put aside. This sermon seeks to accomplish this by showing that such controversies miss the major point of the book and then by moving to the issue that will be the concern of the sermon. The issue is identified as God's concern about Nineveh and Jonah's dislike of that concern. There is a second set of clarifications of the text (over against memories brought to it) in the list of false reasons given for Jonah not wanting to go. In every case, it is the text itself that is used to show that such reasons cannot be true. This helps narrow the focus to the central issue: Jonah did not want to go to Nineveh because he did not want Nineveh to be saved, and was sure that God did want Nineveh to repent.

Therefore, in the face of a familiar passage that the congregation would assume they already understood, some undoing of those false understandings is necessary. Furthermore, such challenges must be from the text itself, not a matter of the preacher's preference for one interpretation, or of a psychological reading into the text of the supposed motives of people in such situations as Jonah's. What is needed is a staying with the text that says why Jonah did what he did and failed to do other things. In addition to dealing with the biblical text, there may also be a need to show how this one passage is related to the central issues of Scripture. In the present sermon, this was made natural by the Gospels' use of the phrase, "the sign of Jonah." Jesus' application of the phrase to his own situation made it possible to show that this strange and controversial book from the Old Testament is directly related to the chief issues of the gospel itself.

Establishing how constantly Scripture shows the relationship between the people of God and the wider social context in which they live serves a twofold purpose. For those who are not yet committed to such a vision, it helps clarify that such involvement is not an optional part of the church's life. For those who are so committed, it reenforces the importance of what they are doing and gives them further theological and biblical support for their work. It may help alleviate the sense of isolation and hopelessness such commitment can engender.

With this as a general background, let us look at the four specific elements of analysis raised in the opening essay.

First is the need to be aware of the dynamics of social status between the preacher and the congregation. On the occasion of this sermon, the preacher was a Hispanic male, with sufficient accent to show English was not his first language. That does not lead to high social status in this culture. The congregation was largely Anglo-Saxon, white, and male. There were some women, and some minorities, mostly black. It was the minorities who had urged that this preacher be invited. Many of the members of the majority culture were committed to evangelism, but not necessarily involved in issues of justice.

With all of this in mind, it was necessary for the preacher to establish that the authority for what was being said rested not with the preacher, not with the power of the minority groups, but with Scripture itself. Furthermore, it would be helpful to show that the existing concern for evangelism and church growth could not be pursued apart from the issues raised by the wider social setting without doing damage to the biblical understanding of mission. This also had to be done from the text itself, and not from any intrinsic authority given by the congregation to the preacher. The preacher sought to do this by trying to be as directly and transparently related to the text as possible.

The second element discussed in the opening essay is the need for catholicity of focus. There may be greater catholicity in church gatherings above the level of the local congregation, and that was the case when this sermon was preached. But even so, it was not fully catholic. In an attempt to provide such a wider perspective, the sermon brought in references to groups not present—especially ethnic minorities not there, other nations whom we view as the enemy, children, and the animals. Since most of these were already explicitly in the text, these references were quite natural. One wonders, however, how often they are present and we do not notice them.

The third element raised was the fear of change, especially, though not only, by those who benefit from the status quo. The sermon points out that God is working for change in the situation of Nineveh, and it is Jonah who wants nothing to do with it. Jonah wishes to maintain the present situation of enmity, and God wishes to end it. The sermon therefore raises quite specifically the choice that faces God's people in every generation: to follow a God who does wish some things to be changed or to try to keep things as they are, even when that is opposed to God's will. Jonah poses the question quite clearly, and the sermon seeks to leave the congregation with exactly the same choice that Jonah faced, though it hopes for a different response.

The last element of analysis has to do with the particular theological heritage that has influenced many of our congregations, especially in regard to two issues. The first is the false spirituality that sees little connection between faith and questions of material well-being, the environment, and so forth. The sermon deals with that by stressing God's concern for all of creation, even the animals. Salvation is physical as well as spiritual. The second issue is a false view of Providence that assumes that whatever is, is God's will, and ought not to be changed. The passage has fairly complex implications for that issue. On the one hand, God is working for change and using a human agent, Jonah, to accomplish this. Clearly, Jonah is resisting God by refusing to be involved in this change-effecting activity of going to Nineveh. On the other hand, however, throughout the whole Book of Jonah it is obvious that God's will is going to be done, whether Jonah likes it or not. Although whatever takes place now is not necessarily God's will, God's will is ultimately going to triumph. The sermon dealt with the first half of this paradox, but not with the second. It may well be that, given our particular theological heritage and the weaknesses that it has, the first side of the paradox is helpful. The second could be too readily misunderstood as implying a kind of fatalism. It could take an entire sermon to deal with that issue.

The function of a sermon in the setting of a worship service is to clarify and confirm our vision of what it means to be the people of God in our present setting. Since that vision includes God's purposes for the whole of creation, it is also a new vision of the context in which we live. The goal, therefore, is not simply to interpret the Bible in the light of our context, but even more, to interpret ourselves and our global context in the light of Scripture.

Notes

1. Transcribed by the authors from a recording of a mass in El Salvador.
2. In The United Methodist Church, the Annual Conference is a governing body, often statewide, composed of approximately equal numbers of ministers and lay delegates.
3. Traditionally, one of the main items of business of an Annual Conference has been the reading of pastors' appointments, usually toward the close of the session.
4. The parallel text is in Matthew 12:41-42.
5. 475 Riverside Drive, in New York City, is the address of the Interchurch Center, where a number of general agencies of The United Methodist Church are located. An Annual Conference is presided over by the bishop, who, jointly with the cabinet, decides on pastoral appointments. The General Conference is the highest governing body of The United Methodist Church, meeting every four years.
6. We often speak or preach together, using a form that we call "dialogue." This term, however, is used rather inexactly, for what we do are really lectures, Bible studies, and sermons in which we speak alternatively to the audience, rather than to one another.

2

Preaching
as the Interface
of Two Social Worlds:
The Congregation as Corporate
Agent in the Act of Preaching

Don M. Wardlaw. Consider a congregation called Faith Church with its pastor, David Landry, in an urban center called Metro City.* A growing number of the members of Faith Church are becoming aware of a dimension of Landry's preaching that they do not find in most other churches. The people at Faith Church are beginning to see themselves as active, corporate partners in preaching with David Landry. They are discovering that preaching is essentially a complex interaction of several social realities.

The Social Realities of Preaching at Faith Church

For one thing, David Landry's sermons have become as much an act of the congregation as they are the expression of one individual. Each week five different small groups in the congregation meet to discuss the passage of Scripture for the sermon two Sundays hence and to explore how the Faith congregation walks the streets of that passage today. Most of the time the groups, whether a Tuesday noon business-person's lunch, or a Thursday morning prayer and Bible

---

*The following description of David Landry interacting with his people in sermon formation and feedback groups is a composite of a number of pastors and congregations I have been privileged to serve in this process.

study group, or a Sunday evening discussion group, meet without David Landry. He is present, however, in the form of a page of exegetical notes or ten minutes' worth of exegetical insights on an audio cassette. Dozens of Faith Church members who do not participate in these groups also study the Scripture for the sermon ten days away. They read David's study notes in the weekly newsletter and then launch into their own exploration of the passage, leaving scribblings and suggestions in a special sermon box in the vestibule. David is never bound to use in his sermons any musings or insights of his members, but while his sermons definitely bear his own style and convictions, they nevertheless carry clear traces of a corporate voice of the congregation. These data from the life of the Faith congregation, rich in the people's symbols and values, assure Landry of sermon materials that consistently hit home with his hearers. In short, David Landry preaches as much *for* the congregation as to it.

Nor do the social dimensions of preaching at Faith Church belong only to the people's participation in sermon formation. While David Landry speaks for the congregation, he also preaches *to* his people as a corporate body. Worshipers cannot listen to Landry's preaching long and remain an aggregate of individuals. The words "we" and "us" pop up frequently in his sermons. Landry regularly raises questions about what difference the scriptural text makes to the hearers *as a community* and constantly envisions how the congregation can react *corporately* to the implications of the Word in Scripture. Worshipers get the impression from Landry's rhetoric that he sees himself primarily as a member of the Faith community and secondarily as one set apart to preach to that body. He has the knack of joining his people in the pew at the same time that he addresses them, and of sharing with his folk in a corporate response to the sermon.

Another corporate body impinges on most sermons preached at Faith Church—Metro City with its politics, economics, institutions, demographics, decision-making, and life-style. Faith Church sits next to the City Hall at Fourth and Central by Market Square. The Faith Church steeple and City Hall tower rise together above this intersection, symbolizing in their juxtaposition the gospel's address of the demonic principalities and redemptive possibilities inherent in corporate human power. Landry's sermons cultivate an image of Christ at work in corporate structures to make life on earth more truly human. A check of Faith Church's activities calendar reveals an outreach program that resonates with Landry's preaching. A halfway house for emotionally disturbed teenagers, tutoring programs for educationally deprived youngsters, a community service program for senior citizens, and a hot-line link with a substance abuse clinic, become, in Landry's sermons, ready references to ways in which Christ intervenes in the corporate life of downtown Metro City, to help translate the powers of death into the vitalities of new life. Nor is the target of Faith Church's mission limited solely to the central sector of Metro City. A hunger task force regularly urges the members to be involved in famine relief for northern Africa. Also, the ruling board of Faith Church is presently studying a recommendation from a dozen members that the congregation serve as a sanctuary for political refugees from Central America. The outreach programs at Faith Church work well because they are owned by the people, generated by the same ongoing dialogue within the community of believers that engenders Landry's sermons.

The social realities that come through preaching at Faith Church do not all belong to the contemporary moment, however. Another kind of community regularly comes alive in David Landry's sermons; the body of believers that either foreshadows or gives rise to the sermon's scriptural text. Landry sees to it that his people in the sermon formation process always ask first what the struggle in faith meant, for instance, to those primitive Christians in Corinth or to the faithful in Solomon's temple. In his sermons, Landry invites his people to walk in the robes and sandals of the ancient community in order to be clearer about how to walk in the dress of a relevant body of believers today. Landry serves as catalyst for an interface of his people with the people who sat by the waters of Babylon and wept, or with the band of faithful who were shipwrecked, stoned, and imprisoned on behalf of the gospel. It is as if the sermon were a transfusion of life blood from an ancient faith community to a modern body of Christians.

The above scenario presupposes preaching as a thorough-going societal event, merging the faith experience of an ancient biblical community with the life of a body of believers today. Whatever is said in this chapter about that boundary assumes a dynamic, multi-dimensional view of preaching that sees in the preaching moment a confluence of peoples, times, and contexts. Such a view of preaching, however, presumes too much when compared with the average parishioner's understanding of a sermon's meaning and function. It is important to step aside to clarify the nature of a preaching moment before exploring how preaching can be the interface of two social worlds. Until the decks are cleared with regard to what a sermon is and does, all that is said about the social reality of preaching will make little sense.

The Questionable Linear Model

Until recently most members of Faith Church, as well as David Landry, brought a rather flat, single-dimensional orientation to preaching. They expected the sermon to function as a static, linear transaction, with the sermon as a message, the preacher as sender, and the congregation as passive recipients. This model presumes that the sermon is an objectifiable message, critical information that, when projected from pulpit to pew, promises to change perspectives, and then presumably, to rekindle wills to change the world.

The model carries with it three basic, but questionable presuppositions that now find little sanction in the pulpit at Faith Church. First, the model presumes that the sermon is fundamentally *data about Scripture* to be shared, truth as treasure buried in biblical soil waiting to be unearthed, delved into, and offered to the hearers. Such a view of the function of Scripture in preaching makes no room for the dynamic of God's Word in Scripture. The Word of God, far from being solely the object of a preacher's analysis, is primarily the subject of revelation. The Word of God is fundamentally God's revealing activity, primarily act and event. The Word happens, does things, makes things

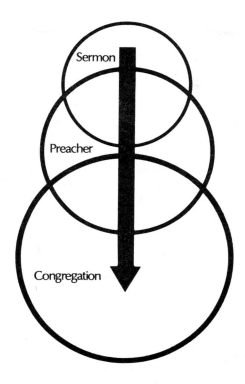

happen. For all their significant differences in interpreting the nature of proclamation, theologians Barth, Brunner, Gogarten, Bultmann, and Tillich agree on one fact that has left a permanent mark on the contemporary Christian consciousness, namely, that in the preaching event God actively engages the world. These theological giants in the early and middle twentieth century rescued preaching from what E. M. Forster once called "poor chatty little Christianity," and, along with their more recent successors such as Ebeling and Fuchs, took Word primarily to be explosive, confrontative power. In David Tracy's summation, this *eventful* Word was

first released in the prophetic and eschatological strains of both Testaments, paradigmatically expressed in the parables of Jesus and the Pauline theology of the cross, retrieved in the word event which was the Reformation and recalled for and in our word-impoverished, wordy culture by those early twentieth-century classic exponents of the power of the Christian proclaimed word as that proclamation disclosed anew the event of Jesus Christ.[1]

While this Word as proclamation event takes on a secondary confessional character as manageable content, it does so only when it is understood primarily as event.

The second presumption about the two-dimensional model is that the preacher most often stands apart from and above the people in the things of the Spirit. This frequently translates into a hierarchical, authoritarian stance in which the preacher, in the language of no less a gathering than Vatican II, "molds and rules" the people. The church for centuries has sanctioned preaching as the expression of a separated, commanding individual. Pulpit and pew alike have been too prone over the centuries to accept as normative for the pulpit a Lone Ranger mentality that elicits visions of an heroic prophet crying from the wilderness of an isolation necessary to maintain prophetic integrity. Admittedly, from such privacy in prayer and study has come profound preaching that at times has sparked visions and started reformations. But how realistic has the church been to assume that the Word in Scripture must depend principally on isolated individuals in pulpits for the communication of its inspiration and wisdom? One of T. S. Eliot's characters, Edward, could as easily be addressing this presumptuous individualism as his wife, Lavinia, when he says:

> One of the most infuriating things about you
> Has always been your perfect assurance
> That you understood me better than I understood myself.

Sometimes this monarchical air and distance is not so much assumed by the preacher as projected on him or her by the people. Pastors in sermon feedback gatherings almost invariably struggle at first to get parishioners to utter any words of evaluation that could be heard as negative. Many people in the pews are so dependent in their faith journey on the preacher's spirituality that they cannot afford to allow their preacher to be reproachable.[2]

Whether this distance between pulpit and pew is assumed or assigned, it violates the identification pastors must have with their people if the Word of God is to come alive in preaching. All preparation for preaching that sensitively tunes into Scripture begins with what Leander Keck calls priestly listening, where "the text confronts the exegete, in solidarity with the congregation, with a word that intersects prevailing understandings and loyalties."[3] When the ministerial identity is anchored essentially in the pew, the preacher stands a better chance to offer an incisive Word from the pulpit. Such an awareness makes a difference in how pastors bear authority in the pulpit and in how pastorally sensitive they are in prophecy, for they are at one and the same time preaching *to* themselves as well as *from* themselves. As Fred Craddock says so well, "If a minister takes seriously the role of listeners in preaching, there will be sermons expressing for the whole church, and with God as the primary audience, the faith, the doubt, the fear, the anger, the love, the joy, the gratitude that is in all of us."[4]

The third presupposition about the linear model sees the congregation as passive recipients of the message. Sometimes this passivity takes the form of a corporate body unquestioningly accepting a denominational party-line from the pulpit. Communions that demand close adherence to detailed doctrinal standards promote this kind of quiescence at sermon time. The congregant's role in preaching is to ingest the weekly dose of doctrine prescribed from the pulpit. This view assumes that the will is harnessed to reason and that a closely honed system of theology is capable of engendering a redemptive life-style.

At other times with this passivity in the pews the listeners function mainly as private consumers, more as an aggregate of individuals than as a corporate body. This privatistic, consumer mentality reflects a predominant ethos of American individualism that takes radical private validation as the only criterion for behavior. Robert Bellah and colleagues, in their book, *Habits of the Heart,* describe this reigning value of American life: "Separated from family, religion, and calling as sources of authority, duty, and moral example, the self first seeks to work out its own form of action by autonomously pursuing happiness and satisfying its wants."[5] This American individualist sits in the pew distrustful of most corporate alignments, listening selectively to the preacher for information and inspiration useful for self-validation. Hence, the silent pew, made up of people who either over-invest corporately or under-invest individually in what comes from the pulpit.

As this chapter continually insists, the congregation, far from assuming a passive stance at the preaching moment, engages God's Word and is engaged by that Word as actively as the preacher. Listen to Craddock again: "Historically and theologically the community and the book belong together in a relationship of reciprocity. This means the church does not sit passively before the Scriptures but rigorously and honestly engages its texts."[6] This also means that the active participation by the members begins with the sermon's conception rather than after its delivery. The preacher is much more interested in inviting the hearers along in a search for the Word's meaning than in declaring in prepackaged fashion the meaning they should have already found. Sermon design and rhetoric will reflect this indicative stance, envisioning the hearers as co-creators of the response to Scripture, as partners in the Word-event. This elevated view of congregational responsibility and participation in the preaching moment presupposes that the people in the pews can serve as active sources of theological insight. Preachers who understand that the Word seeks dialogue with the *body* of the faithful, even in the preparation and delivery of the sermon, will so restructure their sermon preparation regimen and alter their rhetorical strategies that they make room for the whole people of God in the pulpit.

A Dynamic, Multi-Dimensional Model

What, then, constitutes a viable model for preaching that features the kind of dynamic, multi-dimensional approach of a David Landry at Faith Church? The following preaching model encompasses the two sets of social worlds inherent in the preaching moment. Investigation of this model will begin by focusing first on the social realities of the world of today's preacher and congregation. Once the social constructs of the contemporary side of the model are established, then the discussion will turn to the dynamics of corporate life inherent in the scriptural text. The investigation will then conclude with an examination of how the model shows the corporate dynamics in today's preaching situation bringing to fruition the social vitalities of the text.

The preaching model that is faithful to the social worlds inherent in the sermon moment, rather than establishing itself on a line that carries message, preacher, and people in sequence, actually presents itself in a loop of three interlocking circles within an encompassing circle. The diagram on page 64 presents the basic holism of preaching with its integration of scriptural text, preacher, and community of believers, all set in the surrounding social context. The point of confluence at the heart of the model, the dynamic swirl of interaction of Scripture, preacher, and people, *is* the Word-event. A fundamental point this model makes by its very gestalt is that the preaching event consists of a cluster of dynamic interactions. Brandon Scott gets at the interactional character of meaning when he writes, "Even for an author, meaning is not in the mind but is a relation between imagination and text. A writer works out meaning in the act of communication."[7] The meaning that becomes the Word at the preaching moment consists of three key interlocks: the interface of scriptural text with preacher; the interrelation of preacher with people; and the interconnection of the people with Scripture. This loop of threefold interplay, all set in and sensitive to the contemporary social context, constitutes the Word-event. We now look more closely at these three interactions of the preaching moment as a way of unfolding the meaning of the social dynamics of preaching.

Scriptural Text and Preacher

Sermon formation begins when the preacher, in solidarity with his or her congregation, cocks an ear toward the text in

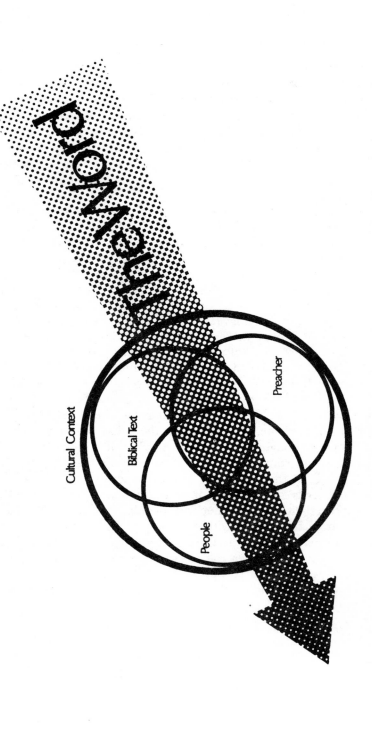

Cultural Context

Biblical Text

Preacher

People

the Word

Scripture. In an enterprise characterized by wave upon wave of words, sermons that become Word-events gestate, ironically, in eerie silence. David Landry sits in his upstairs study in the manse, doing preliminary work on his sermon. He has just finished a second reading aloud of the Scripture pericope scheduled for the first Sunday in November. He leans back and stares out of the study window. A creative silence comes to his soul that belongs to the stillness that preceded the creation of heaven and earth. Landry listens prayerfully and intently to a quiet that almost rings in his ears, a hush of eternity from which will emerge pictures of possibilities from the pericope. Such listening belongs to the nature of revelation itself. As Craddock says:

> A preacher can recover and reclaim the silence that he or she carries within, and out of that silence, speak the Word. It demands the realization that a minister's life does not consist in the abundance of words spoken. But most of all it requires embracing both silence and revelation in one's understanding of God, and developing a mode of preaching which honors that understanding by being in harmony with it.[8]

David Landry will go to the shelves later for help from commentaries and other critical tools in order to grapple with the historical, political, and cultural realities behind the lines of the text, and to wrestle with the literary and structural issues between the lines of the passage. But for now he hangs in suspended animation spiritually, waiting for the wings of the Spirit to give flight to his imagination for the first breakthrough insight that will spark the beginnings of the sermon.

Preacher and People

But listening to God's Word is always a corporate affair. Note how many times in the book of Acts the Holy Spirit gives guidance to the primitive church when the people are gathered *together* in prayerful expectation. Jesus affirmed the importance of the corporate setting for revelation when he said to his disciples, "Where two or three are gathered in my name, there am I in the midst of them" (Matt. 18:20). Sermon formation truly begins, then, when the body of believers, not just the preacher alone, listens for God's address in Scripture. The preacher discovers that this incorporated hearing helps safeguard him or her from forcing truncated agendas on the text. David Landry can testify that his Tuesday noon downtown group or his Sunday evening sermon forum, while not robbing him of his calling to preach the gospel as he sees it, has nevertheless kept him out of many blind alleys in seeking to ride the trajectory of the text into today. When David Landry listens in early morning solitude in the privacy of his study for the dawning of meaning from a scriptural text, he knows he is even then listening in solidarity with his congregation. He knows Andrew Abrams, one of his elders, will have had an ear on that passage the same morning before opening his hardware store and will be responding with insight at the Tuesday noon gathering. Landry also knows that Betty Salinsky will join a circle Bible study at ten o'clock that morning that will seek in holy silence some vision with that same pericope. Landry will open the sermon box in the vestibule on Wednesday and will find among a dozen notes his weekly word on the text from Sid Shoemaker. Landry now knows in ways he could never have dreamed of several years ago that listening for God's Word in the first moments of sermon formation is the province not of pastor alone but of a cloud of witnesses joining their pastor.

For David Landry such an experience of incorporated listening week in and week out has also cast a different light on the meaning of his ministerial leadership. James and Evelyn Whitehead accurately describe Landry's experience when they point out:

> The minister today is seen less exclusively as the one who *brings* God and more as one who helps *discern* God, already present. The minister is a skillful attendant . . . one whose role is to listen for the Lord's presence and to assist other believers in their own attentive response to God's movement in their lives.[9]

Albert van den Heuvel sums up this transformation in Landry's preaching and pastoral leadership when he says,

"The renewal of the preaching ministry is the rediscovery of its communal character."[10]

People and Scriptural Text

The upshot of Landry's seeking solidarity with his people in the first creative silences of the sermon's gestation is that the listeners, in James Sanders' analogy, are being coaxed onstage to participate themselves in the drama of redemption. The spotlight now shifts and the people themselves are entering the plot of the scriptural passage, joining with the characters and living their story. The loop that begins with the interplay of text with preacher in Landry's early morning solitude moves to include the interaction of Landry with his people in order to give integrity to that first hearing. But now the loop closes back upon the text, and in so doing, brings the people into direct interface with the passage. Now the people of God are accountable to the scriptural passage because they know of the tolling of grace firsthand. "Where the Bible's message is preached," writes Leander Keck, "the congregation is invited to appropriate (not merely affirm) its meaning, and so identify itself with the biblical faith and the world church."[11] Anyone can simply nod in assent to the preacher at the door following the sermon. Those who have appropriated the sermon from its inception, however, will more nearly identify with what has been said as direct address from the pulpit.

The Cruciality of Cultural Context

If hearing God's Word is a corporate affair, it is just as importantly a contextual affair. The circle that encompasses the interaction of biblical text, preacher and people, represents the cultural context of the hearers. This outer circle says that God's Word comes to fruition only in terms of the particular cultural setting of the hearers. For Don Browning, culture means "a set of symbols, stories (myths), and norms for conduct that orient a society or group cognitively, affectively, and behaviorally to the world in which it lives."[12] God's Word in Scripture always addresses itself to Israel or to the church at the level of the symbols, stories, and norms that related God's people to the socio-political particularities of their day. In the Old Testament the Word speaks through Israel's day-to-day life and death issues, as in bondage, wilderness, tribal life, nationhood, war, corruption, and exile. And if the Word's target in Scripture was the crucial happenings of God's people, so, too, was the Word's form always in the frame of reference of the people God addressed. God was revealed in Israel's and in the primitive church's history, not ours, and hence spoke the language of their time. Rather than a radar beam, God was cloud by day and a pillar of fire by night; God's prophets spoke in pastoral rather than industrial imagery; God set the drama of redemption in the static three-story language of their universe rather than in the dynamic one-story language of our universe.

The supreme example of the Word's social contextuality is seen in the incarnation. When John, in one of the most penetrating verses in the New Testament, says, "And the Word became flesh and dwelt among us" (John 1:14), he shows the Word seeking its ultimate target and form in the person of Jesus Christ. If the Word's target is always where the action is, John implies the same with his use of the word, "dwelt." The Greek word for "dwelt," *skenow*, is the same word used in the Septuagint for "tabernacle." The tabernacle was for early Israel a special tent for worship and sacrifice that was always set up at the heart of the Hebrew encampment no matter where Israel was in her desert wanderings. The tabernacle was the dwelling-place for the special presence of Yahweh. Thus, wherever Israel went, God was always specially present in her midst. To say, then, that the Word "*dwelt* among us" is to say that the Word chooses as target the heart of the common life of the people of God, wherever that might be in their pilgrim wanderings. The Word, *by definition*, lives in the midst of the cultural context of God's people.

Preaching seeks from the Word it embodies an analogous target and form in the world. As Craddock says so succinctly, "The way of God's Word in the world is the way of the sermon in the world." This means that without the bold particularity of the preacher riding the biblical text's trajectory to direct hits on specific targets today, interpretation of the biblical text has not taken place. Craddock says, "Interpretations and sermons . . . are not sent out to 'Resident' or 'Boxholder' or 'To Whom It May Concern.' "[13]

David Landry does not hesitate to speak directly to corporate social issues about abortion, drug abuse, ecological rape, or minority rights in Metro City and beyond because he understands social contextuality as the norm for the Word realizing itself. Any people and pastor wishing to take God's Word in Scripture seriously, therefore, will regularly be asking what issues or values in the surrounding society are addressed by that Word. A sermon on the parable of the good Samaritan, for example, will dress the priest and Levite in the particular garb of the sermon's social locale if the Word is to hit home. In a racist community in the United States priest and Levite could be prejudiced blue-collar citizens who still fight to maintain closed neighborhoods. In Nicaragua, priest and Levite could be the United States that kept to the other side of the road when this Central American nation languished in the ditch under a dictator's heel. In a South African shantytown, a black preacher might see priest and Levite as Western nations that soft-pedal sanctions against the apartheid government in Pretoria. Without such particular contexts, a sermon remains a collection of useless abstractions, timeless comments that can never be timely. The Bible is its own best witness to that fact in that Scripture came into being through a process of contextualizing interpretation and by its very nature asks for the continuation of that process.[14]

The preacher is constantly challenged, then, to enflesh the sermon in the prevailing symbols of the congregation's culture if the sermon is to be heard. The preacher is the keeper of the store of the people's values and images, the currency with which they trade in meaning. As Brandon Scott says, "The preacher is entrusted with the community's metaphorical stock, its repertoire."[15] Robert Worley speaks of this metaphorical stock as "the manifest culture" of a congregation. "The set of perspectives manifest in a congregation," says Worley, "influences the style and content of sermons, the language of the preacher, the type of illustrations, etc. If a preacher cannot preach in a manner consistent with the set of perspectives that is manifest in a congregation, he or she is in trouble."[16] Many pastors remain in trouble, or are at least ineffectual in their preaching because as keepers of the store they assume sole responsibility for choosing and displaying the people's metaphorical stock. They exercise few options for discovering the range and depth of that repertoire of images and symbols, relying too often on private intuition and guesswork alone to determine how the sermon will dress and walk.

Several years ago, David Landry learned what a friend he has in the social sciences which help him mind the store at Faith Church. He learned from the social sciences how to "read" the environment of Faith Church, all the way from discovering the social networks and patterns in downtown Metro City to learning how such configurations connect with the wars, poverty, political oppression, and inflationary economies that mark the globe.[17]

First, David's faithfulness to the social contextuality of the Word pushed him to reach for some handles for grasping the structure and flow of the neighborhood where he lives and ministers. A week after he moved into his parish he began taking a series of late afternoon walks to acquaint himself with the various social worlds in this inner district of the city. He got into the sights, sounds, and smells of this world. Who's the man with a French pastry who sits by himself in the delicatessen and stares out the window at passersby every afternoon at five o'clock? How will John Donovan's sporting goods store make it here on Euclid Avenue when the new mall is completed four blocks away? Who owns that grand Victorian house that is so neglected and run down?

David Landry also began getting a feel for the delivery of basic services in the central sector. He visited both family practice health care centers in his district, found that AA met three blocks away at First United Methodist Church on Tuesdays, targeted where Big Macs and pizzas waited for his kids' eager grasp, noted the number of shops on Central Avenue that would be difficult for disabled persons to enter and found that there was no clinic for substance abuse and no shelter for the homeless for two miles in any direction. At one of the early meetings of his ruling board, David confirmed these impressions and enriched others from the board members' responses.

Four months after his arrival, the newly formed Long-range Planning Committee at Faith Church, with David's insistence, derived much helpful demographic information about this district of Metro City from the Lake County Planning Board. As the Faith Church committee sought to develop a pathway into the future, it worked with census data on ethnic diversity, household changes, and patterns of age groups in the district. It studied levels of family income, employment patterns, types of housing units, population mobility, and poverty pockets in the area.

One of the members of the committee, Jim Jensen, who teaches sociology at the Lake County Community College nearby, helped David and the committee locate the social classes, ethnic groups, and helping groups in the district and see how much interaction they have with one another and with the power at City Hall and in business.

In addition to providing a technique to grasp the social dynamics of the immediate urban environment, David Landry also learned from the social sciences how to get a feel for the identity of Faith Church. In helping the Long-range Planning Committee get moving, Landry led the members in exercises to identify what Max Weber calls the "webs of significance" of Faith Church, the network of natural awarenesses, beliefs, values, and goals that make up the culture of the congregation. Since a history of Faith Church had just been finished a few months before he arrived, Landry invited the committee to begin its work with a study of this history; the story of the church's founding, its significant experiences in the past, critical turning points, its line of important personages. Landry then helped the committee match its own story with its denominational heritage, noting where the people at Faith Church had cherished its sacred deposit from its total past and where it had gone its own way in the shaping of its local tradition.

Next, Landry helped the committee conduct a series of cottage meetings that uncovered the world view and character of the congregation, along with what symbols and rituals have become important for them. After two months of sifting through the data from the cottage meetings, the committee came up with some interesting conclusions. They discovered that 30 percent of the members think of God's intervention in their lives as only occasional but dramatic. Fifty-five percent feel that God actively engages their lives all the time in the normal processes of human interaction. Fifteen percent believe God is more elusive than engaging, a hidden unfolding reality encountered in meditation, prayer, or altered states of consciousness.[18] David Landry was helped immeasurably by these data in determining as pastor and preacher how to talk with people about how God works in their world. In particular he determined that the half of his congregation who see God as more absent than present in the world, would need help in thinking about God's presence if his preaching to them about God's abiding care for the oppressed were to mean anything.

Landry and the committee also derived help from the questionnaires regarding the character or personality of Faith Church, those traits and dispositions of the congregation as a whole that distinguish it from other parishes. They learned that Faith Church's morale does not easily erode in crisis, that the outlook for the future is almost naïvely rose-colored, and that the manner of doing things at the church is corporately, rather than individually, oriented. The committee determined the controlling symbols and rituals in the congregation's life. The stained-glass windows and the huge wooden cross top the list of visual symbols held most dear. Family-night suppers and Sunday evening hymnfests rank high as symbols of the congregation's fellowship. Some symbols the people struggle with, such as the chandelier in the vestibule that some feel speaks of ostentation, or the stiffly decorated church parlor that many feel is more mausoleum than a meeting place.

The rituals the congregation ranks in preference also proved illuminating. The structure of the Sunday morning liturgy received the strongest affirmation, with the funeral's accent on the resurrection and the wedding's emphasis on worship not far behind. Controversial rituals include the way the sacraments are administered. Members disagree on the use of a common loaf and common cup in the Lord's Supper, or on how water is to be applied in baptism. Some members are restive about seating patterns at worship that are too strung out to express the unity of the worshipers. Some respondents do not care for Sunday greeters who seem too assertive or deacons who would rather count money and gab in the basement than stay with the worshipers at sermon time.

In uncovering this store of information about his congregation's context and identity, David Landry could thank the social sciences for facilitating his entree into the culture of Faith Church. Yet, Landry also knows that societal studies serve only as tools for enabling a people to give meaningful context to the gospel in their lives. The Whiteheads offer a helpful perspective here:

> The . . . findings of social sciences are important tools in understanding the contemporary situation. But it must be stressed that what the social sciences provide for the community of faith is not answers but access to resources. Determining the shape of the contemporary Church remains, under the influence of the Spirit, the task of the believing community.[19]

As social scientists assist pastor and people in developing a rich fund of the stories, traditions, world views, character, symbols, and rituals of a congregation, chances for God's Word impacting the congregation in profound ways are greatly enhanced. The people have made accessible to themselves and to their pastor their metaphorical stock. A wise pastor will use that stock for the currency of his or her sermons, recognizing that such a practice not only ensures meaningful communication, but also improves the chances of God's Word being heard in its depth and power.

The Social World of the Scriptural Text

Up to this point the investigation of preaching as the interface of two social worlds has delved only into the social dynamics of the contemporary preacher, congregation, and social context as they are addressed by the scriptural text for the sermon. These understandings gained from the preaching model should enhance the important remaining task of examining the social realities of the sermon's text. The same social dynamics apply to understanding an oracle of Ezekiel or a pronouncement of Paul as they relate to the moment today when the sermon happens among the faithful. Sensing those ancient corporate realities and learning to bring them into creative correlation with the social factors of Faith Church constitutes one of the most creative challenges in preaching. When the sermon becomes the vital moment of interface between contemporary and ancient social worlds, then the Word of God happens.

The preaching model already established to depict the contemporary social dynamics of a preaching moment serves as a convenient model for the social realities of the scriptural text. This model of the corporate life inherent in a passage of Scripture features obvious parallels with the model of a present proclamation event.

As with preaching, so with Scripture, a biblical passage is as much a communal act as the expression of a single author. The way Scripture itself was born and nourished validates such a claim. The events that became the church's story of salvation happened to a community of believers. Both the old and new Covenants were made with a community *as community*. The story of the holy history of the people of God is cradled in community, shared in community, guarded, and offered to the world by community. The Old Testament prophets, seeming paragons of charismatic individualism, declared the Word of the Lord from within the community as committed members of the community.[20] John the Baptist, often regarded as a loner, proclaimed God's will from within his band of disciples. Supremely, Jesus Christ, the incarnation and epitome of the declaration of God's Word, referred to himself as the Son of man, a term in the Old Testament for the community of Israel.[21] This Son of man surrounded himself with twelve disciples, a deliberate representation of the twelve tribes of Israel, the community of faith he embodied. In short, Jesus embodied in himself communal proclamation. In addition, however individualized is the expression of the authors of the New Testament epistles, what they have to say cannot be understood apart from the

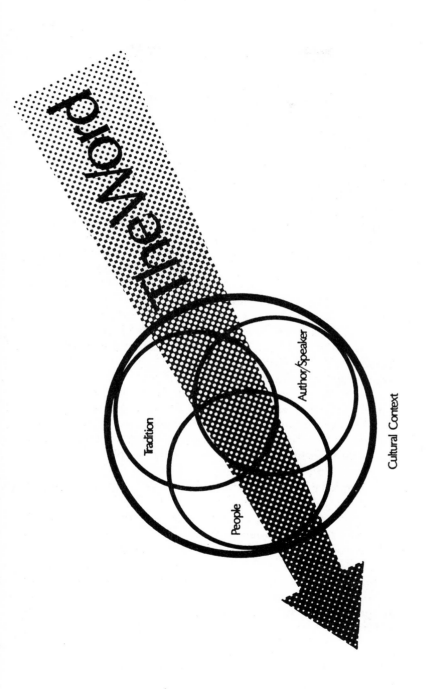

corporate life of the faithful who brought these authors to new life, who put in their hands an established tradition and fueled the passion and agenda of their writing.

From Genesis to Revelation, God is revealed in an unfolding communal dialogue. As Eugene Ulrich and William G. Thompson conclude, "Scripture, which began as experience, was produced through a process of tradition(s) being formulated about that experience and being reformulated by interpreters in dialogue with the experience of their communities and with the larger culture."[22] This tradition, told and retold, shaped and reshaped as world views of believing communities evolved, was heard by these communities as the Word of God.

The model on page 75 of the corporate life in a passage of Scripture carries some of the same important dynamics that emerge from the preaching model. First, the Word of God in Scripture is no more a lodestone to be mined than the Word that comes through the sermon. God's Word as revealing action is just as dynamic a phenomenon in the formation and witness of the Bible as it is in the formation and witness of a sermon. Word happens at the confluence of author/speaker, community of faith, and cultural context.

Second, the author/speaker of the biblical passage is as much a receiver of God's Word as its conveyer. Those individuals who put down on parchment the tradition that the community of believers garnered and protected for them, spoke primarily as a part of God's people even when they sounded as if they stood apart from the faithful. When the prophets railed at and rebuked their people, they nevertheless did so as committed members of those people, willing to join them in the exile of which they warned.

Third, the community of faithful in, or implied by, a passage of Scripture is just as actively engaged with God's Word as is the author/speaker. As with a sermon, so with the formation of Scripture, the people of God as community are co-creators with the author/speaker of the passage of Scripture. Every school of criticism in biblical studies assumes a faith community that cradled the formation of the passage.[23] Form critics now realize with reference to the Psalms, for instance, that the "authors" of the Psalms were more communities than individuals. A canonical approach, in Brevard Childs' words, "interprets the biblical text in relation to a community of faith and practice for whom it served a particular theological role as possessing divine authority."[24] Structuralism, the critical theory that asserts that meaning is a function of the structures of a cultural system, presumes communities that give rise to and nurture the structures of that culture. Structuralist criticism of Scripture looks to structures of a faith community's corporate mind for meaning. Hence, each theory of criticism implies a body of believers actively participating in the formation and perpetuation of that tradition.

Fourth, God's Word is no less contextually oriented in Scripture than in preaching. Biblical scholars have recently turned to the social sciences for clearer insights into the social forces that molded faith communities in Scripture, all in an effort to sharpen the reading and interpretation of the Bible.

"Historical method and sociological method," writes Norman Gottwald, "are different but compatible methods of reconstructing ancient Israelite life and thought."[25] The insights of anthropology, ethnology, social anthropology, ethnography, archaeology, structural anthropology, and psychology are now fair game for students of Scripture in seeking to walk the streets of King David's Jerusalem or the Apostle Paul's Corinth. Wayne Meeks' notable work on the social world of Paul, *The First Urban Christians,* gives the church a fascinating workaday view of its primitive forebears.[26] Examining the Pauline corpus with a sociological eye, Meeks uncovers the earliest Christian community as a scattering of small colonies throughout cities of diverse local character. These local cells of believers, while highly unified, intimate, and exclusive, still interacted routinely with the larger urban society. The social correlate for these early Christians' intimacy was the local household assembly where interpersonal engagement is strong, authority structure fluid, and internal boundaries are weak. Such studies assume an important interface between the words of a scriptural passage and the social reality undergirding those words. Close examination of the social contexts of the various communities of faith in the Bible, therefore, sheds new light on the faith of those believers. What is at stake here is the social contexuality of God's Word in Scripture.

Gottwald stresses the cruciality of this when he writes, "[The biblical] writers lived in an everyday world of their own and many of the topics and interests of biblical texts reflect the conditions and events of that everyday biblical world which it is folly to ignore if we want a well-rounded understanding of ancient Israel." The exegetical approach that attempts to "spiritualize" or "abstract" texts at the expense of social analysis, in Gottwald's words, "flattens and denatures the powerful individualities of style and content that play throughout the rich texture of the Hebrew Bible."[27]

Interfacing the Two Horizons

The preaching moment, therefore, is a time when two social worlds come together in the proclamation of the Word of God. As Norman Gottwald urges:

> We must at one and the same time interpret both the social situations and the literary idioms of the biblical texts and the social situations and literary idioms of *ourselves as interpreters/ actors.* This is the multidimensioned interpretative task now widely called . . . the hermeneutical "fusion of horizons."[28]

The model on page 79 attempts to portray that interface. Here the dynamic world of the biblical text becomes the Word of God that extends itself through the dynamic world of the contemporary preaching situation. As the Word springs forth from the vortex of its ancient setting to express itself through the vortex of text/preacher/people in social context, the Word of God *happens;* it becomes a proclamation event in the lives of the people experiencing the sermon. At this point of confluence in the preaching model, the absolute cruciality of the pulpit makes itself known, for as David Tracy asserts:

> Without the actuality of proclamation, the [New Testament] narratives lose their character as confessing narratives and become . . . quarries for historical reconstruction. Without proclamation, the symbols (cross-resurrection-incarnation)

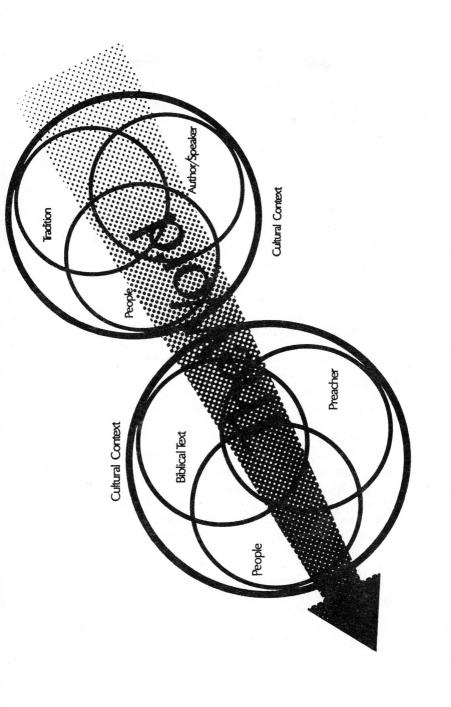

Tradition

Author/Speaker

People

Cultural Context

Cultural Context

Biblical Text

Preacher

People

lose their tensive, religious reality and become occasions for
other kinds of reflection. . . . Only with a sense of the
religious-event reality named proclamation is the New
Testament recognized anew as the Christian classic text, the
scripture.[29]

Where scriptural text, with its own social dynamics,
interacts with preacher and people in social context at the
preaching moment, then God speaks from that swirl as surely
as Yahweh spoke to Job from the whirlwind. In this
harmonious communion of two social worlds the Word of
God speaks meaning to a people and even becomes the
chemistry of change in that people. In T. S. Eliot's words:

> music heard so deeply
> That it is not heard at all, but you are the music
> While the music lasts.

Interfacing the Two Horizons in a Sermon

I preached the following sermon on Pentecost Sunday at a
large suburban congregation outside Chicago. In fairness to
the congregation I shall use fictitious names for this
congregation and community. The congregation shall be
called the Community Church and its town, River Oaks,
Illinois.

Had I been the pastor of the Community Church, I would
have worked with a sermon preparation group from the
congregation in the formation of the sermon. Since,
however, I was a guest preacher that Sunday and had no
access to such a group there, I turned to a group of clergy in
south Georgia with whom I was working several weeks prior
to Pentecost and asked them to be my sermon formation
group. These were pastors I had been leading in a continuing
education venture in preaching over the previous ten
months, preachers who were working with sermon preparation groups in their own congregations.

The Georgia pastors began by imagining themselves as
members of the Community Church in River Oaks. Since I
have acquaintances in the congregation and had preached

there twice before, I felt that I was on speaking terms with the congregation. The Georgia formation group began by assuming the identities of the bankers, lawyers, doctors, and business executives who are in such evidence at the Community Church, successful professionals most of whom work in the Loop in downtown Chicago forty minutes away. The group also identified with the majority of women in the congregation who are homemakers with growing or grown children and with busy schedules in volunteer work and social activities.

The group immersed itself in the ambience of River Oaks, a lovely exurban village with its studied country quaintness, winding wooded drives, and imposing homes. This quiet "edenic" ethos proves an apt setting for people in River Oaks to pursue the dominant, traditional values of marriage, family, and career. Yet this idyllic scene has its dark side. The affluence and power that permeate River Oaks bring with them expected problems of emotional breakdowns, divorce, substance abuse, and a high teen suicide rate. The atmosphere of luxury and ease also makes it difficult to sense the cruciality and immensity of social issues beyond its borders. While the leisure mentality that pervades River Oaks recognizes that a cruel world rages just down the road, it chooses a posture of gentility and repose that seems to ignore that world, a stance that serves as an apparently deserved reward for doing battle in the power corridors of that world during the week.

For two hours my south Georgia sermon formation group worked to connect the world of Jesus' followers at Pentecost with the world of the Community Church in River Oaks. Our text for this Pentecost sermon was Acts 2:1-13, the opening verses of the account of the church's birth amid the dramatic coming of the Holy Spirit. Each of the seven pastors had already done exegetical spadework in the historical-critical issues in the passage. Now, in solidarity with seven colleagues, I listened to these verses for God's Word to the Community Church in River Oaks.

I gained a number of insights from this group exegesis that proved critical in the formation of the sermon. Some new light came to me amid the group's acting out the Pentecost event. Before we turned to any exegetical insights generated by our individual historical-critical investigations of the passage, we immersed ourselves in the dramatic flow of this Lukan account of Pentecost. We left our tables and books and occupied open space in our classroom, imagining we were Jesus' disciples in that upper room in Jerusalem, waiting for his promised Spirit. We sat in a circle and talked about what it must have been like to pray for ten days together for some kind of reunion and renewal with Jesus. Some got into this imaginative identification a little deeper and began to talk about their sense of failure as disciples when Jesus walked with us. It was as if no matter how hard they tried to follow Jesus along those Galilean roads, the Kingdom never took good root in their souls.

Then, we as a group got into the cataclysm of the wind and fire at Pentecost. We determined to see to what extent our bodies could "tell" us things by literally acting out some of the action in the passage. We got down on our knees in a circle, held hands, and "heard" the thunder, "saw" the flames that shook our bodies and souls. Then we were on our feet, spilling out of the room as if we were newly charged disciples tumbling down the stairs to the streets to engage Jewish pilgrims in their own language.

Once we got beyond the uneasiness that we adults often bring to such role play because we feel safer intellectualizing a reality than trying to embody it,[30] two insights struck us that dictated the shape and accent of this sermon.

First, the literal acting out of Pentecost gave us such an awareness of the event kinesthetically that we determined the sermon had to be structured along narrative lines if the hearers in River Oaks were to have much of a chance to taste and feel the coming of the Holy Spirit.

Second, our enactment of the event underscored for us two radical swing points in the story: (1) the *personal upheaval* amid wind and fire that jarred the disciples into new life, and (2) the *movement* of the disciples from the prayerful safety and quiet in the upper room to the hustle and excitement *of engaging other seekers* in the streets below. In its narrative shape the sermon would lead the hearers through a Pentecost that would be grounded in radical, often painful upheaval, and would reach its stride in the missional stance when they shared their new life with others in surprising ways.

When our sermon formation group returned to our discussion table after our role play and shared further insights from our earlier historical-critical homework, two further revelations came into focus for the sermon.

First we were struck by how *middle class* Jesus' disciples actually were. Recent sociological studies of the New Testament suggest that Jesus' band of followers, far from being ignorant peasants, were a group of capable merchants, entrepreneurs, organizers, and motivators, people recruited from the hustle of the business and political world at that time.[31] In this fact I had a crucial point of identification between the power brokers in the pews in River Oaks and the disciples who waited in the upper room for heaven to break loose.

Second, we came into a new awareness of what it can mean to be given the gift of speaking another's language. We had already noted that the miracle of tongues dramatized in this passage in Acts involved the disciples speaking known languages rather than the ecstatic utterances usually associated with glossolalia. Hence, we got into a fruitful discussion of what it means to be given the gift of speaking another's language. We talked of language as the extension of being. Hence, to speak in another's tongue is to be given the capacity to identify closely with the other person and to find the sensitivity to be open to the other person's need. Speaking in the tongues of other seekers at Pentecost, then, means among other things entering deeply into their lives to promote *shalom,* or wholeness. The devout Jews thronging the streets of Jerusalem at *Shabuot,* or the Feast of Weeks, in celebration of the day the Ten Commandments were revealed to Moses, were in one sense not too different from Jesus' followers in the upper room. Both groups were hungry for wholeness, one questing after it in the promise of the Mosaic law, the other seeking it in Jesus' last earthly promise. Pentecost would empower the seekers in the upper room to offer this wholeness to the seekers in the streets below. And

Pentecost would *drive* Jesus' followers to help other seekers find wholeness. Hence, the title and theme of the sermon were born.

With the above insights gained through this corporate hearing of God's Word in Acts, I went to the drawing board to shape the sermon. I would give the sermon the shape of Acts 2:1-13, involving the hearers at the Community Church of River Oaks in the dramatic action of Pentecost. I would begin by assuming that many hearers in the pews at River Oaks find it difficult, by virtue of their education and sophistication, to imagine what the Pentecost of Acts 2 would be like, much less feel any degree of comfort with such a cataclysmic experience. I would plan to spend little time, however, attempting to argue them into a sense of connection with that upper room in Jerusalem. Rather, I would take them to that room and let them experience in a narrative format their own Pentecost with its sense of expectation, its traumatic upheaval, and its drive to help others find wholeness.

One important key in interfacing the two horizons would be the use of the Community Church's metaphorical stock in the representation of Pentecost. I would help the people of the Community Church see themselves in the capable, first-century entrepreneurs who sat in the upper room praying for new life. I would work to avoid trivializing the wind and the fire in that upper room by bringing these primal elements through my hearers' lives as the upheavals in marriage, family, and careers that jar us into new possibilities for wholeness. I would picture their speaking other pilgrims' language as exercising new sensitivities in their professional lives that promote wholeness in the social structures where they work. My concentration would be wholly on images of their witnessing in their work world as a means of counteracting the temptation to believe that God as Holy Spirit is mostly at home in the wooded lanes of River Oaks. In all, I would so refashion the Pentecost experience that the hearers in River Oaks might feel the winds of the Spirit come upon them to claim them, surprisingly, for witness in unlikely places.

Pentecost: Driven to Help Seekers Find Wholeness

And they were amazed and wondered, saying, . . . "we hear
them telling in our own tongues the mighty works of God."
(ACTS 2:7, 11)

I

Your first reaction to Pentecost may well be that
  there's little place for you in that upper room.
Such a scene may offend the sensibility of your spirituality.
Why not just slip quietly out of the room and down the stairs
  and let some holy roller take your place up there.

But there's a deeper sense in which you belong there.
Some spiritual part of you has always been at Pentecost.
Like the genetic pool of your and my spirituality,
  it came into full force and focus that dramatic day.
We were there when all heaven broke loose.

Do you remember that strange calm before the Spirit came?
We sit in that upper room in expectant silence.
Quite a contrast with the hubbub below of milling crowds
  of religious pilgrims, devout Jews from everywhere,
    Phrygia, Egypt, Cappadocia, Judea, Libya—
An estimated one million seekers were down there
    for the annual festival of the Feast of Weeks,
  one million pilgrims choking the streets
     designed to accommodate fifty thousand,
  seekers after *shalom,* God's wholeness and peace.

But above the jostle and hum of the seekers
  we sit in our quiet space.
We're local people, ordinary people. No super spirits.
Over there, Simon Peter, business entrepreneur,
  with his small fleet of fishing boats.
Next to him, Matthew, bureaucrat and tax man,
  on leave from his regional office near Jericho.
Then there's Simon the Zealot, political activist,
  good organizer and motivator.

And on around the room, James, John, Andrew, and the other
    disciples, and the women, and about a hundred others.
Capable, sensible people.
People you might see any morning nowadays at the 7:37 train,
    in business suits with attaché cases, bound for the Loop.
Ordinary people waiting for Pentecost up there above the
    seeking millions.

So we sit and wait.
We sit with Christ's promise, not sure what that
    Spirit will look or feel like when Pentecost happens.
All we know is that Christ promised to empower us for mission
    and so we wait prayerfully, expectantly, silently.

Then, the Spirit breaks loose.
God's order explodes into our order.
A deafening, thundering sound like a Kansas tornado.
A rush of warm wind slams us all into a huddle,
    making our hair stand on end.
Crackling streaks of flame pop and dance about our heads
    as we clutch at one another in fear and awe.
Finally, the swirl of heat and thunder above our heads
    turns into a pressure cooker within us
        that explodes in acts we never knew we were capable of.
Now we're on our feet, tumbling down the stairs,
    driven by the Spirit out into the melee of seekers
    in the streets below.
Surprising words start tumbling from our mouths.
We're talking other people's language,
    standing there eye-to-eye with Parthians, Medes,
        Pamphylians, Romans, Cretans, Arabians,
            telling them about the wholeness God gives,
                putting it in their own thought frame,
                    their own symbol system, their own language.
The Spirit has driven you and me out of our prayer room
    to help seekers find wholeness. That's Pentecost!

II

Now look again today out the windows of that upper room.
The Parthians, the Medes, the Pamphylians are still down

there in our streets, hungering for wholeness,
     pilgrims in search of inner peace.
Up here in this room you and I wait again for the Spirit,
     not really feeling special, spiritually.
We're capable people. But ordinary people—
     in the things of the Spirit.

As you and I sit together in the quiet, you tell me
     your story.
Like Peter, James, and John, you've tried to follow Jesus
     for some time, but only so much of it really "takes."
You've sought Jesus for years in Sunday school.
     You've done time for Jesus on church committees and
          boards.
          You've listened for Jesus in a thousand Sunday sermons.
               You gave money to Jesus, even wrote letters and
                    made house calls on Jesus' behalf.
Still, something's missing.
While He sweats blood at Gethsemane,
     you, with us, still fall asleep at His side.
While He gets crucified again and again at City Hall,
     on Capitol Hill, at Corporate Headquarters,
          or even at your own breakfast table,
     you, with us, only stand at a distance and watch.
At a distance you don't say much. Nor do I.
We simply ease away one more time into our own shadows
     with Peter and weep for want of a Pentecost
     in our own lives.

The wholeness isn't there. We don't really
     have our act together. Our spouses could tell you that.
          Some people at the office could tell you that.
Surely we're capable enough to have enjoyed some
     power in our friendships.
But we know there's a wholeness that's missing.

Where's the Pentecost that will open the flow of personal,
     emotional, and spiritual power within us?
Where's the Pentecost that will so ground us in ourselves
     that we will be less controlled by anxieties and fears?

Where's the Pentecost that will break the dam of distrust
    within us and give us more of a flow of trust
        both of ourselves and of others?
So we sit in the upper room and wait for Pentecost.
And then the Spirit breaks loose.
God's order explodes into our order
    like a tornado rearranging the landscape of our psyche,
    like cleansing fire spreading through our souls.
Wind and fire sweep through this upper room of our habitual
    spirituality to upset the self-protective scene
        we have built around ourselves.
Maybe your Pentecost begins with the wind and fire
    that sweeps through your marriage,
        in some cases destroying the marriage entirely,
    in other cases radically rearranging the relationship.
But in the wake of the pain and struggle, you are
    learning at last how to love and how to be loved.
You are seeing how even through the wind and the fire
    God's Spirit is moving you toward wholeness.

Maybe your Pentecost begins with the wind and fire
    that shakes your family life to its foundations,
        when your son confesses he is gay,
            or when your daughter is hospitalized for depression,
                or when your son can no longer hide his addiction.
But now with professional help and much confrontation,
    and much reconciliation, you begin to see the flames
        that once seemed to sever family ties as the very
            fire that cauterized long-standing wounds.
You are seeing how even through the wind and fire
    God's Spirit is moving you toward wholeness.

Again, maybe your Pentecost begins with the wind and fire
    that leaves your career hopes in rubble,
        when the company power-play leaves you on the street,
            or when the budget crunch cuts all your work away,
                or when the people upstairs plot your demise.
But now, with the help of family and friends, you see
    yourself rise from the career ashes like a phoenix,

not only with a new job, but also with sounder
　　values and your head at last screwed on straight.
You are seeing how even through the wind and the fire
　　God's Spirit is moving you toward wholeness.
However your Pentecost begins, the pattern's so often
　　the same. Wind and fire shake your whole space,
　　　and traumatize you and me into new perceptions.
We're beginning to see what it looks like to be human
　　beings, to respond to God's Spirit in our lives.
We're beginning to see the Spirit move us toward wholeness.

III

Then comes the climax of this contemporary Pentecost.
The swirl of wind and fire above our heads
　　turns into a pressure cooker within us that explodes
　　　into action we never knew we were capable of.
At some point we're on our feet, down the stairs
　　reaching out to seekers in the streets below.
And what's amazing is how readily and naturally
　　you can speak the language of those seekers,
to share with another seeker in his or her own language
　　the gift of wholeness.
What a gift of the Holy Spirit to be able to do that!
Look how speaking in other tongues happens today.
To speak another's language is to enter deeply
　　into that other person's world to promote wholeness.

Maybe you are a surgeon who was once content
　　to use your surgical skills on your cancer patients
　　　to remove tumors while letting the patient adjust
　　　　to the process the best she or he could.
But then the wind and fire of Pentecost comes
　　and now you find yourself driven by the Spirit
　　　to enter much more deeply into your patients' lives.
You start a center for holistic surgery.
You recruit a team of professionals to work with you
　　in promoting peace and wholeness with patients,
　　psychotherapists to help them focus on hope,

physical therapists to help them learn to
be at home in their bodies again.
You are helping seekers find wholeness.
You are entering deeply into their lives,
speaking in *their* language with God's gift of wholeness.
Or maybe you are the first woman executive in a corporation
where the existing idea of management is more a matter
of headship than leadership.
For a while, you are good at rules and regulations for making
the employees do what you want them to do.
But then the wind and fire of Pentecost comes,
and now you find yourself driven by the Spirit
to enter much more deeply into your people's lives.
You find yourself treating your staff as if they have
capacity for creative input into company planning.
You get help in learning really how to listen.
You begin working to reshape policy structures so the workers
can begin owning more of the company work process
and sharing more of the company vision.
You are entering more deeply into your employees' lives,
speaking their language, with the gift of wholeness.

Or, maybe you were once a lawyer who enjoyed a sizable
reputation for ably defending clients
who had the money to pay for your services.
You know how to work the legal system to make things
happen pretty much the way clients want them
to happen.
For you, working for success and working for justice
were not necessarily the same thing.
But then the wind and fire of Pentecost comes,
and you find yourself driven by the Spirit
to enter more deeply into your client's lives.
Your life-style now isn't as important as it used to be.
You surprise yourself by taking on more than a few clients
who hardly have a dime, but who have been unjustly
violated by the system.
You've fallen in love again with justice,
and with the chance to be a part of others'
quest for wholeness.

•

You are entering more deeply into your clients' lives,
   speaking their language with the gift of wholeness.

So, seeker, do you wonder if there's a place for you
   in the upper room?
Well, think again—
   Feel the wind of the Spirit against your face.
    Feel the fire of the Spirit spread through your soul.
And listen, seeker, to how you're beginning to speak.
You're offering the gift of wholeness.
Pentecost has come!
And it comes again and again.

Reflection

The theme of this sermon centers on the reenactment of Pentecost. That ancient event happens again today when the Holy Spirit surprises and empowers expectant Christians to share in depth the ways God brings wholeness with those seeking such wholeness. Many Christians at the Community Church in River Oaks may not see themselves as worthy or capable of being used by God to reach other people in this way. Therefore, the purpose of this sermon is so to involve them in the drama of the Acts 2 account that they will sense the possibilities of their becoming involved as the Holy Spirit's instruments of wholeness.

I begin *with* the congregation and seek to engage and expand their imaginations rather than admonish them. As they move out, I redraw the picture of the waiting disciples so that they are no longer distant images on the horizon. Then I combine the strange experience of wind and fire with the all-too-familiar struggles of many in the congregation until there is a fusion, an identity of the past with the present and the present with the past. The Word of God at Pentecost is a contemporary Word.

The specificity of the examples from personal circumstances, in part two, allows me to particularize about more controversial areas in public life in the final section. If the congregation can recognize that God may be involved in their own lives, they are better able to be led by the Spirit to be

God's instruments in the world where they work and play and vote. Grace that is experienced grounds the call to service. The personal and the social are linked, not through ideological arguments, but in a theological understanding of grace. The affirmation of Pentecost compels a new approach to the world. A social analysis of the world of the biblical text and of the congregation enables a fresh and broader hearing of the Word of God.

Notes

1. David Tracy, *The Analogical Imagination: Christian Theology and the Culture of Pluralism* (New York: Crossroad Publishing Co., 1981), 389.

2. The conclusions from this paragraph are derived from the author's work with dozens of pastors who have worked with formation and feedback groups in their congregations.

3. Leander E. Keck, *The Bible in the Pulpit* (Nashville: Abingdon Press, 1978), 63.

4. Fred B. Craddock, *Preaching* (Nashville: Abingdon Press, 1985), 26-27.

5. Robert N. Bellah et al., *Habits of the Heart: Individualism and Commitment in American Life* (Berkeley: University of California Press, 1985), 79.

6. Craddock, *Preaching*, 129.

7. Bernard Brandon Scott, *The Word of God in Words* (Philadelphia: Fortress Press, 1983), 16.

8. Craddock, *Preaching*, 55.

9. James D. Whitehead and Evelyn Eaton Whitehead, *Method in Ministry* (New York: Seabury Press, 1980), 82.

10. Albert van de Heuvel, quoted in Clyde Reid, *The Empty Pulpit* (New York: Harper & Row, 1968), 67.

11. Keck, *The Bible in the Pulpit*, 107.

12. Don Browning, *The Moral Context of Pastoral Care* (Philadelphia: Westminster Press, 1976), 73.

13. Craddock, *Preaching*, 52, 137.

14. For more on this important subject see Craddock, *Preaching*, as well as James Sanders, *God Has a Story Too* (Philadelphia: Fortress Press, 1979).

15. Scott, *The Word of God in Words*, 77.

16. Robert C. Worley, *A Gathering of Strangers* (Philadelphia: Westminster Press, 1976), 81.

17. For particular help in understanding the social realities of a congregation, see Jackson W. Carroll, Carl S. Dudley, and William McKinney, eds., *Handbook for Congregational Studies* (Nashville: Abingdon Press, 1986).

18. For a helpful chapter on the comic, romantic, tragic, and ironic world views of congregations and how to identify them, see the chapter by Jackson Carroll and James Hopewell on congregational identity, *Handbook for Congregational Studies*, 21-47.

19. Whitehead, *Method in Ministry*, 76.

20. For a helpful survey of the literature on the communal orientation of the Israelite prophets, see John S. Kselman, "The Social World of the Israelite Prophets: A Review Article," *Religious Studies Review*, 11, 1985, 120-29.

21. See T. W. Manson, *The Sayings of Jesus* (London: SCM Press, 1954), 141-42.

22. Eugene C. Ulrich and William G. Thompson, "The Tradition as a Resource in Theological Reflection—Scripture and the Minister," in Whitehead, *Method in Ministry*, 36.

23. For a helpful review of the communal character of different schools of biblical criticism, see John Barton, *Reading the Old Testament* (Philadelphia: Westminster Press, 1984).

24. Brevard S. Childs, *Introduction to the Old Testament as Scripture* (Philadelphia: Fortress Press, 1979), 74.

25. Norman K. Gottwald, "Sociological Method in the Study of Ancient Israel," in *Encounter with the Text: Form and History in the Hebrew Bible*, ed. M. J. Buss (Philadelphia: Fortress Press, 1979), 69.

26. Wayne A. Meeks, *The First Urban Christians: The Social World of the Apostle Paul* (New Haven: Yale University Press, 1983).

27. Norman K. Gottwald, *The Hebrew Bible* (Philadelphia: Fortress Press, 1985), 32, 608.

28. Ibid., 607.

29. Tracy, *Analogical Imagination*, 274-75.

30. For more consideration of the values in such an approach to group Bible study, read Walter Wink, *The Bible in Human Transformation* (Philadelphia: Fortress Press, 1973).

31. For a summary of viewpoints and this consensus, see Robin Scroggs, "The Sociological Interpretation of the New Testament: The Present State of Research," in *The Bible and Liberation: Political and Social Hermeneutics*, ed. Norman K. Gottwald (Maryknoll, N.Y.: Orbis Books, 1983), 341-43.

3

The Preacher
as a Social Being
in the Community of Faith

Edwina Hunter. Social scientists and psychologists have long known the value of telling one's story and of sharing personal descriptive histories.[1] It is essential, historians tell us, to know where we have been in order to project where we want to go. Narrative theology and narrative preaching are opening new vistas in theological education. Theologians and professors of preaching are saying that awareness of our own histories helps us discover how our personal narratives intersect with biblical narratives.[2] We can discover how to "own" the texts we preach as we know ourselves better and discover the journeys that make us who we are.

If we claim our own histories, if we know who we are and why we are, and if we know how to reflect on those influences that have shaped us, then we may be able to initiate change. We may even be able to transform ourselves and our immediate concrete situations.[3] The preacher who undertakes reflective and critical self-analysis may well be on the way to the greatest freedom he or she has ever experienced: freedom to preach; freedom to challenge theologies that would claim God's love is limited to the rich and the powerful while excluding the poor and the powerless; freedom to act out a commitment to social justice; freedom to envision new faith communities and new ways of being faithful to God, to God's people, and to self.

Self-reflection would appear, then, to be a first step for the preacher who is committed to growth. And self-reflection is best begun with autobiography—with the stories of the preacher's existence and formation which will include the actors and the relationships that are a part of that personal history. In order to illustrate this narrative process as graphically as possible, two preachers were interviewed. Both are male; one is black, the other white.

These two persons were chosen for several reasons. The first is that they are both widely regarded as prophetic preachers. The second is that they are well-known to me and an element of trust is needed for more candid storytelling. The third is that they are men and, although I might wish it otherwise, male preachers have been primary role models in my own faith journey.

The interviews took place in offices of the churches where the two men pastor. Both interviews were recorded on cassette tapes and notes were taken as well. They were both asked to speak as fully and openly as was comfortable and to tell and reflect on the stories of their calls to ministry, their formative faith communities, their spiritual formation, and their social consciousness. Only rarely were they asked questions once they had begun speaking, because interruptions tended to break into the flow of images and memories in a way that did not appear helpful to the reflective/analytical process.

Two Journeys to the Pulpit

James Alfred Smith, Sr., is pastor of Allen Temple Baptist Church in Oakland, California, and is president of the Progressive National Baptist Convention. He serves as adjunct professor at three different seminaries in the San Francisco Bay Area. Dr. Smith carries the image of pastor/prophet in his East Oakland community. This image extends well beyond the immediate community because of his leadership in Allen Temple and because he is invited to preach in churches and seminaries across the country. He preaches social justice and leads his faith community to participate actively in many social justice enterprises in East

Oakland. These include: developing prenatal care for expectant mothers, providing low-cost housing for the elderly, forming political coalitions with Hispanics, Asians, and Caucasians, waging war against drug traffic, and conducting a Job Information Center for all unemployed persons.[4] In addition to leading the church to address social justice concerns in such practical and far-reaching ways, Dr. Smith has served a term on the Oakland School Board after being elected by more than 80 percent of the vote.

There is a special mark of this great man that seems unusual in a preacher of his stature. He is totally unselfish of his pulpit; for him, it is truly God's pulpit. He makes a practice of inviting the greatest black preachers (both men and women) of the nation to preach at Allen Temple so his people can hear them. Allen Temple has been host to Bishop Desmond Tutu, as well. Dr. Smith also invites Caucasian preachers to preach, again both men and women. Student preachers find a warm welcome to the pulpit of Allen Temple and response and encouragement from the congregation, which has become a teaching congregation under Dr. Smith's leadership. He always makes a practice of using language inclusive of race and gender and is an advocate for women's ordination.

Dr. Smith's sermons have three primary themes: spiritual and economic liberation for his own people, helping them develop what some would call black pride, but what he terms "self-esteem, a sense of somebodiness"; the church's mission as the Body of Christ in the world; and reconciliation and relationship—"Relationship is what the gospel is all about for me." Sermons on these themes are undergirded by carefully selected biblical passages. Moses and the Exodus event are almost always, explicitly or implicitly, present in his preaching. Closely allied to these themes are the writings of the eighth-century prophets. Luke's Gospel and the Jesus of Matthew 25:35-45 keep his sermons tuned to the mission of the church. A growing edge for him is to be found in Paul's writings ("I used to have a lot of trouble with Paul," he says); particularly important now are such passages as Galatians 3:23-29 and II Corinthians 5:14-20.

When Dr. Smith talks about preaching, it soon becomes

evident that a rich spiritual component supports and permeates all he does and says, and that worship, including music, is the essential framework for preaching. He says the preacher is like a jazz musician who improvises on a theme. The jazz musician receives the signal that it is time to play solo for eight bars or maybe sixteen. He or she must then take the theme and improvise, play out all the feelings and expressions of the theme, letting the music soar into the very beings of those who listen so they are no longer listeners only, but themselves become part of the music. Now, what can we and Dr. Smith discover about how he came to be the preacher and prophet he is? What narratives from his earlier faith communities reveal how this social and theological development has occurred because sociology and theology are inextricably linked? Why does he preach the themes he does? Can we see reasons from experiences in his early faith community? The first theme is, in his own words, the theme of "self-esteem, of somebodiness" preached for his own people.

Young Jimmy Smith was born out of wedlock to a mother who worked as a domestic in Kansas City. His mother, grandmother, and an aunt and her husband pooled resources, shared what they had, and survived—more than survived. It was from his grandmother Jimmy heard the Bible stories instead of nursery rhymes and such stories became the stuff of his childhood imagination. The stories of the Exodus of the children of God under the leadership of Moses were the earliest tales he heard and the most often repeated, and they are central in his preaching today.

His mother's work as a domestic meant that she often had to live away from home during the week, but on weekends she was at home and showered Jimmy with love. As he grew, she also showered him with experiences that pervade his preaching. She purchased black newspapers for him to read, introduced him to black history, and, most importantly, made sure he heard in person all the great black leaders and preachers who came to Kansas City. She encouraged him to keep a scrapbook on these orators and ensured his exposure to the great liberation leaders of his race. He remembers, particularly, Dr. Daniel Arthur Holmes,[5] a Kansas City pastor, whom he describes as a "great giant of a preacher, poet, and scholar." He was a brave man and one of the few black men who could tell racist politicians they *were* racist, and they would not do anything to him. He saw Holmes as the "clarion voice, speaking out on behalf of the black community, pointing his finger at racists." Jim was strongly attracted to the ministry because of the prophetic voice of this preacher.

His community of faith was further expanded in an unusual direction when his mother began working for the family of "a humane Jewish lawyer named Levy." Jim would frequently go to their house with his mother and he worked there helping with parties. Through the Levys he met a rabbi with whom he had a number of conversations. He once overheard the rabbi talking with his mother. The rabbi told his mother of the Jewish teaching concerning the possibility that any son born to Jewish parents may be the Messiah. Then the rabbi told Jim's mother, "Give your son a sense of somebodiness."

That experience, together with one Jim had a little later, increased his own "sense of somebodiness." There was an older man, a Mr. Boswell, in the church he attended. One day, as Jim walked down the street, he saw Mr. Boswell on a porch and he called out a greeting. Mr. Boswell called back, "Jimmy, Jimmy, Jimmy, come here. Jimmy, there's a place in the world for you. You repeat it. There's a place in the world for you." Dr. Smith says, "When I get discouraged now I can hear it—that old man saying it, ringing across the years."

A second theme in Dr. Smith's preaching is that of social justice for all. It is clear that, for him, the preaching of D. A. Holmes and Martin Luther King, Jr., was not just for those members of one church or one race. Through the stands they took and the risks they ran, James Smith has been inspired to work for social justice in the larger community. When his "call to preach" came, it came filled with the content of the totality of the church's mission.

But it is necessary to go back and sketch the setting in which another stage in Jim's call took place. The child Jimmy was so drawn to the great preachers he heard from so many different denominations he would slip out in the backyard and "preach" in imitation of them. However, as a teenager he became disillusioned by what he saw in his own church: a congregation composed of "a young pastor, old deacons, and all women," a congregation that did not sufficiently support pastors and their families either emotionally or financially. He began to rebel. By then he loved jazz and decided to become a jazz musician. Jazz was "the thing" in Kansas City at that time with Count Basie and others making their mark. As a junior and senior in high school, Jim played professionally with adult musicians. In the summer after his junior year, he was invited to play with a band that needed a "good E-flat alto saxophone player."

> Grandmother said it was sinful; I was gonna go to hell. Mother said, you have to live your own life. Go. So I went.
> It was there in that context that all those biblical stories became more than stories. It was there I really understood what sin was. Before then sin was just a Bible verse I had memorized. . . . The prodigal son story was just a story, but playing in a band, being out on the road, one night stands in western Kansas, southern Missouri, and Oklahoma helped me to understand the Scripture. . . . One night while reading the music (down in the pit) and looking at the dancing girls (on stage), I became so unhappy, so miserable, so sick, so joyless, so dull because the Scripture I had memorized in my Sunday School came to me: "What would it profit a man to gain the world and lose his soul?" So, I decided then, I didn't want to be a jazz musician. And I said, I've got to preach the Gospel. But it can't be a sweet bye and bye Gospel. I've got to deal with the problems I see all people facing; basically the problems of injustice in the black community. I knew it was possible for us to live and work for the Kingdom of God.

Then Dr. Smith told of a YMCA conference the year he was a junior in high school. He was the only black student delegate to be chosen from Missouri to attend the conference that met on a college campus in Iowa. He recalls:

> I remember two young white gentlemen saying, "Come on James, let's go to the show." We got down to the movie theatre. They got their tickets and told me to come in. I was still standing there, scared. Then the lady selling the tickets said, "Come on in. You can go. Come get your ticket." And I lived in that integrated environment for a week and I knew the Kingdom of God was possible because of that experience, and so that helped me dedicate my life to the Kingdom of God.

This story bridges themes two and three. Dr. Smith preaches a gospel that takes the church beyond its own walls—to wage war against drugs in the street, to form coalitions of Hispanics, Asians, and Caucasians to work for changes in social systems and structures. He also preaches a gospel of reconciliation and relationship. He knows such is possible because he knew a Jewish family and a rabbi, because he attended a YMCA conference where he knew one full week of integration, because he is able to see with eyes made clear through the preaching of prophet-preachers such as D. A. Holmes, Mordecai Johnson, A. Philip Randolph, Mary Bethune,[6] and because the young pastor who befriended him as a small boy and taught him, "It's all right for a Christian to play marbles." He said:

> Christ has to do with relationship to God, to each other, to self. That's what the Gospel is all about for me. I find that theme in my preaching. For me there is a new family alignment that transcends blood, race, and nationality. Because I didn't know my father, Jesus is my big brother and God is my father. . . . I don't understand the hatred between some blacks and the Jewish community because I remember the Levys and I remember the great rabbi who stood with D. A. Holmes in Kansas City way before Martin Luther King, Jr., brought that kind of ecumenicity.

He went on to quote II Corinthians 5:18 about our being given "the ministry of reconciliation." Then he said:

> You never know where help is going to come from. You never know who your friends are going to be. There was William Lloyd Garrison[7] and Frederick Douglass[8] and all through history you see those parallels. There is Pharaoh but there is also Pharaoh's daughter. And there is Ahab but there are saints in Ahab's palace who have never bowed their knees to Baal. And even Paul said, "The saints in Caesar's household greet you." . . . I preach this: the Pharaoh's very own daughter may be a saint incognito!

And preach it he does! It is a preaching firmly grounded in a family and faith community history that was rich in spiritual elements, where a grandmother prayed aloud and woke him each morning singing a gospel song, and where the whole family prayed together each evening. His social and theological beginnings were woven together in a manner that produced one whole cloth. His seminary education (where "I could concentrate on critical biblical scholarship because I already knew the biblical content and narratives so well") and his later faith experiences and human encounters made it possible for him to analyze and interpret his own history in a way that has freed him to preach from the totality of that experience to the totality of human experience, encompassing as it does suffering and celebration, alienation and reconciliation, sin and redemption.

Dr. Smith's socialization took place in an arena considerably different from that experienced by most Caucasian preachers. From the beginning he knew what it meant to be discriminated against because of his race and because he had no father. He knew what it meant to work in the homes of the wealthy and see his mother cleaning up after them. It is little wonder, then, that he has taken up the cause of social justice and the spiritual and political fight for racial equality. The wonder is that he also loves, that he also preaches the gospel of reconciliation. Somewhere there have been those who served as Pharaoh's daughter to rescue him from the stream of bitterness and the river of hostility that might have flowed toward those who decreed he had no right to live in their world.

The personal story of a white male preacher may demonstrate how a person whose beginnings were in a totally different social milieu may arrive at a strong commitment to and theology of social justice. The story is that of Dr. David L. Bartlett, a former professor of New Testament at American Baptist Seminary of the West, United Theological Seminary in St. Paul/Minneapolis, and the Divinity School of the University of Chicago. He presently serves as pastor of the Lakeshore Avenue Baptist Church in Oakland, California, and as adjunct professor of Preaching and Field Education at Pacific School of Religion in Berkeley.

David was born into a white middle-class preacher's family. Both his grandfathers had been preachers, as was his father. All three demonstrated more social consciousness in their preaching than was typical of American Protestantism of their generations. Dr. Bartlett remembers most vividly his father's strong stand on matters of war and peace. As the elder Bartlett spoke out against the draft and against any form of universal military training, he also took a stand against Senator McCarthy and his anti-communist activities. This resulted in the FBI sending agents to attend worship and monitor his sermons. Dr. Bartlett recalls that his father served as pastor of two churches that integrated white and black people. Both his parents had a strong appreciation for social justice issues. The elder Bartlett had been a student at Colgate Rochester Divinity School after Walter Rauschenbusch[9] was no longer there, but Rauschenbusch's students were still there mediating his influence.

The two congregations Dr. Bartlett remembers best from his early years were "struggling with the whole issue of inclusiveness." The members, in his view, "represented conservative forces who were upholding the best values they saw around them while, at the same time, giving permission to people who were going to be more renegade, so that by and large, the church people I was around growing up were not models of radical social action."

What David learned early from the example of his parents (and the FBI visitation in worship) was that there may well be consequences for taking a stand that goes against societal norms. It was an important lesson and one he was to verify through his own later experience. While living in New Haven, Connecticut, he was involved in the peace movement and became a resister to the Vietnam war. A number of people in the church of which he was a member and of which he had been pastor could not accept what he was doing and so became estranged from him, some of them remaining so to this day. He notes that they felt that it was all right to disapprove of the war but it was not all right to break the law.

Within this framework, it becomes important to discover if there are growing edges for David Bartlett, if there are areas for him that are different from those that concerned his parents. Two primary areas he identifies immediately are the role of women in church and society and the acceptance of gays by the church and their role in the life of the church.

He reports that women students in his classes and women

theologians impressed him with the rightness of their cause and so intellectual assent came early. It took longer to use inclusive language and to internalize the cause of women.

For him, the gay issue was harder. Why? He says, "I think because it was an issue that people had not thought about very much and I came to it without any mentors or forebears to help me think it through, whereas in issues such as race relations and war and peace, there were a lot of folks of my father's generation who pointed the way."

This thought led him to recall a third growing edge:

> The whole move from acceptance of black people to the Black Power concept came when I was active in New Haven as the Executive Secretary for the Black Ministerial Alliance; that forced me to have to rethink where I stood, whether a white person had any right to have that job in the first place and what Black Power meant vis-à-vis those of us who were part of the white establishment. That's one that I'm still working out. As long as we are freely associating, both in my present position and my theological position I think the fact that we have white churches and black churches is a scandal. I understand that the black experience is rich and important, but I think, somehow, that ought to be brought into the mix and not segregated and separated. I know a lot of my black brothers and sisters stand against me on this one.

When it was suggested to him that too often when churches integrate, the white mode of worship dominates, he replied, "I admit the puzzlement. We've thought, if we move, one thing we would like to do is to be white members of a black church since we have always seen it the other way."

Asked if he considers himself a prophet, Dr. Bartlett answered, "Only on the days I feel despised and rejected—which aren't many." He recalled a "prophet" he knows who is never happier than when stirring up people, and added:

> I don't particularly like conflict and I don't particularly enjoy controversy. When I get up and say something controversial I do it dreading the consequences rather than kind of reveling in them. So I need to be on to myself to make sure I don't back off. . . . No, I don't see myself as prophetic. I see myself more as a traditional preacher in the Reformed mode who tries to interpret Scripture to the needs of the congregation. But

there is no way you can do that without getting involved in social and political concerns. You just can't. If you pretend you can, you haven't really dealt with the Gospel and significant issues.

It became evident in further discussion that Dr. Bartlett sees his attitude toward, and use of, Scripture as a primary difference between him and his father as preachers. Whereas his father's training was shaped in the classical liberal tradition and his sermons tended to be topical, Dr. Bartlett's training at Yale and his own experiences have moved him to ground his preaching more directly in the Scriptures and, as he said, "When you do that, you have to get involved in social and political concerns."

Analysis of Personal Histories

The first step for the preacher who is committed to growth is personal reflection—remembering and telling the stories of call to ministry, formative faith communities, spiritual formation, and social consciousness. The second step is to analyze *how* these experiences have shaped the preacher's spiritual and social consciousness. Joe Holland and Peter Henriot, two practitioners of social analysis, put it this way: "Effective pastoral planning necessarily involves this movement *from anecdotal to the analytical.*"[10]

Call to Ministry. Both James Alfred Smith and David L. Bartlett grew up in Christian families. Both were members of a larger faith community from an early age. The economic circumstances of the families and the nature of the faith communities were different and yet both acknowledge the role of family and faith community in creating the framework in which a call could be heard. Dr. Bartlett's call appears to have been a gradually emerging consciousness that the path his father and grandfather had walked was a good path for him. Dr. Smith, on the other hand, while deeply influenced by the strong, prophetic black preachers his mother made sure he heard, exercised considerable resistance to the call initially. He clearly saw what a young black pastor's life was like. He saw how poor pay and living conditions affected not only the preacher but the preacher's family as well. Scripture verses were the seed that had been planted in him; at the right moment they burst into growth and opened his heart to the call of God.

But the whys must be asked. Why did these two respond as they did? Other young men have grown up as David did, the sons and grandsons of preachers. Many have been embittered by the experience. Many have left the church refusing to return. And how many young black men reared in similar conditions to those of young Jimmy Smith have found their way to education and ministry and the respect of so many people that he has? Why was J. Alfred Smith called to preach and led by God to the place he is now when so many in like beginnings have fallen by the wayside?

Faith Community. It is impossible to ignore the role of cultural socialization experienced by J. Alfred Smith. That culture was transmitted to him by every member of his immediate family and by the music that was a way of life, by all the preachers he heard, by the very nature of the family structure, and by the society in which he lived. He received all sorts of messages from that cultural milieu. Some of these directly contradicted others. Some messages said, "You are poor and black and illegitimate—not much of anybody." But the contradictory message was louder because it *was* different and because it offered hope. The rabbi, his mother, Mr. Boswell, and all those brave black leaders he heard gave him the message: "You are black. Be proud of it. You are somebody. You can do something." And in one week at the YMCA Youth Conference he discovered the possibility of becoming bilingual and bicultural—of living in a wider world than the one he had known.

He attended an all-white seminary where his black culture was considered something to rise above. He was taught to think critically and rationally and in an orderly way. He was taught to "preach white." He left that seminary having lost the immediacy and power of his "native tongue." He could no longer speak the language of his own people. It took self-analysis and great intentionality for him to relearn his native tongue and to rediscover his cultural roots and embrace his cultural heritage. Now he is proficient in the language of his own culture and people. Now he is truly bilingual.

As a bicultural, bilingual person he is well-equipped to fulfill a much more clearly defined call than that which he originally received. He is now a molder and shaper of a faith community that affirms and celebrates rich traditions of black worship, music, and preaching but also lifts up the equality of men and women in the sight of God and the liberation of all oppressed people—particularly people of color.

It is equally impossible to ignore the role of cultural socialization experienced by David Bartlett. He grew up in white middle-class America, a "preacher's kid." Family members were well-educated, and David had role models to follow which pointed him to liberal and just causes and the best education possible. His study of the Bible particularly, and his capacity to interpret Scripture in the light of contemporary social movements and political and world events have sensitized him to the need and demands of persons very different from himself.

David Bartlett has discovered multiple ways of living in a faith community. In his own family he and his wife are truly partners, collaborators in writing and creating, joint caretakers of their children. In the church in which he is minister, an ethnically mixed church, he is pastor to all and is guide to a faith community that seeks to invite and acknowledge the full and equal participation of all persons: men, women, straights, gays, people of color, and whites. He preaches the gospel with integrity and he challenges the faith community to be a community of justice.

Spiritual Formation. Here again, culture plays a strong role. Prayer for Dr. Smith comes as naturally as breathing. From earliest childhood his grandmother prayed aloud and the family prayed together daily. Black church tradition, when untampered with, encourages the expression of feelings. Joy and sorrow are equally expressed. The dialogue of the sermon with the people vocally encouraging and affirming the preacher is a spiritual movement all its own. Celebration is an extremely important part of worship because hope is seen as both a gift of God and a way of keeping faith with God. What is overtly present and observable in the black worship experience of Allen Temple is also present in Dr. Smith. His spiritual formation, his way of relating to God, is both a personal and corporate manifestation.

Rarely can Christians from white middle-class North America claim the same sort of relationship with the spiritual life of the corporate body. Individualism[11] plays a more decisive role for us in all parts of our lives and is, unfortunately, manifest in the way we function in church as well. So many hymns of the less liturgical churches are filled with singular personal pronouns. Even though they are sung collectively, they are the expression of personal individual piety.

David Bartlett's spiritual formation was affected by this individualistic tradition. Prayer had certainly been a part of his personal life; however, personal and faith community experiences of crisis are now making the corporate dimension more important. By his own testimony, time in prayer and a deepening spiritual life provide both courage and energy to preach publicly what he believes to be the Word of God on matters of social justice.[12]

Social Consciousness. It is clear that early childhood experiences helped shape the social consciousness of both Dr. Smith and Dr. Bartlett. What is equally clear is that injustice and oppression continue to call forth deep commitment from both of them. Each has developed a facility for self-reflection and critical analysis. Each has the spiritual integrity to deal honestly with difficult questions. Each reads widely and places himself deliberately in situations where personal biases can be challenged and critiqued. Each has become skilled in asking himself the "why" questions that challenge the status quo. They know that "we must move from issues . . . to explanations of *why* things are the way they are."[13] They have learned what Robert McAfee Brown calls "hermeneutical suspicion."[14]

Here is where the preacher who is committed to growth begins a third step—asking the why questions that help us understand who we must be and how we must act to challenge the status quo. We have done the reflection. We have told the stories of call and faith community, of spiritual and social consciousness. We have attempted to analyze how these experiences have shaped us. Now we ask the questions that will reshape us and re-*call* us.

What if, in our own development, we have resisted becoming involved in social justice issues? Brown asks: "How adequate is our hermeneutics, our method of interpretation, if it leaves us complacent with the way things are, or committed only to tepid changes that fall far short of the Bible's radical demand for justice? Must we not engage in hermeneutical suspicion?" If an anecdotal analysis of our social consciousness and spiritual formation leaves us with the realization that, as Brown says, "there are some selective lenses by means of which we read Scripture, and . . . those lenses need to be torn from our eyes,"[15] then how do we tear them away? How do we change and develop a radical social consciousness? How do we even begin to want to change?

If preachers have been socialized in ways that blind them to the reality of social injustices, then healing of sight can best come through personal exposure to these realities. Just as our earlier personal experiences and the persons we knew shaped who we are now, we need to expose ourselves to new experiences and persons. We need new stories to tell. So many preachers have returned from El Salvador, Nicaragua, or the Philippines having experienced a social and theological conversion. Closer to home, many have shed their blindness when confronted directly with the homeless on the streets of their own city or with the emotional and physical deprivation to be found in nursing homes throughout our country. Many others, reared to believe in an exclusivistic "god" at the beck and call of the white race only, have had their eyes painfully pried open when the social situation demanded a one-to-one encounter with a person of color who grew to be a friend. Books can help; listening to others who "have been there" can bring intellectual assent; but once we have met the Jesus of Matthew 25:35-45 and Luke 4:18-19 in the hovels and barrios and streets of our own and others' lands, we can never again read the Bible in the same way.

We may say, "Sometimes I wish my eyes hadn't been opened; sometimes I wish I could no longer see," but once our eyes are opened, once we do see, we are forever changed. We cannot go back. We must then begin to ask the "whys" that challenge the systems of our world and the world of those we have come to care about. Why are people hungry? Why are so many living in poverty? Why does our government spend billions on weapons of war while so many go homeless and without the bare essentials of life? Why do we give millions of dollars to other countries for weapons? Why do Americans expand multi-national corporations abroad and exploit the poor and suffering of other countries? Why are there still pockets of hatred and oppression of Blacks and various other ethnic groups within our own society? Why do some churches still refuse to ordain women or grant women full equality before God? Why do so many Christians hate gays and deny them full fellowship and personhood in the community of faith? Why—? Why? "Whys" are dangerous questions for preachers to ask.

The Sermon: Preparation and Setting

Nowhere are preachers more a part of their faith community than at the time they are preaching in those communities. I have, therefore, chosen to include a sermon that has been preached in two different settings, with two different faith communities, and with different illustrations.

The first setting was Senior Chapel, the final chapel of the 1985–86 year at Pacific School of Religion. I believe preaching is at its best as a dialogue and the listeners and setting are vital parts of the preaching moment. For this reason, the primary setting visualized for this final written version is the PSR chapel and the listeners are the members of the PSR community, persons with whom I have almost daily contact.[16]

A committee from the senior class planned the worship and selected the theme of "Holy Ground." As is true for most preachers, this theme was not a new one for me. Exodus 3:1-15 had furnished the inspiration for more than one sermon because my own history causes me to identify with the entire Exodus event. However, the Senior Chapel setting affected me deeply. Here were persons I knew and loved who had already made firm commitments to God regarding social justice issues. There were those among them who had been arrested because of civil disobedience in protest against nuclear research or U. S. involvement in Nicaragua. Now many of them were about to graduate and go out from seminary to God knows what! Not only did I know them but they knew me. Most had taken at least one class with me. Almost all had heard me preach before. "Holy Ground" was an excellent but scary theme. I did not want to speak in clichés. To preach dialogically and with integrity was extremely important to me.

The choice of Acts 7:17-34 as the primary text rather than Exodus 3 helped *me* look at the original story in a new way. I saw Moses' story through *Stephen's* eyes and experience.

It is altogether probable that Luke composed Stephen's sermon and we have no guarantee that the results of that sermon were those recorded in Acts. However, in the world of Luke's narrative, Stephen preached to a hostile crowd. He reviewed the history of the Hebrew people and he recalled for his listeners Moses and Moses' call out of a burning bush. He told how Moses led the Hebrew people forth from Egypt. Then he reminded those who listened how the people refused to obey Moses and longed to return to Egypt. He used this example to accuse his listeners of even more reprehensible actions. They had rejected Jesus, murdered him, and betrayed him. Stephen's direct preaching inflamed his audience; they were angered to the point that a kind of savagery was unleashed. They reacted in a manner that calls to mind the image from network television when people, similarly enraged, turned dogs loose on Martin Luther King, Jr., and his followers as they knelt in prayer. The mob stoned Stephen to death.

The second text, Exodus 15:22-25, 27–16:3 is the narrative reminder of the kind of behavior about which Stephen spoke. It relates graphically the very human tendency to blame all adversity on the one who leads. The people had cried out for deliverance, for freedom, but in the wilderness they decided that the price was too high and turned in wrath to blame Moses for their predicament.

"Burning burning burning burning"[17]

EXODUS 15:22-25, 27–16:3; ACTS 7:17-34

It is both a joy and an honor to participate in this Senior Chapel. You see, however aware or *not* aware of this fact you seniors are, I entered Pacific School of Religion as a full-time faculty member three years ago. So this class may well be my class in a way no other ever can be. Yes, this is special *and* difficult. Something tells me that I have led preaching classes in critiquing too many of your sermons to be other than vulnerable standing here right now!

In addition,
> you have given me the theme of *Holy Ground.*

I don't know about you, but when I hear the words "holy ground," I don't have to be skilled in word association to think immediately: "Take off your shoes!" Now *that* is an occasion for vulnerability. I remember a little poem written some years ago about a child who ran in crying from play, having stumped his toe while running barefoot. The poet listened while he cried out his distress and then told him if he wore his shoes he would not stump his toe. She watched while he considered this for a long moment. She rejoiced when suddenly he dried his tears, turned, and ran back outside—still barefoot. Her comment was,

> "He ran back to the grass
> > *and* the rocks, *vulnerable*
> > but free!"

I know something personally about how vulnerable being barefoot can make me. A couple in a church I served did not want a woman pastor—not at all! They told me so in no uncertain terms, and then added, "Not only are you a woman, but you're too short!" There are a few of you here my height or even shorter. And *you* know, and *I* know, that we need our shoes, especially shoes with heels when we stand in some of these massive pulpits. But what if, when you stand there—all poised and proud because you look taller than you are—what if the voice comes,

"You are standing on Holy Ground.
Take off your shoes!"

*(At this point I do take off my shoes and drop my
height some two or three inches, rendering me
almost invisible behind the pulpit.)*

Well—

Perhaps you can see me better—
or hear me better—
if you take off your shoes, too.
Go ahead, try it if you want to.
Take off your shoes.
Now, will you stand up, barefoot?

While you stand there, think. Taking off your shoes is what
you do on holy ground. Is this holy ground? Where we stand
right now? Why, we have classes in here and all kinds of
programs in here. How can it possibly be? How can it possibly
not be?

I can remember sitting right back there just a few rows from
the back in worship when there was a time of silence, and all of
a sudden I knew I was on holy ground—such a glow within me
and around me as I became aware of the invisible presence of
all those who have stood in this place and heard God's call, of
all those who have made life-changing decisions right here.

I remember a young man who used to sit in preaching class,
right back there, just a short time ago. Already he is being
spoken of as "the most loved gringo in El Salvador."

I remember a Good Friday when Bob Brown and Daniel
Berrigan led a day of prayer and education concerning U. S.
involvement in the nuclear arms race.

I remember a preaching class making a decision that they
did not have to complain and wait for someone else "to do
something" but *they* could reserve this chapel and set a time
and plan a worship experience that permitted the community to
come together to grieve and share concerning the U. S.
invasion of Grenada.

I remember that I was one of the many who, at different
times, were commissioned and prayed for and sent out from
this community to Nicaragua and the Philippines for exposure
to the pain and poverty lived every day by our brothers and
sisters in those countries.

I remember some of the dreams that have been dreamed

here and the innumerable times God has spoken saying, "I have seen how my people are treated; I have heard their groaning, and I have come down to deliver them. I will send you—or you—or you—to Egypt."

But sit, sit again. It is allright to sit on holy ground, too, *if* you continue to see and hear!

> *(The congregation sits down again. I leave it up to them whether or not to remain barefoot but I remain without my shoes in the pulpit.)*

See what? A burning bush. Now that's attention getting! Burning that will not be consumed. Hear what? What God has to say out of the burning bush. What are the requirements of this God who speaks out of a burning bush?

To go where we are afraid to go.

To go where we do not want to go.

To go back to the people of God, wherever they are, and lead them to freedom.

That's what Moses found out and he tried to get out of it. God, why? Why do you ask this?

Because I have seen my people and heard their cry!

But God, why *me*? I mean, I can't talk as well as my brother, Aaron. And you ought to see my sister, Miriam—how she can sing and dance. God, I don't know how to sing and I sure can't dance. God, why me?

Because *you killed someone.*

Because you ran away.

Because you are in a desert.

Because you were reared a stranger to your own people.

Because I killed? God, none of this makes sense.

Why? Why me?

Because you had the capacity to see a burning bush.

Because you had the curiosity to turn aside.

Because you took off your shoes when I told you to.

Because *you are arguing with me!*

Because I have heard my people.

Because I AM.

Because you are.

But, I AM, what can I expect? I mean, *if* I do what you say, what can I expect?

You can expect to be ignored,
         to be challenged
                  to be lied to,
   to have to repeat the same actions, protests, demands,
         WORDS
   over and over again in order to be permitted to do what I
      have called you to do.
And, when you are finally heard, finally doing what I call you
   to do, finally released, and are leading the people toward
   freedom and new vision, you can expect to be rejected by
   them, by the very people you seek to lead—the very ones
   I heard crying out for deliverance. Many will want to go
   back.
      Back to captivity.
            Back to Egypt.
   They will tell you freedom is too hard—too painful.
   They will tell you to be vulnerable if you want to, but leave
   them alone.
   Free people starve for food,
      for a place to be still in,
         a place to know security,
            a place that is *theirs.*
   Free people starve for roots, they will say.
   They will tell you, "You're the preacher, the prophet, the leader;
   do it yourself. Go on if you want to, but take us back first, or just
   leave us—alone."
   It's easier just to stay in a seminary classroom,
                        or chapel,
                        or church,
      than it is to journey in the desert,
                  in the wilderness,
                     in the world.
   Wait!   Are you equating the church
            (surely not the *seminary*)
                        with Egypt?
   Maybe, maybe. If people are bound there.
   Maybe. If the food they get there is so precious they are sure
   God cannot feed them in the desert, on the journey, but only in
   the seminary community—only in the church.

Maybe. If every time God tries to call the people forth, they run and hide—beneath a pew—or in a pulpit—or in the library—and cry, "We are so comfortable here, so safe. Here we are learning so much!

Here we can pray and sing and talk about God and how much God loves the world!

Here it is (mostly) easy to tell the truth and be kind
   and generous and loving and ethical.

Don't make us try to be Christians in the world.

It's a desert out there!   It's a wilderness!

There's no water!

There's no food!"

H O L Y   G R O U N D   ! ! !

Why me?

Why am *I* standing here barefoot on holy ground?

Stephen, you did it, too. Moses wasn't the only one. You stood on holy ground. They set you aside to wait tables because the apostles were too busy preaching!!! Wait tables, indeed! As though you were not capable of doing anything else. As though you, too, were not called by God, even if you weren't an apostle. Stephen, your problem was you remembered Moses. You remembered Abraham and Sarah and you remembered Moses and Moses' burning bush and how he stood barefoot on holy ground and listened to God. Stephen, be careful. You've found a burning bush, too. You are listening to God, too. And that's dangerous. You know it's dangerous, if you're really listening to God. You, too, are standing on holy ground.

   Barefoot,
        vulnerable,
             on *holy ground.*

But *free!!!!!!!*   Free—

Stephen, is that why you had the courage to preach as you did? The courage to say what you had to say? Is that why your face shone as you stood there?

Is that why they killed you?

In the name of God, look at all the burning bushes! Look at all the people standing barefoot on holy ground. I don't have to name them. You know them. Like a great roll call. But why? Why Moses? Why Jesus?

Why Stephen?

Why Martin Luther King, Jr.?

Why Oscar Romero?

Why *Karl Gaspar?*[18]

Let me tell you about Karl Gaspar. He was a college professor, quite ordinary, somewhat committed to Christianity. But one day he saw the burning bush of his people's oppression. *His people,* Filipino people, were shut up in Egypt, in the captivity of poverty and hunger, in prison for daring to criticize the Marcos regime, because of false accusations when they had done nothing. And Karl Gaspar, Christian teacher and layman, brought some of his college students together and began teaching them how to do improvisational protest drama. The result? Karl Gaspar spent twenty months in prison as a political detainee. He said, "It is long past the time for the church to do acts of charity. It is time for the church to challenge the system that makes acts of charity necessary."

Why Karl Gaspar?

Or why Robert McAfee Brown, theologian and seminary teacher?

Why did he see a burning bush? Why was his life turned upside down? By his own telling, for a long time he saw himself "as a middle-class, white Anglo-Saxon Protestant male, born and reared in the United States—a vintage WASP."[19] He tells how his entire socialization was shaped by his life experience: the son of a clergyman, he grew up in suburbia, attending predominantly white schools, including both high school and college, and then what was considered a "liberal" Protestant seminary. He knew himself to be part of the majority and was comfortable in all he had "absorbed" from his various communities—none of which included more than the token presence of

Catholics   Blacks   Jews

and members of ethnic minorities.

His burning bushes came gradually, distances between each. They came with "World War II, seeing Nagasaki after the bomb, participation in the Freedom Ride, various acts of civil disobedience in response to racism and Vietnam resulting in brief spells in a variety of jails, and other events that shattered my comfortable world."[20] He became increasingly aware that there is not yet true freedom for Blacks in America, that "the land of the free and the home of the brave" is not truly free for black people, not yet. And he drove across the United States and, again, a bush caught fire and blazed as he saw what we have done to Native Americans. By now bushes seemed to be catching fire from other bushes: women and their stories, the stories of Vietnamese and Chileans, the stories of Nicaraguans—bush after bush after bush burning for one whose eyes have been opened.

Why Bob Brown?

    Or why a second career minister
       new to the role of parish pastor,
         why a burning bush for her?

Why did she come to believe that God wanted that church to offer full equality under God to Christian gays and lesbians? Why did she have to preach it? Why did she have to challenge that church to fulfill its own statement of purpose:

    "As a church we will know no circles of exclusion,
       no boundaries we will not cross,
         no loyalty above that which we owe to God."

Earlier she had asked the diaconate of that all-white church in a town 98 percent white to invite a black seminarian to become a student assistant and worship leader every Sunday for a year. And they voted to do it. *And* he accepted. Many people grew to love him. But many people she loved, and had listened to, and had sat down to table with, left that church for another and tried to convince others to leave with them.

Why that particular pastor?

And why Maria?

Maria was a sixteen-year-old girl from a country in Latin America. Bob Brown tells about her in his book *Unexpected News.*[21] Maria was a member of a Base Christian Community and there she studied the Bible with many others; with them she learned to pray; with them she came to know Jesus Christ. She also came to participate in social action with her friends in the community. Maria came to the time when she wanted to be baptized and confirmed but the priest thought she should wait a while until she fully understood the risks of being a Christian in that country. The priest said, "I'm not sure Maria is ready to die for her faith." Before her eighteenth birthday, she *had* been baptized and confirmed, and *had* died for her faith. Why Maria?

Why you, Joy?

Why you, Steve?

Why you, Karen? Tom? René?

Why any of us?

Because when you stop for the fire that burns outside you, and you take off your shoes and you stand there vulnerable on holy ground and you hear God's words clear and ringing:

My people.   My people crying out in captivity, in *any* kind of captivity.

Then—   then— somehow the fire gets *inside* you.

It got inside Moses.

It got inside Jeremiah.

A fire shut up in my bones!

I *have* to speak!

It was inside Jesus.

And at Pentecost, the fire came in tongues and rested on heads.

It got inside.

Holy Spirit fire power got inside

Peter and all the rest of the disciples,

men *and* women,

people of every color and race.

Holy Spirit poured out on all,

inside all,

on the whole people of God!

The whole people of God.

Fire burning inside.

Are you standing on holy ground?

Staring at a bush burning?

Burning just for you?

A bush that will not be consumed?

Then beware.

Be prepared.

Be ready to confess with the poet:

"Burning burning burning burning
O Lord Thou pluckest me out
O Lord Thou pluckest
burning."   *T. S. Eliot*

Reflection

As noted earlier, the theme of "Holy Ground" was selected by the seniors who planned the chapel service but the Exodus event had come to mean a great deal to me in my own life and so I welcomed the choice. This is also a story on which I have done considerable theological reflection. Recently, I have been engaged in a study of 1987 lections from *Acts* which include the portion of Stephen's sermon in which he retells Moses' burning bush experience. It seemed appropriate to use as the Scripture for this sermon a portion of another sermon, especially one that had resulted in the stoning of a preacher!

The context of the sermon is extremely important for every sermon and this one is no exception. I have kept the opening remarks as they were at the time of delivery, because they reflect the closeness of my relationship with these seniors and to demonstrate how these remarks weave together an awareness of the setting, the experience of the listeners, and the specific concept of vulnerability. Clearly, then, a part of my purpose was to acknowledge relational elements and to speak personally. That desire helped set the tone and encouraged the taking-off-of-shoes section which was received with general laughter and great good humor.

How does the sermon reflect my theological stance? I believe deeply in God's call to some persons to preach, as well as to all Christians to minister in many different ways. I have a strong commitment to social justice, particularly in the matter of inclusiveness of all persons in the community of faith. I most profoundly believe God's love is for *all* persons. I believe that God calls us and uses us *because* of, and not in spite of, our past experiences of failure and sin. I maintain a clearly held conviction that God is with us. I also believe that the stands we take for justice are scripturally mandated and can set us free to do what God calls us to do. I believe that for the one who is called, the ongoing activity of the Holy Spirit within compels him or her to speak. This compulsion *is* like "a burning fire shut up in my bones" (Jer. 20:9).

How does this sermon reflect my socialization? I am a woman who grew up as a Southern Baptist in Louisiana. The call I experienced at twelve years of age was a call to preach, but there was no way I could understand that or claim it, even for myself, until I was forty-three years of age. I am divorced. The process of ending a marriage is much like death, perhaps even like "killing" someone or something. During the final year of the marriage, I ran away from my friends and my community of faith because of the pain and shame and the feeling that, if I even considered divorce, no one would trust that I still belonged, or had the right to belong, to the faith community. After the divorce was final, I knew the personal meaning of being in a desert, a wilderness, and that I was being led to a "promised land" and a new beginning.

My ordination means that my hometown church, where I first heard God speak to me, made my profession of faith, was baptized, and made my commitment to vocational Christian service, will not permit me even to speak to a Sunday school class, much less preach. This is not because I am divorced, but because I am an ordained woman.

I grew up in a racist community of faith. (How *can* those two concepts exist together?) Members of my immediate family were taught to be racist by a Bible-quoting, Bible-justifying community of faith. Black people had their place and were supposed to stay there. It was preached from the pulpit and practiced by the pastor. My entire family subscribed to this. Why have I come to such a social justice stance so that I feel I was "reared a stranger to my own people"? Not that I am *now* a stranger, but that I was reared a stranger, because now I feel my "own people" are black and brown and all the people of color, and all those Christian gays and lesbians who struggle for acceptance—all those who know what it means to be discriminated against because of who they are, where they were born, or how much money or education they have. The story of the gray-haired, second career, woman pastor in the sermon is my story. This is an area in which I *must* speak; I have no choice, whatever risk is involved.

Other faith communities and experiences have contributed to my socialization as revealed in this sermon. For example, I worked in a Hispanic community as student missionary when I was nineteen years of age and made a number of close friends my age. I dated a Korean man from Hawaii. When I was twenty-five, I worked under a black woman supervisor at Northwestern University library. Throughout my life I have attended black churches and heard the sermons and music of these churches. For the last several years I have known the friendship of Dr. Alfred Smith, as well as of Allen Temple Baptist Church as a whole. My present church membership is in the integrated faith community of Lakeshore Avenue Baptist Church in Oakland. Since 1976 I have been associated with the faculty, students, staff, and administration of Pacific School of Religion, where an entire academic community is also a faith community struggling with a multitude of social justice issues in personal and corporate ways. Eight students from PSR and I traveled to the Philippines in January of 1986 for a seventeen-day intensive exposure tour. I am now an American Baptist, a member of a denomination whose membership, nationally, is more than 39 percent non-white. As a denomination we are struggling with what it means to be fully inclusive and to take dangerous stands on matters of social justice.

How did the sermon minister to the community of faith? The PSR community, particularly students, were addressed as co-ministers; their journeys were recognized, as were their calls, their fears about the future, their need for courage, and their compulsion to speak out for social justice. Out of a biblical mandate, the sermon challenged them to respond fully to God's call to them, to hear, with God, the crying of God's people. It reminded them that it would not be easy, that some people would not want to be free, and others would even protest the preacher's right to try to set anyone free. It sought to shake them loose from a felt need to stay in the safety of the seminary community, and it reminded them of God's ability to provide nourishment for the journey.

Notes

1. For a recent example of narrative method employed by a social scientist see Robert N. Bellah et al., *Habits of the Heart: Individualism and Commitment in*

American Life (Berkeley: University of California Press, 1985). For an example of narrative method employed by a psychologist and pastoral counselor see Archie Smith, Jr., *The Relational Self* (Nashville: Abingdon Press, 1982). Karen Lebacqz, a Christian ethicist, uses a single narrative as the unifying thread in her *Professional Ethics: Power and Paradox* (Nashville: Abingdon Press, 1985).

2. James W. McClendon, Jr., *Biography as Theology: How Life Stories Can Remake Today's Theology* (Nashville: Abingdon Press, 1974). This book has become a standard work in the growing area of narrative theology. A more recent work in this vein is C. S. Song, *Tell Us Our Names: Story Theology from an Asian Perspective* (Maryknoll, N.Y.: Orbis Books, 1984).

3. Smith, *The Relational Self,* 86-88.

4. For more information on the involvement of Smith and Allen Temple in social justice concerns see J. Alfred Smith, Sr., *For the Facing of This Hour: A Call to Action* (Elgin, Ill: Progressive National Baptist Publishing House, 1981). This book also contains sermons and lectures delivered by Smith in a number of contexts.

5. The Reverend Daniel Arthur Holmes was born September 22, 1876, in Macon, Missouri. His parents were former slaves in Randolph County. He was licensed to preach in 1889 and ordained in 1901. He earned a B.Th. at Des Moines College in Iowa and a B.D. from the Divinity School of the University of Chicago. He was pastor of Paseo Baptist Church in Kansas City for forty-six years.

6. *D. A. Holmes,* see Note 5. *Mordecai Johnson* was a graduate of the University of Chicago and the first black president of Howard University. He was an eloquent Baptist preacher who often held business people spellbound by sermons of over an hour in length. Martin Luther King, Jr., said he was the single individual who influenced him to study Gandhi. *A. Philip Randolph* was born in Crescent City, Florida, the son of a circuit-riding African Methodist minister. He was founder and president of the Brotherhood of Sleeping Car Porters and urged the major black organizations of the country to organize a march on Washington, D.C., to spur Congress to immediate enactment of Kennedy-administration civil rights legislation. In 1941, he exerted pressure on President Roosevelt that resulted in the creation of the Fair Employment Practices Commission. Later he was instrumental in persuading President Truman to order desegregation of the U.S. Army and, ten years later, he met with President Eisenhower to impress upon him the need for greater speed in enforcement of civil rights laws that brought about integration of the schools. *Mary McLeod Bethune* was a black American educator who dedicated her life to helping her own people. She taught in mission schools and founded schools for black children. One school she founded bears her name. Bethune-Cookman College in Daytona Beach, Florida, is an accredited co-educational college. From 1936 to 1944 Mary Bethune served as the director of the National Youth Administration's Division of Negro Affairs. In 1945, she was a consultant on interracial understanding at the San Francisco Conference of the United Nations.

7. William Lloyd Garrison was an American newspaperman who worked against slavery. In 1833, he and others helped organize the New England Anti-Slavery Society. He was outspoken in his denouncement of slavery as a moral wrong and may be considered a pioneer in the area of civil disobedience. He publicly burned a copy of the U. S. Constitution because it did not denounce slavery. Until his death in 1879 he also crusaded for women's rights and for other causes.

8. Frederick Douglass, born about 1817, was a Negro slave who learned to read and write as a child. He escaped and went to Massachusetts where he became prominent in the Anti-Slavery Society founded by Garrison. He made public speeches against slavery and published an autobiography. This book became known in England where he spent two years lecturing against the evils of slavery. British sympathizers raised money to buy his freedom and to establish an abolitionist newspaper that Douglass published for over ten years. In 1889, he was appointed U.S. Minister to the Republic of Haiti.

9. Walter Rauschenbusch was an American Protestant theologian, an American Baptist minister, and a leader of the Social Gospel movement in the United States before World War I. He applied Christianity to the social and economic ills of his day and wrote several books including *Christianity and the Social Crisis* (1907), *Christianizing the Social Order* (1912), and *A Theology for the Social Gospel* (1917). He taught at Rochester Theological Seminary in New York.

10. Joe Holland and Peter Henriot, S. J., *Social Analysis, Linking Faith and Justice,* rev. ed. (Maryknoll, N.Y.: Orbis Books, 1983), 10. This entire book is recommended.

11. See Bellah, *Habits of the Heart,* particularly pages 142-63, for an extensive discussion of individualism. He identifies four traditions of individualism: biblical, civic, utilitarian, and expressive. He says, "Individualism lies at the very core of American culture" (142). His discussions of "Communities of Memory" and "Community Commitment" are especially relevant to our discussion of the preacher as a social being in the community of faith. See also Archie Smith, Jr., *The Relational Self,* 49. Smith states:

> Sociological information and social analysis have not played a strong enough role in preparation for ministry. . . .
> Individualism and individual salvation have been a pervasive theme in American Protestantism. True, there have been strong advocates of a social gospel orientation. But the social dimension has been a minority position within mainline Christian denominations and has been effectively countered by a very strong individualistic strain in American Christian life.

12. For an entire book that deals with the interconnectedness of spiritual life and active participation in matters of social justice, see Gustavo Gutierrez, *We Drink from Our Own Wells: The Spiritual Journey of a People* (Maryknoll, N.Y.: Orbis Books, 1984). For a moving and unique approach to interpretation of Scripture by persons most involved in social justice issues, see Ernesto Cardenal, *The Gospel in Solentiname,* 4 vols. (Maryknoll, N.Y.: Orbis Books, 1982).

13. Holland and Henriot, *Social Analysis,* 10.

14. Robert McAfee Brown, *Theology in a New Key* (Philadelphia: Westminster Press, 1978), 81.

15. Ibid., 82.

16. The second setting was the "National Pastor's Convocation: Empowering the Whole People of God for Ministry," a conference at Green Lake, Wisconsin, in July 1986. The congregation was composed of approximately one hundred pastors and twenty-five spouses.

17. The title of the sermon is taken from T. S. Eliot's *The Waste Land,* III, "The Fire Sermon," lines 308-11.

18. I met Karl Gaspar during an "Exposure Tour" to the Philippines in January of 1986. He has written a most provocative book, *How Long? Prison*

Reflections of Karl Gaspar (Quezon City: Claretian Publications, 1985).

19. Brown, *Theology in a New Key,* 136.

20. Ibid.

21. Robert McAfee Brown, *Unexpected News: Reading the Bible with Third World Eyes* (Philadelphia: Westminster Press, 1984), 152-53.

4

The Social Nature
of the Biblical Text
for Preaching

Walter Brueggemann. The preacher
stands midway in the process of the biblical text. The process
of forming, transmitting, and interpreting the biblical text is
a creative process at its beginning, midpoint, and ending.
The creative dimension of the process means that the text
and its meanings are always being produced. They never
simply exist. They are not just "there," but the community is
continually engaged in a willful act of production of
meaning. That is what is meant by "the social nature" of the
text. It is the community at work with the text.[1]

The Textual Process

The textual process has three identifiable points, each of
which is creative, that is, productive. First, it begins in *the
formation of the text,* that is, the way in which the text has
reached its settled canonical form. Historical-critical methods
of study are concerned with the ways in which the
community, through editors, redactors, scribes, and tradi-
tionists, has put the text together. Whatever view we have of
the creation of the text, we know that human hands and
hearts have been at work in its formation.

Second, the end of the textual process is *the reception and
hearing of the text* which is done by the congregation. We know

that such listening is a complex matter, because communication in general is exceedingly complex, and reception of the text is a specific moment of communication. No one can any longer imagine that the preaching of the text is heard by members of the community just as it is spoken, or just as it is intended by the preacher. The listening is done through certain sensitivities that may distort, emphasize, enhance, or censor, depending on the particular situation of the listening community. The listening community is engaged in a constructive act of construal, of choosing, discerning and shaping the text through the way the community chooses to listen.[2] The text thus construed may or may not be the text that is the one offered by the speaker. That is, the text heard may be quite different from the one proclaimed.

It is the third identifiable point, *the midway process of interpretation*, that interests us in this paper. Interpretation is all the action between formation and reception that seeks to assert the authority and significance of the text. This interpretive step includes the classical creeds and commentaries, the long history of theological reflection, contemporary scholarship, and contemporary church pronouncements. Above all, it includes the interpretative work of the preacher in the sermon. It is in the sermon that the church has done its decisive, faith-determining interpretation. The sermon is not an act of reporting on an old text, but it is an act of making a new text visible and available. This new text in part is the old text, and in part is the imaginative construction of the preacher which did not exist until the moment of utterance by the preacher.[3] Like a conductor "rendering" Beethoven so that that particular music exists only in that occasion, so the preacher renders a text so that it only exists in that particular form in that particular occasion of speaking.[4]

These three dimensions of the textual process—*formation, interpretation, reception*—are all creative acts in which the text and its meaning are not only an offer made to the community, but are a product generated in the community. Interpretation and listening, as well as formation, are creative acts of construal. This creative aspect of the text is unavoidable and should be welcomed as an arena in which faith is received, discerned, and made pertinent. Some may think such creative possibility in interpretation is an aberration to be avoided. It cannot be avoided. Nor should it be avoided, because it is the way in which God's Word is alive among us. Interpretation can and must be creative and imaginative if it is to be interpretation and not simply reiteration. Listening is inevitably an imaginative act of response in which the listener does part of the work of rendering the text.[5]

This entire creative process consists of two factors which are in tension and which make our topic both important and difficult. The textual process is at every point *an act of faith*. In faithful interpretation, the entire process is governed by the work of God's Spirit of truth. It is this that permits interpretation to be an act of faith. The promise of faith is the conviction that in its formation, interpretation, and reception the text is a word of life that makes a difference. No part of this process is undertaken on the pretense that this is objective or neutral or a matter of indifference.

Those who formed the text did so because they knew the traditions to be important and they judged them to be true and urgent for the ongoing generations of the community. That is the theological meaning of the canon. The subsequent interpreter who received the text has labored diligently over the text, as does the contemporary interpreter, because faith requires interpretation. Interpreters in every generation, even those who have exercised enormous freedom, have intended their work as an effort in fidelity. Finally, those who receive the text, the assembled community of listeners, gather in an act of faith. The church gathers around the text because it takes the text seriously. It listens eagerly (and therefore imaginatively) to try to hear the nuance in the text that is God's live Word now. Participants at every point of the textual process are unembarrassed about the premise of faith. All parts of the textual process are undertaken primarily to ensure the powerful, authoritative presence of the Word among members of the community.

It is also the case, however, that every part of the textual process is *an act of vested interest*. Exegetical study is now learning this insight from sociological criticism.[6] The textual process does not proceed objectively or neutrally, but always intends to make a case in a certain direction. Just as there is no "exegesis without presuppositions,"[7] so there is no textual activity that is not linked to a vested interest. The formation of the text itself has been an act of vested interest. Certain pieces of literature are selected, gathered, shaped, and juxtaposed in different ways to argue certain points. We know, for example, that the early community around Moses authorized certain texts that served the interest of liberation.[8] The Exodus narrative is surely put together by proponents of a radical liberating faith. In the time of Solomon, other texts were celebrated because they legitimated the concentration of power in the monarchy and served to enhance the inequality of the status quo.

In like manner the interpretive act is notorious for being an act of vested interest. There is no doubt that "liberation communities" in the Third World approach every text with an inclination that tilts interpretation in a specific direction. We are coming to see that even what we regarded as the objective scholarship of historical-critical method has not been objective, but has served certain social interests and enhanced certain epistemological biases.[9] We are coming to see that what we thought was objective has in fact been the "class reading" of male Euro-American theology. Richard Rohrbaugh has offered stunning and convincing evidence that many of the great American preachers of the last generation handled texts so that the sharp and disconcerting social dimension that questioned our economic commitments was ignored. As a result, the text was interpreted in other directions that probably were serious distortions.[10] This was not intentional distortion on the part of the preacher. It is simply that our faith is regularly embodied in a vested interest that we ourselves are not always able to discern.

Finally, listening to the text and its interpretation is an act of vested interest. Over time we select the mode and substance of interpretation that we want to hear. We select our interpretive tradition. We read certain books, subscribe to certain journals, even join or avoid certain churches in order to find a textual interpretation congruent with our vested interests which we can receive and hear and to which we can respond.[11]

The textual process of formation, interpretation, and reception is therefore always a mixture of faith and vested interest. To study "the social process" is to pay attention to that vexed combination. That the textual process is skewed by interest requires a hermeneutic of suspicion.[12] That the textual process is an act of serious faith permits a hermeneutic of retrieval. Despite the identification of these two hermeneutics, the matter remains complicated and problematic because we cannot practice one hermeneutic first and then the other. We cannot first sort out vested interest and then affirm faith, because vested interest and faith always come together and cannot be so nicely distinguished. We must simply recognize the fact that the two always come together, even in the midst of our best efforts of discernment and criticism.

The creative act of formation-interpretation-reception *produces a text*. As it produces a text, it forms an imaginative world in which the community of the text may live. That production of a text is a willful, intentional act generated by faith and vested interest. That the text is "produced" means a *different* text could have been formed, interpreted, or received. This means that the produced text is never innocent or disinterested. But it is this text, never innocent or disinterested, that we take as the normative text for our faith. The text that has been produced and made canonical is the only one we have. It is to that text we must obediently and critically attend.

When the community has thus produced a text, it is the task of the community to *consume the text,* that is, to take, use, heed, respond, and act upon the text. The entire process of the text then is an act of *production and consumption* whereby a new world is chosen or an old world is defended, or there is transformation of old world to new world.[13] The purpose of using the categories of production and consumption is to suggest that the textual process, especially the interpretive act of preaching, is never a benign, innocent, or straightforward act. Anyone who imagines that he or she is a benign or innocent preacher of the text is engaged in self-deception.[14] Preaching as interpretation is always a daring, dangerous act in which the interpreter, together with the receivers of the interpretation, is consuming a text and producing a world.

The world so produced is characteristically a world made possible by faith, but it is a world mediated through vested interest. Thus the text never only says, but it does. What it does is to create another world of perception, value, and power which permits alternative acts. Great attention must be paid to vested interest and its impact on perception, value and power, because vested interest has an enormous power to guide the textual process in certain directions. It is this dangerous, inevitable drama of the text that is referred to under the rubric "social nature." As both member and leader of the community, the preacher is necessarily involved in this dangerous, problematic production and consumption of texts through which worlds are chosen and life is transformed.

The Classic Tradition of Sociology

The classic tradition of sociology illuminates the lively shaping action of the community upon the text.[15] It is important to recognize that sociology arose as a distinct discipline in response to a specific social crisis. That is, sociology is not simply the general study of human community, but from its beginning was a discipline preoccupied with a particular set of awarenesses and problems.[16] The startling changes in human consciousness that came in the seventeenth, eighteenth, and nineteenth centuries which are associated with the Enlightenment and modernity have made us aware that the world in which we live is a social contrivance that carries with it important costs and gains. Sociology is essentially a critical discipline that has exposed the deceptive notion that the social world is an absolute given arrangement, by bringing to visibility the ways in which society continually constructs itself. At the outset sociology as criticism was aimed against traditional notions of the absolute givenness of social life which were legitimated by religious orthodoxy. These notions, as sociological study made clear, also brought with them the legitimacy of an absolutist economic and political orthodoxy.[17]

Sociology was therefore initially addressed to the mystification of a religion that claimed and pretended the world was a given. At the same time, however, sociology tended to be blind and inattentive to a scientific orthodoxy that posited a new social given; this time, objective, rational, neutral, and technological—all the things we have come to label as positivistic.[18] Critical sociology emerged to deal intentionally with the naïve positivism of much social science; it has become clear that the new "objective" world is as confused as the old religious world, and as incapable of seeing as operative its own ideology.[19] Critical sociology can help us see that the vested interests and ideological defenses of "scientific objectivity" are as dangerous and dishonest as the old absolutes of religion.

This shift from the old world of religious tradition and convention to the new world of technical control is a theme that has preoccupied the classical tradition of sociology. This theme has been articulated in various forms. We may mention its appearance in the three progenitors of the classical sociological tradition.

1. Karl Marx addresses the social alienation caused by capitalism and the role of religion in legitimating social structures that are exploitative and dehumanizing.[20] Marx's great insights are that economic arrangements are decisive for all social relationships and that religion functions primarily to legitimate economic arrangements. Clearly Marx was preoccupied with the shift in economic relations that tore the economic dimension away from the general fabric of social life.[21] He saw that this shift was deeply destructive of the possibility of human community. The emergence of alienation as a central product of the modern world is at the center of Marx's analysis. The textual tradition entrusted to the preacher has as a task the discernment of that alienation and the consideration of alternatives to it. The preacher must pay attention to the ways in which the text and its interpretation participate in the process of alienation.

2. Max Weber sought to provide an alternative to Marx that did not identify economics as the cause of everything.[22] Weber paid particular attention to the new forms of social control and administration and the emerging power of

bureaucracy. It would be a mistake, however, to interpret Weber (against Marx) as a friend of modernity. Like Marx, Weber saw the heavy toll that the structures and values of modernity would continue to assess against the possibility of humanness. The emergence of new forms of rationality preoccupied Weber. The emergence of destructive forms of rationality is also a struggle in the Bible, where covenantal modes of rationality are regularly offered against the temptations of naturalism and nationalism. In our present social situation, the connections Bellah has made concerning managerial rationality offer a suggestive critical insight for the preaching office.[23]

3. In a more conservative mode, Emile Durkheim was interested in the requirement of social cohesion for the survival of society.[24] In his classic study of suicide, Durkheim observed what happened in societies where the fabric of value and cohesion is exhausted and persons must live in a context of normlessness.[25] Durkheim's critique can cut two ways. Ours is a society that lives at the edge of normlessness, and on the other hand, we are a society that reacts to normlessness with a heavy-handed emphasis on conformity. The crisis of normlessness and conformity in our culture sounds strangely reminiscent of the Mosaic crisis about freedom and obedience and the problematic of the law as Paul understood it. The preacher is cast in a social role as a voice of normativeness, in a society bereft of norms.

There are great differences among these three spokespersons for social possibility and pathology, but they all focus on the fact that societies have ways in which to articulate and distort certain kinds of truth that make human life possible or problematic. Social structure, order, and value are not objective givens. But they also are not simply connections that can be willfully and artificially wrought. They are, rather, the slow, steady work of formation, creation, and transformation by which a community orders its life of perception, value, and power.[26]

Interpretation as Social Construction

The act of interpretation takes seriously both the old treasured memory and the new demand of the situation.

Interpretation seeks to mediate between tradition and situation. On the one hand, interpretation is always *responsive* to the situation, that is, commenting on the new social realities that are already established. On the other hand, interpretation is always *assertive,* saying something genuinely new and challenging the community to rethink and reperceive the newly established reality in light of the tradition. In modes of both response and assertion, interpretation is an imaginative act which articulates reality in a new way that had not been possible until the moment of speech. It is the speech that creates the possibility.

Sociology shows us that society is constantly reconstructing itself. While great attention therefore needs to be paid to the manipulation of power and the management of economic and political forces, we know that the primary mode by which a community reconstitutes itself is by its interpretation, by its reflection on ancient memory and tradition, and by its recasting of that memory and tradition in new ways that are resonant with the new situation.[27] All communities are always engaged in the process of interpretation. This is what ideology, propaganda, mass media, and civil religion are about. They are responses and assertions that are more or less creative, which seek to mediate a newness juxtaposed between tradition and situation.

In order to arrive at a better understanding of interpretation as a social act of reconstruction, several dimensions of critical exposition are peculiarly important.

1. Interpretation is unavoidably a communal activity. The whole community is involved in the process. Interpretation must take place if the community is to live and continue. Interpretation inevitably does happen because it is a main activity of the community. Sociology has helped us see that communities are always engaged in interpretive acts of reconstitution and reconstruction. That act of interpretation is characteristically a mixture of faith and vested interest.

With the coming of the Enlightenment and the rise of modernity, many have failed to understand the inevitability of interpretation. The fascination with so-called objectivity led to the mistaken notion that reality did not need to be interpreted. As reality did not need to be interpreted, it was mistakenly concluded that the biblical text could be read in a straightforward manner without interpretation. This is also the mistaken notion of those who want the U.S. Supreme Court to be "strict constructionists," that is, not to engage in interpretation. The kind of interpretation that denies it *is* interpretation is the most dangerous kind, because it is not then available for criticism.

2. The interpretative act of social reconstitution is what the biblical text itself is all about. That is, the text is not simply a factual reporting about what happened. In each of its statements it is an act of interpretative mediation whereby ancient Israel and the early church seek to reconstitute the community in the face of a new danger or crisis.[28] In ancient Israel the new situation is characteristically the new concentration of power and knowledge in the monarchy or the loss of monarchial power and knowledge in the Exile.[29] In the New Testament the characteristic new situation is the interface between Jewish and Gentile Christians and the derivative problems of ethics and organization. In each case the new situation requires a total recasting of the memory in order to sustain the identity of the community.

The texts are not only response, however. They are also bold assertions in the face of the new situation. For example, in the Old Testament the Yahwistic theologians do not simply conform to the new social reality, but make a strong case that in the new situation Israel must understand itself as the bearer of a blessing.[30] In the New Testament, for example, Luke-Acts offers bold suggestions about how the church must understand itself and order its faith. That the Old and New Testament texts are both responsive and assertive means that they are deeply imaginative. They proclaim a social reality that did not exist until that moment of articulation. Moreover because the text is deeply imaginative, it is probable that each such requesting of social reality is a mixture of faith and vested interest. Thus the J writer is concerned to maintain a human vision against a monarchial enterprise of self-aggrandizement. Luke seems to have been concerned lest the early church become a sect aligned against the Empire. The community over time has judged the vested interests of the texts (for example, J and Luke) to be faithful vehicles for faith and not acts of distortion. As a result, these specific texts have been judged authoritative and designated as canonical.

In the Pentateuch the documentary hypothesis of JEDP has been much misunderstood and maligned. It is an attempt to characterize the ongoing interpretive act of mediation that was underway in ancient Israel.[31] The J material, according to the dominant hypothesis, is an attempt to mediate the old memory in the affluent situation of Solomon. Similarly, the P tradition is an attempt to mediate the old memory in the despairing situation of Exile.[32] These two moments, United Monarchy and Exile, require fresh interpretative acts or the old tradition will have been in vain. In the cases of both J and P, one can detect that this interpretive act is indeed a response to a social crisis, is an assertion in the face of the crisis, and is a remarkable act of imagination. It takes very little insight to see that in each case the mediation is a mixture of faith and vested interest.

In like manner the Synoptic Gospels are mediations of the old memory of the early church.[33] The Gospel of Mark faces the challenge of Roman imperialism; Matthew takes up the question of the relationship between Christians and Jews, or perhaps Jesus and the Jewish tradition; and Luke struggles with the Gospel in a Gentile world. These Gospel statements are clearly not theological absolutes (or we would not have these three variants), nor are they factual descriptions of what happened, but they are mediations that make available a new world in which the community may live joyously and faithfully.

3. In the creative, imaginative act of construction of reality, the interpreters, those who process the text, are dangerously engaged in two ways.[34] On the one hand, they are so engaged because they inevitably make responsive, assertive mediations in the midst of their own mixture of faith and interest. Interpreters are never interest free but always present reality in partisan ways and, indeed, cannot do otherwise. On the other hand, in the act of interpretation they also have their own world remade. They do not stand outside this process but are being self-interpreted in the very act of biblical interpretation. In this act of mediation

hermeneutics then makes a new world possible. In hermeneutics as mediation, we thus bring together the "process of
the text," which includes formation, interpretation and
reception, and the sociology of world-making through which
the community reconstructs itself.

The key hermeneutical event in contemporary interpretation is the event of preaching. The preacher either
intentionally or unintentionally is convening a new community. This recognition will help us see why preaching is such a
crucial event not only in the life of the church, but in our
society. We must interpret to live. There is almost no other
voice left to do interpretation on which society depends that is
honest, available, and open to criticism. Most of the other acts
of interpretation that are going on in our midst are cryptic
and therefore not honest, not available, and not open to
criticism. The preaching moment is a public event in which
society reflects on what and who it will be, given the memory
of this church and given a post-modern situation in society.[35]

4. In the handling of the text by the preacher as
interpreter and by the congregation as receiver, the
hermeneutical work of world-constitution is going on. The
interpretive work is done through the preacher's mixture of
faith and interest while the congregation is listening and
responding in its mixture of faith and interest. All parties to
this act of interpretation need to understand that the text is
not a contextless absolute, nor is it a historical description, but
it is itself a responsive, assertive, imaginative act that stands as
a proposal of reality to the community. As the preacher and
the congregation handle the text, the text becomes a new act
that makes available one mediation of reality. That new
mediation of reality is characteristically an act of fidelity, an
act of inventiveness, and an act in which vested interest
operates. Moreover the preacher and the congregation do
this in the midst of many other acts of mediation in which
they also participate, as they attend to civil religion,
propaganda, ideology, and mass media. They are incessantly
involved in a complex of various interpretive, constructive
acts, while claiming the interpretive act authorized by the
Bible to be the normative one.

The Congregation and the Crisis of Modernity

The congregation that engages in interpretation (and with the interpretation embraces a certain refraction of the text) is not a contextless, undifferentiated entity. The congregation, as a community in crisis, gathers to decide one more time about its identity and its vocation. The people gathered have been bombarded since the last gathering by other voices of interpretation that also want to offer an identity and a vocation. In what follows I am focusing broadly on the typical main-line North American congregation, either Protestant or Catholic. I assume such a congregation, because that is the context in which I characteristically do my interpretation. Certainly other congregational settings could be assumed, and I do not imagine that this one is normative, or even preferable.

A different statement might be made in a different context, such as in post–Christian western Europe, in totalitarian East Germany, or in oppressive El Salvador, but our congregation is not yet post–Christian, not in a totalitarian context, or faced with direct oppression. This congregation is a gathering of people who have been largely enveloped in the claims of modernity. It is a community with a memory and with a present reality. In the midst of this memory and this reality, the act of interpretation is undertaken one more time.

The memory is the memory about God and God's people, about the summons of ancient Israel and the baptism of the early church, about Jesus and the people of Jesus from his time until our time. That memory is about births given to barren women, bread given to desperate peasants, shepherds given to scattered sheep, forgiveness given to those immobilized by guilt. It is about deep inversions and strange power for daring obedience. This memory and the text that conveys this memory are the source and subject of our preaching.

But the memory around which the congregational gathering takes place is also somewhat distorted. In my own work I have studied the memories of David to show how those memories have been variously cast and how they have been articulated to accommodate various social settings and social possibilities.[36] The memory may be enmeshed in a nostalgic longing for normalcy and "the good old days," when life was simple and agrarian, settled, and well-ordered. That nostalgia is all intertwined with evangelical memory, so that the nostalgia has a vague religious feeling about it. There is a need to sort out the normative memory from this other vague yearning.

The present situation of the congregation needs careful attention. It is usually a situation of considerable affluence (even if some present are not affluent). The affluent ones are the ones who are competent and know how to generate income and move through the chairs to the seats of power. But the affluence and competence we treasure so much is matched by a profound fear—that the dollar will collapse, that the bomb will explode, that the Communists will attack. The affluence-competence factor invites us to "stand tall" and be secure; the fear syndrome undermines our confidence and we live our days in an inarticulate uneasiness. This interface of affluence-competence and fear distorts public issues. The matters of compassion and "justice for all" that are embedded in our public conscience have become shriveled. Our fear drives us to selfishness, greed, and vengeance. Along with public failure, we find an erosion of our personal sense of life, a restlessness that generates anxiety that drives us to greed, and finally to despair that it won't really work out. Our actual experience of our common life is not remote from the alienation of Marx, the technical rationality of Weber, and the normlessness of Durkheim.

There are many things to celebrate in this new world of competence and technical security. It boggles the mind to think how different we are from our grandparents and how much better off we are. But we are dimly aware that this new mode of life we value so much has caused us to jettison much that we previously valued. It is odd that the old festivals of solidarity wane, yet there is a persistent hunger for such occasions of solidarity. Old patterns of familial and liturgical gatherings are less and less compelling in our society. Our young people ask about roles and careers, but vocation seems like an obsolete idea. We surprise ourselves when we entertain brutality as a policy option in the world, and vengeance now seems acceptable if aimed at the right people. We have become people we did not intend to become, and we are not fully convinced that this is who we want to be. Given our perception of the world, however, that is who we need to be if we are to "succeed" according to the norms we have embraced.

Such a community gathers for the act of interpretation. Even if we have never heard of the word "modernity," we sense in inarticulate ways that we embody much that is "modern." Much has been lost to us, even if much is gained. We gather to see if we can hold the gain and yet recover what is lost. We gather to see if the world of vocation and tradition, of birth and bread, of shepherds and forgiveness can be mediated to us in the midst of our disproportionate affluence and fear. We do not want to discard the old memory, as our modern world wants to do, but we do not want a flat reiteration of the old memory that pretends we are not affluent and not afraid. We do not want simply a nostalgia that does not touch any of the real problems, the ethics of our affluence and the moral dilemma of our fear. We yearn for a responsive, assertive, imaginative act of interpretation that recasts the memory in bold ways that will transform our situation.

Our discussion thus far suggests a convergence of four major factors in the act of interpretation. These reflect, on the one hand, our present general intellectual situation and, on the other hand, the specific situation of the church. I find it remarkable that these four factors, which are drawn from very different aspects of contemporary thought and life, should so powerfully intersect in relation to our interpretive responsibility.

1. *The textual process* itself is an act of regular recasting that includes both faith and vested interest.

2. *The sociological tradition* in its classic presentations concerns the problem of alienation (Marx), the problematic of rationality (Weber), and the emergence of normlessness (Durkheim). All of these conditions are part of the modern world, and we know them all firsthand.

3. *The task of interpretation* is the task of the community
to mediate the tradition in ways that construe a new
world, that permit a new ethic among us.

4. *The congregation is gathered* to see if the old memory
can be articulated in ways that reconfigure our present
social reality of affluence and competence, of fear and
brutality, of restlessness and despair.

The preaching moment is a moment of great complexity,
great danger, and great possibility. Present in that moment
are the textual process, the sociological realities, the act of
interpretation, the waiting congregation. Such a moment
requires a strategy through which a new community might be
summoned to a fresh identity and a bold vocation.

Options in Social Construction

The preacher in the act of interpretation and proclamation
of the text is engaged in world-making. I find it most helpful
to appeal to the phrase of Berger and Luckmann, "the social
construction of reality."[37] The community authorizes special
persons to head and oversee the process of social construction. In our context, the minister (usually ordained) is
authorized to lead the community of faith in its construction
of reality. Such an act is an ongoing process of education and
nurture, especially in liturgy.[38] This liturgical articulation is
presented as objectively true. When it is also received in this
way, this liturgically presented world may be internalized by
members of the community as "mine." Thus the process of
appropriation includes the public action of the community
and the personal internalization by the individual members
who participate in the liturgy.

The second awareness from Berger and Luckmann is that
the "life-world" so constructed is always underway and must
be modified. New data, fresh perspectives, new experiences,
and changed circumstances require recasting the life-world
to keep it credible. If it is not regularly recast, the "old world"
becomes disengaged from experience so that it either must
live in protected, uncritical space (where it will be irrelevant),

or it will be jettisoned as dead. It is the ongoing act of interpretation that recasts the life-world to keep the text credible. The preacher is engaged with the biblical texts in both elements, to sustain *the act of appropriation* and to engage in the ongoing *recasting* to keep the text credible.

This means that the purpose of interpretation and preaching is to present a life-world that is credible, that can be appropriated, out of which the community is authorized and permitted to live a different kind of life. As the text itself is a responsive, assertive, creative act, so the interpretation of the text is also a responsive, assertive, creative act. The purpose of the sermon is to provide a world in which the congregation can live. Indeed, the preacher is intentionally designated precisely to mediate a world that comes out of this text which endures through the generations. That world which the preacher mediates is one possible world out of many that could be offered. The offer of this world competes with other offers made by capitalism, by militarism, by psychology of various kinds, by health clubs, by automobiles, by beers, and so on. Moreover it is a possible world among many which might be articulated out of the Bible, so it makes a difference if the text mediated is a Mosaic or a Solomonic text.

Scholarship has found it helpful to speak of a typology of interpretative postures. We may speak of a primary decision, so that the interpretive act is either transformative or stabilizing, in the service of discontinuity or in the service of equilibrium.[39] The basis for that model is rooted in the social history of ancient Israel and is evidenced textually in the Old Testament tension between the transformative vision of Moses, which belonged to the earliest voice of liberated Israel, and the stabilizing tendency of royal theology which sought to build institutions and establish a reliable social structure.[40] When the texts are read sociologically, this interpretive issue of transformation-equilibrium is enormously helpful. This Old Testament paradigm (as Gottwald has shown)[41] has important parallels to a Marxist class analysis, to Weber's construct of charisma and bureaucracy, and I should suggest, also to Toennies' typology of *Gemeinschaft* and *Gesellschaft*.[42] The text itself in the Old Testament reflects this tension. The radical vision of Mosaic faith is in deep tension with the royal enterprise subsequently developed.

The tension exists between texts with different social locations.[45] The act of interpretation can and inevitably must deal with the ways in which the text destabilizes and transforms, or the way in which the text stabilizes and gives equilibrium. How the text is interpreted by the preacher and how the text is received in the congregation may depend on the vested interest of both preacher and congregation, which may or may not adhere to the position of the text itself. Texts may transform *and* stabilize. Sometimes the same text may function either to transform *or* stabilize, depending on context, interest and interpretation. Text and/or interpretation offer a world of transformation or equilibrium that enhances or diminishes a particular view of social reality. It is in the nature of the act of interpretation and therefore of preaching to participate in these world-making acts, either knowingly or unwittingly.

In what follows, I am presenting a typology of texts through which various texts will be interpreted. It is, of course, the case that the texts themselves are never as clear and unambiguous as is the typology. The typology is useful only to the extent that it helps us see specific texts afresh; it should never be imposed on texts.

The text can be an act of good faith, because both transformation and stabilization are faithful acts of God and both meet deep human yearnings, but the mediation of either comes through the vested interest of the preacher. Whether the preacher will mediate a world of transformation or equilibrium depends on many things, including what the preacher reads, with whom the preacher eats, the economic history of the preacher, and much else.

The texts will be received by the congregation as an act of faith. People do come to church to hear and respond. The reception of a mediation of either transformation or equilibrium happens through the interpretive receptivity of the congregation. What happens, what the text can "do," depends on the propensity of the congregation. That will be determined by many factors, but they include where and how the congregation is socially situated, what travels have been taken, what part of the world has been seen, how many members have experienced poverty, unemployment, crime, and all sorts of social disruption—or conversely how strong is the social equilibrium in the experience and horizon of the congregation. All of these factors impinge in powerful, subtle, and complex ways upon the interchange of text, preacher, and congregation. In the midst of the interchange, a new world may be mediated.

In presenting the world of the text to the congregation, the preacher has, according to this typology, four possible strategies. The typology assumes that the text may be an offer of transformation or stability and that the congregation is likely to be in a situation of transformation or stability. The available strategies in establishing an interface between the text-world and the congregation are these:

1. To present "a world of transformation" to those who yearn and hope for transformation. This is done when oppressed or marginalized people are invited to hope for the basic changes of social reality that are given in the texts of transformation.

2. To present "a world of equilibrium" to those who wait and yearn for transformation. This is done when oppressed or marginalized people are invited to accept and participate in the present regime as their proper duty and their only hope. The present order is then presented as the best chance for any change, but it will be change within that order that is accepted as non-negotiable.

3. To present "a world of transformation" to those who value the status quo and do not want the world changed. This is when those who benefit from present social arrangements are called, in the face of that benefit, to submit to change as the will and work of God.

4. To present "a world of equilibrium" to those who crave equilibrium and regard the present social world as the best of all possible worlds, a world decreed by God. This is done when religion becomes a comfortable endorsement of the status quo.[44]

Each of these strategies is possible and each reflects a decision about the thrust of the biblical text and how that thrust is to be related to the actual situation of the church.

Each of these four strategies is possible and on formal grounds, each is biblical. It is equally clear that the gospel gives criteria to sort out the various strategies and to see that all the possible strategies are not equally legitimate for genuine evangelical proclamation. The preacher is summoned by the gospel to present an imaginative Word that lives "out beyond" and challenges the taken-for-granted world of the congregation.

In presenting this typology, I am aware that the actual situation of any congregation is enormously complex. In every congregation there are those who welcome change, those who resist change, and those who are unsure. Moreover, there are various kinds of changes, each of which needs to be critically assessed. In addition, various preachers and pastors are inclined either to welcome or resist change and that helps shape interpretation and preaching. My discussion intends not to deny or disregard all of that complexity which must be honored and taken seriously.

For purposes of clarity, however, in what follows, I have chosen to deal only with the third and fourth elements of this typology. My sense is that these dimensions of interpretation bear particularly on the typical North American congregation. A church that does not want the world changed will either be offered a text-world of transformation that calls the present into question (#3 above), or a text-world that celebrates equilibrium (#4 above). To be sure, there are times in such a congregation when equilibrium is legitimate and a genuine offer of the text, but for now we have posed the question in another way. The preacher thus may appeal to texts that offer either equilibrium or transformation and in doing so must pay attention to the possible hearing of the gospel that will occur in the congregation if the text is heard as an abrasion or as an assurance.

The important interpretive point is that the text should be kept in conversation with what the congregation already knows and believes. At times, the purpose of interpretation is to evoke fresh faith for another world from that which the community already knows and believes. In the typical North American situation, it is often the case that the text should be interpreted to make available an imaginative world out beyond the one to which the congregation now clings. More often this is so because such congregations tend to be ideologically trapped in a social world at odds with the gospel. But this interpretation that calls for newness may, nevertheless, appeal to the deep and serious faith latent in the church.

In a world of war and violence, for example, equilibrium is not objectively true, but is in fact an imaginative act of interpretation that has been established and accepted as true. The interpretive issue is whether to ally the gospel with that already accepted mediated world or to propose an alternative that may "ring true" but also will surely evoke conflict.

The strategy of the preacher then is to use texts in ways that legitimate the present perceived life-world, or to present a life-world that puts people in crisis by offering a challenge to their present view and posing an alternative. Both are needed, but different emphases probably need to be made in various circumstances.

Whatever strategy is undertaken, it is most important that the preacher—and hopefully the congregation—is aware that good preaching (which is an act of inventive world-construction) is fundamentally opposed to two tendencies in our culture. It is opposed to a false kind of objectivity that assumes the world is a closed, fixed, fated given. That assumption of objectivity is a great temptation to us, whether the claim is given in the name of religious orthodoxy or in the name of technological certitude. An evangelical understanding of reality asserts instead that all of our presumed givens are provisional and open to newness, a newness that may be enacted in the event of preaching.

The other tendency to which good preaching is opposed is a kind of subjectivity that assumes we are free or able to conjure up private worlds that may exist in a domesticated sphere without accountability to or impingement from the larger public world. Such a powerful deception among us seems to offer happiness, but it is essentially abdication from the great public issues that shape our humanness.

The preaching task is to be critical and challenging in ways that expose our present life-world as inadequate, unfaithful, and finally flat. This is to be done, however, in ways that neither become ideological nor simply terminate the conversation. Preaching is aimed not simply at this or that ethical issue, but seeks to cut underneath particular issues to the unreasoned, unexamined, and unrecognized "structures of plausibility" that are operative in the congregation. Such preaching is also to offer reassurances about the coherence of reality, but a reassurance that is not a legitimation of present arrangements, but an act of hope about another life-world available in the gospel. That life-world could offer the joy for which we yearn, which the present life-world cannot give. This offer of another world is the primary work of the gospel, for the gospel is news of another world. The articulation of that other world is unavoidably a critique of and challenge to every present world. This "other world" which is announced in and mediated by the gospel is not "other-worldly" in the sense that it is in the remote future, in heaven, after death, or "spiritual." Rather, the "other world" is now "at hand" (Mark 1:15). It refers to the present Rule of God that calls us to a new obedience now and that releases us from every other obedience in the here and now, for the sake of God's sovereign rule.

Texts of equilibrium are important to the formation of a new life-world. The creation narrative-liturgy of *Genesis 1:1–2:4*a is such a text. It asserts that the world is ordered, good, belongs to God, and is therefore reliable. When according to critical study, that text is set in the Exile as an affirmation to Israelites and a polemic against Babylonian imperialism and Babylonian gods, the social function of that equilibrium emerges. The Genesis text asserts that the world belongs to God and therefore not to Babylon, not to their gods or their rulers. Moreover God rests and Israel is mandated to rest. In that mandate it is asserted that Israelites in exile need not be endlessly anxious and frantic to become secure or to please Babylon, but can rest in God's sure rule. Thus the text offers a world of well-ordered stability and equilibrium, in which Israel is invited to live. That well-ordered stability is not neutral, however, but is a counter-equilibrium that invites Israel to break with seductive Babylonian offers of stability and equilibrium that cannot be true because the world does not belong to them. The community that lives within this text is given stability but also is summoned to a freedom outside Babylonian definitions of reality. That is, by an act of imagination, creation theology becomes a warrant for what the Empire would regard as civil disobedience.[45] The capacity of exiled Israel to act freely depends on its acceptance of the world of this text. The text responds to exile, asserts against Babylon, and imagines an alternative world of faith in which life is possible. The congregation may be invited to sense what an uncommon act of imagination this text is which dares to say that the world belongs to Yahweh who is a God of rest and order, dares to say it even to exiles whose life is disordered and restless.

Texts of transformation are equally important for a new life-world. The healing-feeding narrative of Elijah in *I Kings 17:8-24* is such a text.[46] It is a text of disruption. It tells about this strange formidable man of inexplicable power who comes into the life of a poor widow. He deals with her poverty by giving her food. He deals with death by raising her son to life. He is perceived by the widow, by the narrator, and finally by us, as a bearer of the power for life. This text evokes a question about this power, where it is available, and on what terms. The narrative asserts that power for life is not given through the royal regime but by this uncredentialed outsider.

This story destabilizes. It shatters the poverty-stricken, death-ridden world of the widow. It breaks her assumptions and her habits. If we listen attentively to the story when it is well told, it will also break our conventional assumptions, for it announces that the world is not the way we thought it was. The critical effect of the narrative is to delegitimate the king and his deathly rule and to invite us to another rule under the God of life. But the story of disruption also turns out to be a story of affirmation. It asserts that power is available, that life can be given, that food is offered.

Thus the story responds to the failure of Ahab and his governance. It asserts an alternative reality against Ahab's world. By an act of imagination, a story of feeding and a story of healing have been mobilized as vehicles for a different life-world. The narrative invites the listening community into a new arena of existence in which God's power for life has enormous vitality for new possibility, even though it is untamed and unadministered and we cannot harness and manage it on our terms.

Every text proposes a life-world that may counter ours. Texts of equilibrium are needed to give people a sense of order, but such texts as Genesis 1:1–2:4a turn out to be invitations to transformation. Texts of transformation are needed to give people hope that there is possibility outside present circumstances. But such texts as I Kings 17:8-24 turn out to be invitations to a new equilibrium wrought only by the gospel. Texts of both equilibrium and transformation are needed. In both cases it requires not only the capacity to respond and assert, but also the capacity for imagination in order to let these texts become truly effective. Characteristically they invite the listening community out beyond the presumed world to a new world of freedom, joy, and obedience.

Exegetical Comments: I Kings 8:1-13, 27-30

The text we will consider in detail in relation to the social nature and function of interpretation is I Kings 8:1-30.

1. The literary delineation of the text is complex. We may, however, make three preliminary, critical judgments:

a) The text contains very old materials. Verses 12-13 in particular probably go back to the actual liturgy of dedication in the time of Solomon and reflect uncompromising, uncritical temple theology.

b) The text contains later Deuteronomic theology.[47] Verses 27-30 contain a critique of temple theology that had too easily assumed God's presence.

c) The completed form of the text is likely an exilic construction (which becomes more explicit in verses 31 ff.) and reflects the theological agenda and interests of the Deuteronomists. As exilic theology, it reflects on the old claims of the temple to be God's place of presence in the sober context of the Exile of 587 B.C.E. and the destruction of the temple.[48] The grand claims of the temple turned out to be not true. It is not the case that God dwells there forever, for now the temple is destroyed and the community, including its priests, is displaced.[49]

Thus the text is a reminiscence of temple theology that is critically assessed even as it is knowingly appropriated. The text continues to hold on to the temple as a central source of hope for Israel, but it also knows that temple hope is profoundly problematic because it makes assumptions about God's availability which crowd God and cannot be sustained. The reality of God's presence is now seen through the prism of exile which must face the experienced reality of God's absence.

2. The sequence of the text is as follows:

a) Verses 1-13 is a narrative account of the actual liturgy of dedication and the movement of the ark, Israel's most sacred symbol, into the temple. Noteworthy are the prominent role of the priests and the careful attention to the details of liturgical propriety. These verses reflect uncritical confidence in the liturgic claims of the monarchy.[50]

b) Verses 14-26 are a reflective statement, placed in the mouth of Solomon, concerning God's commitment to the Davidic dynasty. The promise asserted here refers back to II Samuel 7:11-16, but in I Kings 8:25 the unconditional promise of II Samuel 7 has become conditional by the introduction of "if."[51] One can detect a restless awareness in Israel of unconditional and conditional assurances from God. The facts of the Exile qualify the unconditional character of the promise.

c) Verses 27-30 are a statement of sober reflection on God's presence in the temple which critiques the confident claims of verses 12-13. One can discern here the voice of exilic Deuteronomic theology that proposes that it is not God's self, but God's name that is in the temple.[52] The solution may seem to us not very persuasive, but it is at least evidence of the honest, profound, and imaginative wrestling with the problem of God's presence among banished exiles.

3. In its completed form, I Kings 8 stands as the pivotal text in the long Deuteronomic history from Deuteronomy through Second Kings.[53] That interpretive reflection on the history of Israel with God concerns (a) God's goodness to Israel, (b) Israel's recalcitrant response to God, and (c) the delayed but heavy judgment of exile. Immediately after

I Kings 8, the Deuteronomist begins the downward tale to the year 587, destruction, and exile.

Deuteronomic theology is complex.[54] For our purposes, it is sufficient to observe the tension between temple and Torah as a central motif.[55] The temple functions ideologically as a guarantee of God's presence in Israel; thus it is a legitimating part of the royal-temple establishment. The temple is a visible embodiment of self-assertive ideology by king and priest that makes God a sure patron. In tension with that is Torah theology which asserts that obedience is the prerequisite for presence. Disobedience will evoke God's absence. This is the context in which the "if" of I Kings 8:25 is to be understood.

This tension can be discerned historically as a live dispute in exilic Israel that trusts in God's presence but knows well about God's absence. This tension can be discerned literarily in the contrast of verses 12-13 and verses 27-30. It is this tension of temple and Torah, of conditional and unconditional, of presence and absence that I have taken as the theme of the sermon that follows. This sermon has been preached at the Iliff School of Theology, Wesley Theological Seminary, and First Congregational Church, Swampscott, Massachusetts.

A Footnote to the Royal Pageant

I KINGS 8:1-13, 27-30

While the choirs processed, the choirmaster sat nervously and proudly holding his baton, posed for the moment of his new anthem. The king sat complacently, too satisfied in the royal box, too confident of all that he now controlled. The procession was long and colorful with all the great men and sheep and oxen and incense—and the ark and the priests and the cherubim. Perfectly rehearsed, perfectly implemented. Everywhere splendor and elegance—and glory. When all were in place, the choirs sang what had never been sung before in Jerusalem, a genuinely new song:

The Lord has set the sun in the heavens,
    but has said that he would dwell in thick darkness.
I have built thee an exalted house,
    a place for thee to dwell in for ever. (I Kings 8:12-13)

God was there. The temple was dedicated. The king was legitimated. The order of temple and monarchy was sanctified. God was present now, for time to come, forever and ever, world without end.

1. This is a sermon about God's presence and the legitimacy that comes from it. The high claim of presence made in this text is not different from the claim with which most liturgies begin—assured, umambiguous, settled, "God is with us." The problem, of course, is that this is a theme in a royal pagaent. It is done for reasons of state. The music is crafted by state employees whom we call temple singers. The theology is worked out by royal ideologues who never forget the name of their true patron, and his name is Solomon and not Yahweh. In the end it is all too neat. Of course God is present. That has been the promise and claim for Israel since the burning bush when God came down to sojourn in the slave camp. But then the presence was awesome, inscrutable, and terrifying. But kings manage things better than slaves. Now the presence has become settled and reassuring and enduring. Moses may have trembled, but the king only smiles benignly, without trembling, because the resolve of God to dwell in this place—that is what the liturgy affirms—means that God is present, always present, ally, patron, guarantor, a social functionary. The choirs may sing, but it will not be that simple to reduce God to a character in the king's drama. It couldn't be that simple, but the king is not vexed by that problem, as indeed kings never are.

This is a sermon about God's presence because theologians and pastors, theological teachers and theological students now have to think more seriously and more critically about God's presence than we have had to do for a long while. They must help the whole church think how and in what ways God is present and how and in what ways God may be absent. We have grown up in our culture sure of God's attentiveness and availability. Notions of God's abrasive freedom are almost gone from our vocabulary. It all seems so cozy. Pastors and seminarians in Clinical Pastoral Education are paid to let God be present, because it seems to give reassurance. But life is not all a royal pageant. Life is also a social revolution. It is a long slow dying in the night and a waiting for the phone to ring. Such living (and dying) happens for some, more in the absence than in the presence of God. There are signs as we think about the Christian West and the rise of Islam and oil that seem to indicate that the glory may have departed, and the liturgy may be a lie over which the king still presides benignly. The question requires us to be tough and honest about the text and about the texture of our life that is more problematic than the king's pageant intends or acknowledges.

2. After the three-hour liturgy (for royal pageants tend to last that long), they had a luncheon in Jerusalem and then a panel discussion reflection on the liturgy—what it meant, what we learned from it, how we ought to think about it. The heavies were all there with their prepared seven-minute responses which panels always require. And as is the case with such panels, some responses were more clever than others. The panel is never as powerful as the liturgy, for we are always too self-conscious and game-playing on such panels. But there was one urbane, candid, unencumbered voice that day. It was the Deuteronomist. He was tenured and had no fear of royal theologians. He could say things that the choirmasters might not like, or that had just never occurred to them, because they were so caught up in aestheticism that they lacked critical distance. He spoke with clarity and with some indignation:

Will God indeed dwell on earth? Behold heaven and the highest heaven cannot contain thee, how much less this temple! God dwells in heaven, not here, God watches from heaven and hears from heaven. God is attentive, but not available, not on call, not patron, not guarantor.

There was a stunned silence when he finished. Astonishingly, it is an exegesis of the second commandment! I thought for one day we could be free of that heaviness for the sake of the king's program. But Israel never quite gets free of the second commandment. The Deuteronomist always makes sure of that, sounding it again and again. There is a strange distance maintained between heaven and earth. The one who is sovereign might for a moment be mistaken for patron, but this God really does not "do windows," even the windows of the king.

It must have been a stunning moment in the day of the dedication of the temple to have this statement dumped in the middle of Jerusalem, because it has the effect of delegitimating all the proud claims of the day. It abruptly empties Jerusalem of its claim to heavenly significance. It warns against absolutizing any project, any scheme, any formula. It makes clear that we come as expectant but unsure supplicants, that the initiative for our life is held by God who will not easily fit into our models, political, economic, and moral. Every religion, ancient or modern, has a God who is a willing patron. Every religion but this one—and we are cast into the world without a patron, only with a Sovereign who listens and who hears, but who will not be administered.

3. So the panel ended. The folks went home. The king retired to his quarters exhausted and satisfied. He was only mildly alarmed by the Deuteronomist, for who listens to such abrasive theology? And anyway, that guy always said the same thing and people no longer paid him any attention. Everybody went home, except of course the janitors. A big crew had to clear up the litter. It was everywhere. Old bulletins of the service were even left around the ark. The ark had been the focus of the service. It was the oldest, most honored symbol, kept over from the days of the revolution. It was said to be God's special place. One of the young custodians, who had become cynical by living too close to "holy people," thought he would take a peek. He did not believe much about God's presence, but he did not have the skill or ability to doubt the claims of the throne very critically. It just seemed to him it was all more mundane than the liturgy suggested. His cynicism had helped him notice that the ones who believed all these liturgical claims so deeply were also the ones who seemed so well-off and secure. Perhaps such self-contained, excessively reassuring liturgy is more compelling when one has more of this world's goods. He suspected the claims might not convince so easily if one were not so well-off.

So he took a look into the ark. He did not touch it, for his cynicism had not advanced that far. Nor was he that jaded. He did not know what he expected to see. But he was shocked when he looked. What he saw was not God, but two tablets.

There was nothing in the ark except the two tablets of stone which Moses put there at Horeb, where the Lord made a covenant with the people of Israel when they came out of the land of Egypt. (I Kings 8:9)

The words said nothing mystical or enigmatic or eloquent or supernatural about God's presence. Only the old simple words first uttered to the liberated slaves:

No other gods,

No graven images,

You shall not steal,

You shall not commit adultery,

You shall not covet.

Kings have better words, more syllables, smoother, more reassuring, not so costly, but slaves and peasants tend to get down to basics. The janitor, at the end of the pageant, was driven back behind the pageant to the liberating miracle and the moment of bonding when Israel's life was changed and Israel's identity was set for all time in obedience against all the rulers of this age. The janitor was not a sophisticated theologian, or he would not have been messing with the litter. He never made the choir. He never participated in a theological forum, but it dawned on him that simple folk have found God's presence in the daily radicalness of holding to a covenantal ethic. Obedience is the shape of God's presence.

Moses had put obedience and presence together:

What great nation has a God so near,
What great nation has a torah so righteous. (Deut. 4:7-8, author's translation)

The Deuteronomist loved that word remembered from Moses. Moses did not have in mind the triviality of morality, but the deep vocational embrace of covenant. The janitor had a hunch that day that God's presence would not be found in the large, eloquent liturgies. He sensed inchoately that most of that was for reasons of state, contrived to enhance security and legitimacy. One must not be deceived and God must not be mocked.

4. The temple was empty. The lights were out. Every one was gone. Except *there* in the shadow outside was an old woman. She must have been a widow, for she was all in black,

stooped from having carried too many jars of water. Her gnarled hands caressed the stones of the temple where she was not permitted to enter. She caressed, she believed, she trusted and there she found a little peace. There are little old women and other rejected powerless people everywhere around temples and churches and such holy places. I saw one in Spain. She looked so beaten, but she was waiting. She had enough faith to be there. This one in Jerusalem heard ringing in her ears, going over and over it in her head, the anthem she had heard from inside the building:

The Lord has set the sun in the heavens,
but has said that he would dwell in thick darkness. (I Kings 8:12)

She held on to the building. She believed and trusted. She knew. The anthem is true. The temple stands making God available in God's gracious abiding splendor. The widow comes there to grasp life desperately one more time.

A pastor I know reports on a trip to Russia. He was in a crowded Orthodox Church in Moscow. Amid all the pageantry, at a point in a service he did not notice, the little old women, wearied with their life, wearing babushkas, began mumbling in a language he did not understand. It was a sing-song chant they all understood. He found out later they were, as they do each Sunday, quietly and defiantly reciting the Beatitudes:

Blessed are the poor . . .

Blessed are the meek . . .

Blessed are the pure in heart . . .

Blessed are the peacemakers . . .

The old widows believed the promises of the liturgy and they came to the temple as the place to reenact the hope that kept them free and sane.

All of these may come to the same temple room together: the king who counts too heavily on his liturgical legitimacy, the Deuteronomist who knows better and debunks, the janitor who finds only Torah tablets and seeks to obey, the little old lady who has nowhere else to turn, and holds desperately to the place of the liturgy which she regards as the place of presence.

It occurs to me that the king and the black-dressed, stooped widow follow the same liturgy. It was true for her, desperately true. She found there sustenance in a world that was shaped like starvation. But it was not true for the king who controlled it all. For the king it was a lie. He needed to heed the Deuteronomist. Or better, he needed to consult with the janitor who knew more.

We are left with the text, the temple, and the liturgy. We have a yearning for presence. Only a few of us have been driven with the widow to find the liturgy true. To arrive at such guileless certitude requires fingering the tablets with those ten liberating words. The church in the West—and we in theological study—have this old liturgy and a new awareness that God among us is sovereign and not so easily available. We are driven to question behind our conventional legitimacy the character of the God who is not contained.

Our struggle with the God of the Bible is that God's presence is real, but never on our terms.[56] In God's presence we are more surprised than assured, more shattered than accepted. But how our meeting with God turns out will be a gift from God, never designed by us.

Listen to this exegesis of the text from I Kings 8.

He also told this parable to some who trusted in themselves that they were righteous and despised others: "Two men went up into the temple to pray, one a Pharisee and the other a tax collector. The Pharisee stood and prayed thus with himself, 'God, I thank thee that I am not like other men, extortioners, unjust, adulterers, or even like this tax collector. I fast twice a week, I give tithes of all that I get.' But the tax collector, standing far off, would not even lift up his eyes to heaven, but beat his breast, saying, 'God, be merciful to me a sinner!' I tell you, this man went down to his house justified rather than the other; for every one who exalts himself will be humbled, but he who humbles himself will be exalted" (Luke 18:9-14).

We have the text, the temple, the tablets, the ark, the liturgy. Our life-work is in sorting it out. The royal pageant is important. But God is not a mere footnote.

Reflection

I have taken the text of I Kings 8:1-13, 27-30 for a sermon because the theme of presence is important in our society.

Obviously God must be present or we will die (Ps. 104:29-30). False forms of presence will deceive us and destroy us, however. One false form of presence among us is the therapeutic, in which a subjective, individualistic model of reality assumes that we can have a private relationship with God without reference to social reality. A second false view is in degenerate modes of civil religion which regard God as a patron and ally of Americanism in all its forms. Moreover the public practice of civil religion and personal therapeutic propensity are mutually reinforcing. Together in the name of freedom they encourage the most destructive, stultifying kind of conformity. That false practice of God's presence, in both of its forms, is untrue and unbiblical because it reduces God to our ally and denies God's sovereign freedom. That false practice of presence seduces us into idolatrous worship of self, of nation, of ideology, so that the courage to lead a life of tough dignity and serious accountability disappears. It is my judgment that the theme of presence must be critically addressed, because a presumed, uncritical presence functions to legitimate and sanctify much that is false and destructive in our common life. This sermon intends to surface that issue.

I have constructed the sermon around four voices, through which I intend to suggest four social practices, four social functions, and four social possibilities. The first (verses 12-13) is *the voice of official religion* which uncritically celebrates the status quo and understands God to be its legitimator.

The second (verses 27-30) is *the voice of Mosaic theology* which sounds the second commandment through the Deuteronomist. In ancient Israel and in our preaching, this theological voice functions to criticize easy religion.

The third voice (verse 9) which I have placed in the mouth of the janitor is *a voice that debunks* and in rather simple form returns to obedience as the center of biblical faith. This voice is congenial to that of the Deuteronomist, but the text (verse 9) bears none of the marks of that theology.

In the fourth voice, that of the widow, the *voice of hopeful marginality,* I have obviously exercised homiletical freedom. I have done so to form a sharp contrast with verses 12-13 and

have done so on the strength of the parable in Luke 18:9-14. I
did not want simply to dismiss the liturgical claim of verses
12-13. That would be too easy, too abrasive, and not faithful
to the text. Instead of dismissal I suggest rather that verses
12-13 may be true faith or false ideology, depending on the
social situation of the believer. What functions as faithful for
"have-nots" may be false for "haves." Obviously I have made
an interpretive decision informed by a conviction of "the
preferential option of the poor." By going in that direction I
hope to raise questions for future conversation among the
listeners.

The sermon intends to do four things.

1. To suggest that the issue of God's presence is urgent
and complex. It is a complex issue with which the Bible itself
struggles. Implicit in that affirmation is the suggestion that
the issue is not settled even for us settled secure North
Americans, but is an open question with risks. We need to pay
attention also to other voices that are alive and involved in the
conversation.

2. To enact the notion that our practice of faith is a
conversation of many voices, some of which are congenial to
us and some of which are not. We must be full parties to the
conversation. Partly that conversation is a public, external
one going on in the world church. Partly it is an internal one,
because in our seasons of honesty we are all these voices and
we are not of one mind and do not experience God's presence
in one single mode.

3. To engage the congregation in an imaginative act of
interpretation. The sermon intends by inference to open up a
suggestive critique of American civil religion and to suggest
that as the church holds to the second commandment, we
may notice idolatry in peculiar places. The urge back to the
commandments suggests that in our cultural exile, if we sense
that the glory has departed, a return to obedience is a clue to
our future. To raise the question of obedience in the midst of
American civil religion is a hazardous enterprise, but that is
precisely what the Deuteronomist has done in the midst of
temple ideology.

4. To offer through the text an alternative life-world. The
life-world offered here is a world other than the Western

imperial world of control, security, and affluence. It is a world of exile in which many voices compete, in which God's presence is an open question, in which the poor are visible and vocal, in which the cynical must be heeded, in which the commandments may prevail. It is a world in which presence may be true—or a terrible self-deception. New decisions are possible for Western Christians in this life-world, but they will be possible only if widows and janitors are included in the conversation. The text, set in the Exile, dreams of a homecoming and restored well-being, only if there is obedience. Such obedience is only possible, however, when the question of presence is honestly faced. The God disclosed here commands. This God also cares, but will not be our ally in the things of the world. Imagine that widows and orphans have access to the very God whom the heavens cannot contain! Much less can our impotent ideologies contain this God.

This text reflects a situation similar to our own, one in which royal liturgy regularly guarantees our world. The text asserts a situation radically in tension with that royal promise. Thus, in a shrewd and delicate way it both affirms and questions, assures and debunks. Such a text may gain a hearing, because there is a hunch even in the royal pageant that more needs to be said about God. More needs to be said about God for God's sake, and for our sake.

Notes

1. On the work of the community in generating the text, see Michel Clevenot, *Materialist Approaches to the Bible* (Maryknoll, N.Y.: Orbis Books, 1985), esp. chapters 12-15. Leonardo Boff, *Church, Charism and Power* (New York: Crossroad Publishing Co., 1985), 110-15, has seen the critical implications of this insight of production concerning the ideological control that the interpreting community exercises over the text.

2. On the freedom exercised and the choices made in such construal, see David H. Kelsey, *The Uses of Scripture in Recent Theology* (Philadelphia: Fortress Press, 1975). On a "canonical construal" of the Old Testament, see Brevard S. Childs, *Old Testament Theology in a Canonical Context* (Philadelphia: Fortress Press, 1986).

3. Michael Fishbane, *Biblical Interpretation in Ancient Israel* (Oxford: Clarendon Press, 1985), has shown in a compelling way the dynamic relation between *traditum* and *traditio*, i.e., the tradition and the ongoing traditioning process. It is often the case, clearly, that the *traditio* becomes the new *traditum*. See also his more succinct statement of the matter, "Torah and Tradition," in

Tradition and Theology in the Old Testament, ed. Douglas A. Knight (Philadelphia: Fortress Press, 1977), 275-300. In this latter work he comments: "Hereby the danger inherent in the dialectical process between a divine Torah-revelation and a human exegetical Tradition has been disclosed. Tradition has superseded the Torah-teaching and has become an independent authority. Indeed, in this case, Tradition has replaced Torah itself" (294).

4. In the "rendering" of the text, one "renders" God in a new way. On the theme, see Dale Patrick, *The Rendering of God* (Philadelphia: Fortress Press, 1981).

5. On the methodological possibilities in "reader response," see Wolfgang Iser, *The Act of Reading: A Theory of Aesthetic Response* (Baltimore: Johns Hopkins University Press, 1978), and the collection of essays, Susan R. Sulieman and Inge Crosman, eds., *The Reader in the Text* (Princeton, N.J.: Princeton University Press, 1980).

6. For brief introductions to this method of study, see Robert R. Wilson, *Sociological Approaches to the Old Testament* (Philadelphia: Fortress Press, 1984), and Norman K. Gottwald, "Sociological Method in the Study of Ancient Israel," in *Encounter with the Text,* ed. Martin J. Buss (Philadelphia: Fortress Press, 1979), 69-81.

7. See Rudolf Bultmann, "Is Exegesis Without Presuppositions Possible?" in *Existence and Faith* (Cleveland: World Publishing Co., 1960), 289-96. Given our current sociological inclination, the formula has come to have different, and perhaps more radical, implications than originally suggested by Bultmann.

8. This is a central argument of Norman K. Gottwald, *The Tribes of Yahweh* (Maryknoll, N.Y.: Orbis Books, 1979). See, for example, chapter 13 where he speaks of substructure and superstructure and narratives as "objectifications of the tradition superstructure."

9. This point has been well argued by Elisabeth Schüssler Fiorenza, *Bread Not Stone* (Boston: Beacon Press, 1984). For startling examples of tendentious interpretation, see Robert Ericksen, *Theologians Under Hitler* (New Haven: Yale University Press, 1985).

10. Richard L. Rohrbaugh, *The Biblical Interpreter* (Philadelphia: Fortress Press, 1978).

11. On the neutralizing effect of much scholarship, see Jose Cordenas Pollares who has observed the power of "guild scholarship" to avoid the central interpretive issues. He writes, "Today, Sacred Scripture is studied with the benevolent approval of the *pax imperialis;* no exegetical activity disturbs the tranquility of the 'empire' for a single moment. What biblical periodical has ever fallen under suspicion of being subversive? Biblical specialists have curiously little to suffer from the Neros and Domitians of our time." *A Poor Man Called Jesus* (Maryknoll, N.Y.: Orbis Books, 1986), 2.

12. The notion of a hermeneutic of suspicion has been normatively presented by Paul Ricoeur, *Freud and Philosophy* (New Haven: Yale University Press, 1970). See the programmatic use made of it by David Tracy, *The Analogical Imagination: Christian Theology and the Culture of Pluralism* (New York: Crossroad Publishing Co., 1981), 346-73 and passim.

13. On production and consumption in relation to texts, see Kuno Füssel, "The Materialist Reading of the Bible," in *The Bible and Liberation: Political and Social Hermeneutics,* ed. Norman K. Gottwald (Maryknoll, N.Y.: Orbis Books, 1983), 134-46.

14. The preacher characteristically and by definition uses words in a

performative manner. Cf. J. L. Austin, *How to Do Things with Words* (Cambridge, Mass.: Harvard University Press, 1962). On the definitional impossibility of a "neutral pulpit," see Brueggemann, "On Modes of Truth," *Seventh Angel*, 12, March 15, 1984, 17-24.

15. C. Wright Mills, *The Sociological Imagination* (New York: Oxford University Press, 1959), exhibits the categories of discernment that have been generated and nurtured by sociology.

16. See Robert A. Nisbit, *The Sociological Tradition* (New York: Basic Books, 1966), for a survey of the characteristic themes of classical sociology.

17. This is of course the focus of Marx's critique of religion. It is important that his critique be taken in a specific context and not as a general statement. For a positive sense of Marx's critique of religion see Jose Miranda, *Marx Against the Marxists* (Maryknoll, N.Y.: Orbis Books, 1980).

18. See Robert N. Bellah, "Biblical Religion and Social Science in the Modern World," *NICM Journal for Jews and Christians in Higher Education*, 6, 1982, 8-22.

19. See Alvin Gouldner, *The Coming Crisis of Western Sociology* (New York: Basic Books, 1970).

20. The writings of Marx are complex and not easily accessible. The best access point I know is the introduction by David McLellan, *The Thought of Karl Marx* (New York: Macmillan, 1971). On alienation in Marx in relation to religious questions, see Arend van Leeuwen, *Critique of Heaven* (New York: Scribner Book Companies, 1972), *Critique of Earth* (New York: Scribner Book Companies, 1974), and Nicholas Lash, *A Matter of Hope* (Notre Dame, Ind.: University of Notre Dame Press, 1982). See most recently, Rene Costi, *Marxist Analysis and Christian Faith* (Maryknoll, N.Y.: Orbis Books, 1985).

21. On the emergence of "laws of the marketplace," which are regarded as detached from social pressures and values, see Karl Polanyi, *The Great Transformation* (Boston: Beacon Press, 1957).

22. Weber's works are scattered, but a useful sourcebook is *From Max Weber: Essays in Sociology*, ed. H. H. Gerth and C. Wright Mills (New York: Oxford University Press, 1946). For an accessible introduction to Weber, see Frank Parkin, *Max Weber* (London: Tavistock Publications, 1982).

23. See Robert N. Bellah et al., *Habits of the Heart: Individualism and Commitment in American Life* (Berkeley: University of California Press, 1985), 44-51.

24. Robert King Merton, *Social Theory and Social Structure* (New York: Free Press, 1957), chapters 4 and 5, has well articulated Durkheim's attentiveness to the crisis of normlessness.

25. Emile Durkheim, *Suicide: A Study in Sociology* (New York: Free Press, 1951). More generally on Durkheim, see Kenneth Thompson, *Emile Durkheim* (London: Tavistock Publications, 1982).

26. For a more general critical survey of recent sociological thought, see Robert W. Friedrichs, *A Sociology of Sociology* (New York: Free Press, 1970).

27. See Fishbane, *Biblical Interpretation*, 1 and passim.

28. Narrative is essentially this act of recasting and interpreting the memory to meet a new crisis. Unfortunately narrative theology has been frequently presented as a sense of relief at being delivered from Enlightenment modes of historicity, without attention to the dynamic, positive act of reconstitution. On the power and significance of story, see James Barr, "Story and History in Biblical Theology," in *The Scope and Authority of the Bible* (London: SCM Press, 1980), 1-17, and Tracy, *Analogical Imagination*, 275-81. On the cruciality of narrative, see Fred B. Craddock, *The*

Gospels (Nashville: Abingdon Press, 1981). "A writer has in the sources available the sayings and the events for a narrative about Jesus Christ. A church has needs to be addressed. The intersection of the two is called a Gospel, a literary work of immense courage and freedom," 27.

29. Gerhard von Rad, *Old Testament Theology I* (New York: Harper & Row, 1962), 36-85, has shown how these two crises are pivotal for Israel's interpretive action.

30. See Hans Walter Wolff, "The Kerygma of the Yahwist," *The Vitality of Old Testament Traditions,* Walter Brueggemann and Hans Walter Wolff (Atlanta: John Knox Press, 1975), 41-66.

31. See more generally Brueggemann and Wolff, *The Vitality of Old Testament Traditions.*

32. On the Exile as a situation requiring and permitting bold interpretation, see Ralph W. Klein, *Israel in Exile* (Philadelphia: Fortress Press, 1979).

33. On the canonical process and its significance in the New Testament, see James D. G. Dunn, "Levels of Canonical Authority," *Horizons in Biblical Theology,* 4, 1982, 13-60.

34. For a formidable introduction to the issues see Anthony C. Thiselton, *The Two Horizons* (Grand Rapids: Wm. B. Eerdmans Publishing Co., 1980). See also Richard E. Palmer, *Hermeneutics, Interpretation Theory in Schleiermacher, Dilthey, Heidegger, and Gadamer* (Evanston, Ill: Northwestern University Press, 1969). Unfortunately both Thiselton and Palmer are confined to the tradition of Heidegger. This tradition needs to be carefully critiqued by a political hermeneutic rooted in Marx as suggested by Ernst Bloch and the Frankfurt School. A more balanced view that takes into account the liberation trajectory is offered by David Tracy, *Analogical Imagination,* chapter 5 and passim.

35. On the shape of religious problems and possibilities in a post-modern context, see William Beardslee, "Christ in the Post-Modern Age," in *The Post-Modern Condition: A Report on Knowledge,* ed. Jean-Francois Tyotard (Minneapolis: University of Minnesota Press, 1984) and Mark C. Taylor, *Erring: A Postmodern, A-Theology* (Chicago: University of Chicago Press, 1984).

36. Walter Brueggemann, *David's Truth* (Philadelphia: Fortress Press, 1985).

37. Peter L. Berger and Thomas Luckmann, *The Social Construction of Reality* (New York: Doubleday, 1966).

38. On constructive work in education, see Jack L. Seymour, Robert T. O'Gorman, Charles R. Foster, *The Church in the Education of the Public* (Nashville: Abingdon Press, 1984), 134-56. More generally on the constructive work of imagination see Paul W. Pruyser, *The Play of Imagination* (Madison, Conn.: International Universities Press, 1983), chapter 4 and passim.

39. Friedrichs, *A Sociology of Sociology,* shows how the tension of transformation and equilibrium has operated in sociology. Concerning Old Testament study, see Walter Brueggemann, "A Shape for Old Testament Theology, I: Structure Legitimation," *Catholic Biblical Quarterly,* 47, 1985, 28-46; "A Shape for Old Testament Theology, II: Embrace of Pain," *CBQ,* 47, 1985, 395-415.

40. See Walter Brueggemann, "Trajectories in Old Testament Literature and the Sociology of Ancient Israel," *Journal of Biblical Literature,* 98, 1979, 161-85.

41. See Gottwald, *The Tribes of Yahweh,* chapter 50, on the interface

between his method and the classical traditions of sociology. See my presentation of the paradigm of the two trajectories in tension, Walter Brueggemann, *The Prophetic Imagination* (Philadelphia: Fortress Press, 1978).

42. Ferdinand Toennies, *Community and Society* (1887), trans. C. P. Loomis (New York: Harper & Row, 1963).

43. Robert R. Wilson has pursued the same textual paradigm with a typology of central and peripheral prophets. Following Wilson's language, one may say there are texts that are "central" and those that are "peripheral." *Prophecy and Society in Ancient Israel* (Philadelphia: Fortress Press, 1980).

44. The presentation of a religious world of equilibrium to those who crave equilibrium is what Marx referred to by his famous characterization of religion as "the opiate of the people."

45. Fishbane, *Biblical Interpretation*, 322-26, has shown how Second Isaiah is a reinterpretation of Genesis 1 for quite specific purposes in a polemical situation.

46. On the text, see Walter Brueggemann, "The Prophet as a Destabilizing Presence," in *The Pastor as Prophet*, eds. Earl E. Shelp and Ronald H. Sunderland (New York: Pilgrim Press, 1985), 48-77.

47. See Martin Noth, *The Deuteronomistic History*, JSOT Sup. 15 (Sheffield: University of Sheffield, 1981), 60, and Jon D. Levenson, "From Temple to Synagogue: I Kings 8," in *Traditions in Transformation*, eds. Baruch Halpern and Jon D. Levenson (Winona Lake, Ind.: Eisenbrauns, 1981), 143-66.

48. For an influential proposal on the editorial history of Deuteronomy, see Frank Moore Cross, *Canaanite Myth and Hebrew Epic* (Cambridge, Mass.: Harvard University Press, 1973), 274-89, and Richard D. Nelson, *The Double Redaction of the Deuteronomistic History*, JSOT Sup. 18 (Sheffield: University of Sheffield, 1981).

49. See Klein, *Israel in Exile*, esp. chapters 2 and 6.

50. On the crisis in the theology of presence evoked by the loss of the temple, see T. N. D. Mettinger, *The Dethronement of Sabaoth: Studies in Shem and Kabod Theologies* (Lund: CWK Gleerup, 1982).

51. See Fishbane, *Biblical Interpretation*, 386.

52. On name theology, see Gerhard von Rad, *Studies in Deuteronomy*, SBT 9 (London: SCM Press, 1953), chapter 3.

53. On this chapter in relation to the governing structure of Deuteronomy, see Dennis McCarthy, "II Samuel 7 and the Structure of the Deuteronomic History," *JBL*, 84, 1965, 131-38.

54. The classic statement of Deuteronomic theology is that of von Rad, *Old Testament Theology I*, 69-77, 334-47. See also Wolff, "The Kerygma of the Deuteronomic Historical Work" in *The Vitality of Old Testament Traditions*.

55. Reinhold Niebuhr, "The Ark and the Temple," in *Beyond Tragedy* (New York: Charles Scribner's Sons, 1937), 47-68, offered a sermon contrasting the notions of presence and legitimacy in the temple and the ark. Since Niebuhr's time, scholarship has redefined the functions of these various options, but his general point remains valid and suggestive.

56. See Samuel L. Terrien, *The Elusive Presence* (New York: Harper & Row, 1978).

5

The Social Function
of Language in Preaching

Ronald J. Allen. At the seminary where I serve, the classroms are spacious, open, and light. The white walls and ceilings are pure and warm, broken only by a simple chalkboard, a large piece of colorful textile art, and a wide window that goes from floor to ceiling. The carpeted floor of the classrooms is two steps below the hallway so that entering the room gives the effect of being gathered into a place of safety. The seminar tables and chairs are handcrafted from oak and are centered in the middle of the room to encourage conversation. A faint yellow glow in the ceiling lights makes the room feel alive. To walk in is to feel purified, welcome, secure, and focused.

In these rooms, as in all rooms, the design has a significant effect on the ways in which we feel and act. The shape of the room, the color of its walls, even the placement of the furniture can encourage us to feel welcome or unwelcome, to seek people or to avoid people, to be open to new ideas or to be suspicious of them.

In much the same way, language shapes the ways we think, feel, and act in the world. From the basic "master story" of a culture or community to the tiniest metaphor, our language results in social attitudes, behavior, roles, and structures. Indeed, to use language is to create, or recreate, a world.

Christian preaching seeks a world that is shaped by the gospel. Therefore, preachers who become conscious of the social function of the language of the sermon can use language in such a way as to encourage social effects that are appropriate to the gospel.

Language Creates World

A community designs and furnishes its own world. That is, a community decides what is good, what is bad, what is important, what is unimportant, and who should behave in certain ways. The tornado dropping out of the sky, the immersion of a person in water, words spoken by a person in a white alb on Sunday—these have no meaning apart from the value given to them by the community and its individual members. Thus, we say that a community creates its own *interpretation* of life, its own view of the world.[1]

The world view of a community has three important functions. (1) It provides the community with a sense of order and security in the face of chaos and death.[2] The Christian community, for instance, confesses that God has overcome chaos. (2) It answers the questions of identity, Who am I? Why am I here?[3] I am a person who has been brought by Jesus Christ into covenantal relationship to the God of Abraham and Sarah. (3) It orders social life.[4] The conviction that God is by nature just, causes the Christian community to seek justice in *all* social relationships. The human family contains as many world views as there are human communities. And, despite a probable core of commonly held convictions, each community contains as many variations of its world view as it has members.

The most important way in which this view is communicated is through language. The foundational expression of the world view is a story, often mythic, which explains how the community came into being and what the purpose of its life is.[5] The master story gives the community a living memory and instills it with hope for the future.[6]

This master story also provides paradigmatic instances of the world view in operation, especially through stories of exemplars whose lives illustrate the best of the world view and through stories of those who forsook it and fell into trouble. Laws and regulations provide for its social institutionalization.

To tell the story, and for later generations to interpret it, is to constitute (or reconstitute) the world view of the group, to renew its sense of identity and purpose, to reinforce its pattern of social life. *To tell a small part of the story, sometimes even to use a single word or image, is to evoke the meaning, memory, and power of the whole.*

One of the most important functions of language is the giving of names and the assigning of value to persons, events, experiences, objects, and places.[7] Giving the thing a name places it into a world view so that the community and its members can respond to it (and manipulate it) appropriately. The name bestows to the community the value of persons, events, experiences, objects, and places. Is it good and to be valued and honored? Is it bad and to be rejected?

Different names for the same thing can lead to quite different social effects. A parade by a small group of people in response to an act of the government can be named an act of faithfulness. But if the same act is labeled unpatriotic, even illegal, the effect is quite different. Indeed the latter name can lead to prison.

Closely related to the giving of a name is the use of metaphors and images. These figures of speech are much more than decorative flowers that brighten the garden of language; for the use of a metaphor or image can evoke the power of the world view to make it legitimate or illegitimate. In this light, Kenneth Boulding speaks of behavior depending upon the image,[8] and an important recent work is entitled *Metaphors We Live By*.[9]

The social effect of metaphors and images can be seen also in select and specific ways. To speak of the "right hand of God" as the hand of power and authority is to relegate left-handed people to secondary social status. In line with recent research, Gibson Winter finds that "certain metaphoric networks become dominant in a total society, shaping modes of thought, action, decision and life."[10] The root metaphor of an earlier time was organic. In the metaphor of organic process, the pattern and meaning of life is understood in terms of birth, growth, and decay. But in the

West, in particular, this metaphor has been replaced by the mechanistic metaphor. This way of thinking about life is basically mechanical, linear, and quantified. Winter asks, "How much of life in this highly technological society is calculated . . . by years of work, annuities, retirement dates, eligibility for military service, weeks of unemployment insurance or years of accumulated pension credits?"[11] The mechanistic metaphor causes Westerners to regard cultures that live on the basis of organic metaphors as "ignorant and confused." Yet mechanism as a root metaphor has resulted in a cold, exploitative, individualistic, quantified world. Winter seeks a new organizing metaphor in the artistic process. For central to the artistic process is the resolution of contradiction in fresh and startling ways which result in fresh and startling understanding.[12]

In religious discourse, the names and metaphors used for God deserve the most careful attention. For God is the center of the Christian world view and the Christian world view ultimately takes its shape and character from the nature of God. For instance, the bald and uninterpreted metaphor, "Lord of Hosts," *implicitly* sanctions militarism, since the noun "hosts" is derived from a Hebrew verb that means "to make war."[13]

In this respect the images we use to describe the sermon are critical.[14] Different images lead to different ways of conceiving the sermon; they also lead to different relationships between speaker and hearer and to different social effects. When one conceives of the sermon as an "argument" (even a lover's quarrel), it is quite different from the sermon seen as "therapy." The sermon as a "polished essay" is quite different from an "oral event." The sermon as "exhortation" is not the same as the sermon as "story." A congregation, which week after week is brow-beaten, soon begins to droop like a cornstalk in an August drought. A congregation that is nurtured in love and grace soon begins to ask, "How can we respond to so great a gift?"

Much of the language of the United States that is used to refer to people of color, especially the black population, presupposes (and creates) a world view in which people of light-colored skin are more highly valued than people of dark-colored skin.[15] Words like nigger, coon, jungle bunny, jig, and darky evoke this world view and (at least implicitly) legitimate practices of discrimination.

The issue is complicated by the fact that the English language gives a negative value to dark colors, especially to black.[16] White is clean and pure, while black is dirty, sinister, and evil. In this milieu, Ossie Davis declares, "The English language in which I cannot conceive myself as a black man without at the same time debasing myself . . . is my enemy, and with which to survive I must be constantly at war."[17]

Much of the language about women in the United States explicitly evokes their secondary location in this world view, for example, the little woman, girl, babe, chick.[18] Many male designations are positive, whereas their female counterparts carry a negative evaluation. The words master and bachelor are much more positive than mistress, spinster, and old maid.

Until the mid-seventies, dictionary entries for terms associated with women cited as attributes for women such characteristics as gentle, affectionate, domestic, fickle, and superficial. Male characteristics included vigorous, courageous, and strong.[19] Even now this world view is called to mind by expressions such as "a *lady* minister" (instead of just "minister"). A study of school textbooks found that the pronouns he, him, and his occurred four times more often than the pronouns she, her, and hers.[20]

Professional advertising intentionally uses language and imagery to associate a product with a world view. The consumer is not motivated to buy the product on the merits of the product per se. Rather, the advertisement associates use of the product with the world view it has created. Television advertising is so sophisticated that it can create a world view in thirty seconds. A classic commercial, now happily departed from the airwaves, sold a soft drink as "the real thing." If a soft drink is *the real thing,* civilization is in trouble.

Leaders of social movements often carefully calculate the social effect of their language. Joseph M. Scheidler, a leader in the movement to halt abortion, recommends the use of inflammatory rhetoric; thus, abortion is a "holocaust." Abortionists are baby killers and murderers. Letter carriers, telephone installers, and other public utility employees, and the maintenance staff of abortion clinics are to be advised that they are servicing "death camps." Garbage haulers are to be told that they are carrying the corpses of babies.[21]

Few institutions in the United States seem more aware of the social effects of language than the federal government. Where once we had a Department of War we now have a Department of Defense. The neutron bomb is called by the much more innocent name, nuclear enhancement device, while a missile is designated the Peacekeeper.[22]

Just as language can create and sustain a world view, it can also cause members of a society to see the world in new ways. At its most potent in this role, language can cause listeners to think afresh about the meaning and organization of their lives. The parables of the Synoptic Gospels, for instance, are more than memorable illustrations of religious truth. They are assaults upon consciousness which are intended to jar the hearers and readers into seeing the world in new ways. The parable commonly known as the good Samaritan causes the reader or listener to reevaluate the social value and role of Samaritans.

The classical prophets who spoke immediately before the Exile often used the language of the social traditions of Israel in ways unfamiliar to the people in order to get them to interpret their situation anew. The prophet Amos, for instance, gives new meaning to the metaphor "the Day of God." This Day was believed to be the time of the manifestation of God's ultimate *blessing* on the community. Yet, in light of the prevailing world view in which it was completely permissible to manipulate, cheat, extort, and rob (especially the poor), Amos sees the Day of God as a day of *judgment* because the community has debased its covenantal relationship with God. In language that causes the community to see itself in a new way Amos says:

> Woe to you that desire the Day of the Lord!
>   Why would you have the day of the Lord?
> It is darkness, and not light. (Amos 5:18)

Thus Dwight Bolinger describes language as a *loaded weapon.*[23] For virtually all language is loaded (biased) and tends to picture things in such a way as to elicit a specific evaluation from the community, usually an evaluation of approval or disapproval. The stories we tell, the metaphors and images that we use, trigger the master story and cause the community to act or think in some traditional way. On the other hand, these may challenge the master story and ask us to think and act in a new way.

The Language of the Sermon Elicits a Social Response

The sermon posits the perspective of the gospel as the basic world view out of which the congregation understands the meaning of life. This stance orders the congregation's social attitudes, roles, behavior, and structures, and it helps the congregation understand its place amid the other world views that are a part of its time and place. In the best preaching, the sermon becomes both an explanation of and apology for the Christian world view. The sermon can also become a metaphor to live by.[24]

In a primary mode of Christian preaching, the preacher takes a biblical text and interprets the gospel as it (the gospel) is refracted through the text. In an earlier day, many scholars believed that interpreters could suspend their values and prejudices and distill the pure, uninterpreted meaning of the text. In an impressive essay Rudolf Bultmann showed that such exegesis without presuppositions is impossible.[25] More recent writers have emphasized even more the ways in which the political, economic, social, and theological positions of interpreters function as vested interests that shade the way in which people read the biblical text and the way in which they understand the gospel.[26] In particular, interpreters will often take the biblical text in such a way as to protect their own places in society. Because such interests inevitably become lenses through which interpretation takes place, it is important for preachers to become aware of them. Only when preachers are aware of philosophical, theological, and social presuppositions can they become critical of them.

The exposition of the gospel through the text presents a world view and results in a social effect.

Text → Theological
and Social
Position → Sermon → Social Effect
of the
Preacher

Sometimes the sermon will call for an overt social program, behavior, or action. At other times, the sermon will result in the formation of attitudes that yield social effects.

The centrality of the Bible in Christian preaching calls for three comments about its potential social effect. At one end of the spectrum of authority, popular religious circles use the Bible as an imprimatur on whatever is said from the pulpit.[27] At the other end of the spectrum, the Bible has little inherent authority, so that any claims derived from it must be justified. In order for the sermon to achieve its intended effect, preachers will want to know the attitudes the congregation has about the Bible. They will then be able to help the congregation develop approaches toward the Bible that are consistent with its role as a witness to the gospel.

Further, the Protestant canon historically has been divided in two parts called the Old Testament and the New Testament. This nomenclature has contributed, and continues to contribute, to the devaluation of the first thirty-nine books of the Bible and to a sense of discontinuity between the two parts, as if the New Testament is in contrast to the Old. In modern culture, especially, the word "old" has come to be associated with the decrepit and outmoded whereas the "new" is fresh and exciting. These factors have contributed in a direct and forceful way to anti-Semitism. In light of the recently reemphasized continuities between the parts of the Bible and between Judaism and Christianity, and also under the impetus of the awful memory of the Holocaust, many Christians are seeking words for the two parts of the Bible that will replace the terms new and old. For example, one may speak of the sacred Scriptures of Judaism, the Hebrew Bible, Canonical Jewish Literature, the Canonical Literature of the Apostolic Church, or simply, the Bible.

Finally, care needs to be given to the translation of the Bible made or used by the preacher. For the English words and idioms chosen to render Hebrew, Greek, and Aramaic have a social effect. For example, in Genesis 2 the word *'adham* is usually translated "man" when the word itself means the more inclusive, "human being." The translation thus contributes to the notion of the superiority of men over women. Again, the Hebrew notion of justice is fundamentally concerned with relationship, with putting relationships in their right order in the light of the covenant. But at the popular level in the United States, justice is associated with legal judgments and often with retribution. When a murderer is electrocuted, someone inevitably appears on a television news program applauding the fact that "justice has been done." The implication is that retribution is justice. For a last example, the translators of the Authorized Version of the Bible rendered many of the Greek words for "servant" and "service" by the word "minister," thereby reinforcing the place of ministers in society.[28] Thus the preacher needs to be suspicious of the social implications of biblical translations.[29]

In order to make a theological analysis of the text and the appropriateness of its world view to the gospel and to the situation of the congregation, it is important for the preacher to determine that world view and its social effects.[30] Indeed, throughout the process of going from text to sermon, the preacher makes several critical decisions. The sermon will be strengthened if these decisions are made clearly and critically.

A fundamental theological evaluation relates to the text itself. Is the world view of the text—and of the elements within the text—consistent with that of the gospel? Most often the answer will be in the affirmative; but in some cases it will be in the negative. Representative of such cases are the household codes of the Epistles (for example, Col. 3:18–4:1), the pleas for divine retribution against enemies (for example, Ps. 137) and the caricature of the Jewish community as exponents of evil (for example, John 8:39-59). Sermons on these texts may take the form of preaching against the text—or against some element of the text. The social effect of these sermons is to cause the congregation to think critically about the Bible and about social attitudes and practices related to the Bible that it has taken for granted. For instance, the disparagement of the Jewish community is called into question by a sermon that challenges the portrait of the Jews in the Fourth Gospel.

It is equally important to identify the world views (and their social effects) that are held by the congregation. Are these views appropriate to the gospel? Schutz points out that for most people these attitudes and actions are largely taken for granted. They are seldom the result of stringent critical reflection, but just because they are taken for granted, they are deeply ingrained.[31] The preacher who plays fast and loose with such fundamental realities will meet strong resistance.

With a clear exegetical and theological understanding of the text and a clear identification of the situation of the congregation, the preacher makes the critical correlation of the text and the congregation.[32] In what ways is the world view and social situation of the congregation similar to that of the community to whom the text was addressed?

Given this correlation, the preacher determines the appropriate social strategy for the sermon. The decisive factor is the content of the text. If the situations of the two communities are similar, the social strategy of the text may be appropriate for the sermon. Given the peculiarities of culture and congregation, the strategy (or some part thereof) may be appropriate even if the circumstances are different. Even when situations vary, a theological theme and its social effect, or a particular image with its social effect, may rise up to address the congregation.[33]

The form and function of the text, viewed in the light of the specific content of the text, may also be suggestive for the social strategy of the sermon. A saga, like the ancestral narratives of Genesis, is intended to locate the community in relationship to time, place, purpose, and the divine. At the time of the Exile in Babylon, the exiles were confused about their place in the world. For them, the stories of Genesis served to renew the community's sense of identity and confidence. If the text is a saga, the preacher determines the degree to which the congregation needs to have its identity renewed.

A parable, as mentioned above, is intended to explode a prevailing world view so that the community can see the world in a new way. If the text is a parable, the preacher decides whether the world view of the congregation is in need of being exploded.

Apocalyptic texts come to expression in times of extreme social distress. The community for whom the text is written is usually in the midst of some form of oppression. In this context, an apocalyptic text has two important functions for the community. In a grim and desperate situation it offers hope in God. It further functions as a principle of social criticism; any idea or social reality in the present social order that does not conform to the vision of God's reign is to be rejected. The ultimate social goal of the apocalyptic text is a new social order. Is the community for whom the sermon is to be preached in a minority situation and/or in need of an affirmation of hope? Can the text function as a principle of criticism by which the world of the congregation can be evaluated?

When the social strategy of the sermon is set, the preacher seeks a homiletical strategy to help the sermon achieve its intended effect. *How* can the preacher say *what* needs to be said in such a way that the sermon will have the best possibility of fulfilling its purpose? In resolving this question, two factors come into prominence: (1) the overall genre of the sermon, (2) the specific language and imagery of the sermon.

Studies in homiletical form are extremely helpful at the first point. A sermon is generally structured along one of two forms of logic: deductive or inductive.[34] In sensitive and skillful hands, either form can perform the social task assigned to it. However, the two forms do have advantages and limitations that fit them especially well for different purposes.

In the deductive sermon, the proposition of the sermon is stated at the outset and the sermon develops and/or defends the proposition. One of the great strengths of this approach to preaching is its clarity. The preacher paints the major points in bold and unmistakable strokes. Further, the line of reasoning in the sermon can be laid out lucidly and persuasively. At its best, the deductive sermon defines a situation with dictionary-like precision.

In the deductive sermon, the speaker's relationship to the

congregation is often hierarchical: "I, the preacher, have something you need and I am going to persuade you that you need it." The congregation sits in evaluation and judgment on the message. This makes the deductive approach somewhat better-suited to sermons whose purpose is to build up or renew the congregational world view than to sermons that challenge it. When a listener's world view is challenged head-on, the listener tends to be defensive and to resist the challenge.

The inductive sermon, in which the preacher begins with the elements of experience and, in the course of the sermon, brings them into a theological perspective, works well for both the affirming and the challenging sermon. But it has a distinct advantage over the deductive form when the purpose is to challenge. For the inductive sermon works by inviting the listeners to identify sympathetically with the data of experience. The sermon brings this data into conversation and confrontation with appropriate theological resources. On the basis of this interaction, the listeners draw theological conclusions.

The inductive sermon helps overcome the initial defensive reaction that often accompanies a direct attack on a world view or social practice. The preacher is in a relationship of collegiality with the congregation. By working through the problem with the preacher, the conclusion arises internally from the life of the congregation. At its best, the inductive sermon evokes a world view in the listener.

Yet the inductive sermon is often difficult to construct. If the movement of the sermon is not sharp and clear, coming deftly to the major conclusion, it is difficult for the congregation to follow. While this kind of sermon can be extremely artful, the preacher must exercise care to see that the congregation "gets the point" and understands the reasons for it. In the worst abuse of inductive preaching that I have heard, the preacher adopted an approach that might be called "stream of consciousness."

These considerations have a theological corollary. When the sermon is rambling, confused, and pointless, the congregation can easily assume that God is rambling, confused, and pointless. By implicitly suggesting that the nature of God is chaotic, the sermon pictures the world itself as a place of chaos. But when the sermon is purposeful and compelling, the congregation begins to think that God may be much the same.

In actual homiletical practice, few sermons will be of a purely deductive or inductive type. Most sermons will include elements of each. A sermon may introduce a problem inductively, gathering the congregation's sympathetic identification and then deal with the problem deductively. Elements of deductive reasoning may appear here and there in the inductive flow of a sermon. By recognizing the social force of the forms available, the preacher can make a conscientious selection for the purpose at hand.

Likewise, careful attention to the social function of the materials in the sermon will enhance its result as a whole. This is true of larger units of material and of individual words, images, and metaphors. For instance, preachers have long known that stories have unusual power to hold listener-attention and to move listeners deeply. It is, therefore, important to remember that stories function on the basis of sympathetic identification. The listener identifies with someone (either in the story itself or with the storyteller or with something else associated with the story) and follows the plot to its climax and completion. With whom will the congregation identify when this story is told? What will be the social effect of that identification?

Furthermore, different stories serve different social functions. Some stories, for instance, assure the listeners that all is well. In the 1984 campaign for the office of President of the United States, Ronald Reagan repeatedly told stories that said, "Things are O.K. No need to be afraid." Other stories serve explicitly to raise the consciousness of the community to the situation and meaning of particular persons, groups, and institutions. The story of acceptance (or rejection) of a homosexual by family and friends can cause people to look again at the phenomenon of homosexuality.

Exhortation in preaching seeks an overt response in the listener. For instance the community may be exhorted to believe something such as the proposition that Jesus is indeed the Christ. Or the congregation may be exhorted to do something, such as boycott the products of a multinational corporation, but much exhortatory preaching fails to produce the expected result. Among the reasons for failure, two deserve mention here. Exhortation typically calls for a change of *behavior* without offering the congregation a *new metaphor* by which to understand the world. A change of behavior is usually the result of a change of metaphor.[35]

Further, in the exhortatory sermon, the indicative and the imperative dimensions of the gospel may be out of balance. Theologically the indicative—the announcement of the grace of God as already given to the world—comes first. The imperative, the command to respond to the gospel in certain ways, follows from the indicative, but in the exhortatory sermon, the indicative is typically diminished or even forgotten. People are asked to do something or to believe something without being given an understanding of its basis. This is like trying to start an automobile when the gasoline tank is empty. And it can leave the congregation with the impression that the love of God is earned on the basis of response to the imperative. "If I do what the preacher said, *then* I will be worthy to receive God's love."

Smaller units of expression—for example, sentences, individual words, and metaphors—can result in social effects as well. For, as noted earlier, these can push buttons in the minds of the members of the congregation that release world views. It is, therefore, imperative that the preacher have a clear and accurate understanding of the relationship between the language and imagery of the sermon and the language and imagery of the congregational world views, for the preacher wants to evoke what is intended.

Even the smallest parts of speech and matters of grammar can have a social effect, for these, too, can exhibit bias.[36] A noun, for instance, is more evocative than an adjective in a comparable expression. Compare the following:

> He's a Turk (noun).
> He's Turkish (adjective).

The noun more strongly calls forth the social stereotype.[37]

In the conventional use of the adjective as the modifier of a noun, the carefully selected adjective can strengthen (or reduce) the world view called forth by the noun, as is "The Lord is a *very great* God, a God above all gods." The same thing is true of the adverb, in "You gave *only* ten dollars?"

According to Dwight Bolinger, the verb is "the least hospitable to bias." Yet verbs, too, are loaded. The use of direct action verbs makes subjects and their actions clear, but in passive constructions, the agent is hidden, and responsibility for the action is thereby diffused. For example, in the statement, *"This information was not meant to be divulged,"* the question is raised as to *who* did not divulge the information. Was it "a bureaucrat who might be embarrassed by it?"[38]

Further, active verbs are more suited to oral discourse; they cause the sermon to feel alive and moving. They are easy to follow; they engage the mind of the listener, and they suggest that God is active. Passive constructions, on the other hand, are not well-suited to oral discourse; they are difficult to follow and they are less mentally stimulating. They cause the sermon to feel slow and nonassertive, and they suggest that God is passive and only indirectly related to the cosmic drama.

In most of the sermons I hear, questions are used in the sermon as rhetorical devices to win the attention of the congregation, but when carefully focused, placed, and delivered, non-rhetorical (that is, real) questions can perform social functions. For instance, in the proper context a question can raise a doubt in the minds of listeners about the adequacy of their world views. The preacher has the opportunity to step into the distance between the listener and the world view that was created by the question. An interesting afternoon for those who save their sermon manuscripts or who make tape recordings of their sermons would be to review the sermons and to note the loaded expressions in a month's sermons. What biases are revealed?

Thus, a basic rule for the use of language and imagery in the sermon is this: *take nothing for granted.* Words, images, and ideas must be evaluated from the perspective of the congregation in order to know what social world they will evoke. And those words, images, and ideas that appear in the sermon must be given the flesh and blood the preacher intends. If the preacher is speaking of love in the framework of the steadfast covenant loyalty of the Hebrew Bible, that needs to be made clear. Otherwise someone is going to think that the preacher is referring to a cozy emotional feeling.

The illustrations and references to people and groups in the sermon have a particularly important social function as well. Those who appear, and do not appear, signal to the listeners who is important, who is not, who is valued, and who is ignored. The manner in which people and groups are pictured sends a clear message as to which social behaviors are approved and which are not.

Three considerations enter into the use of illustrations and the references made to people and groups. First, illustrations and references that reflect the composition of the community to whom the sermon is given say to that community, "You are important. The Christian world view has a word for you."

Second, because the Christian world view transcends local culture, illustrations and references to people from beyond the local situation help the congregation enter into the fullness and inclusivity of that world view. Preachers will want regularly to include material in the sermon from racial, ethnic, and national groups other than those that predominate in the congregation.

Third, the preacher will want to give careful attention to the ways in which people are pictured in the illustrations and references so as not to repeatedly reinforce negative stereotypes but to offer positive images that will result in positive social effects. A sermon contradicts itself when it announces the liberating power of God but at the same time consistently pictures women doing menial jobs and speaks of Blacks on welfare. Especially helpful are illustrations that picture in a positive light people who have been caricatured negatively.

Preachers may find it useful to make a grid that can record the references and illustrations that are included in their sermons. Such a grid might be modeled on the following:

	Children	Youth	Young Adult	Middle Adult	Senior Adult
White Females					
White Males					
Native N. American Females					
Native N. American Males					
Afro-American Females					
Afro-American Males					
Asian-American Females					
Asian-American Males					
Hispanic Females					
Hispanic Males					
College Graduates					
High School Dropouts					
Etc.					
Etc.					

Such a grid, kept over a two-month period, would reveal those persons and groups who are most prominent, and most neglected, in the world view of the sermons.

The delivery of the sermon has a social effect.[39] Indeed, the mode of delivery embodies both the content of the sermon and the way in which people relate in the Christian community. Just as children learn acceptable behavior by observing the behavior of family and friends, so the congregation learns important clues to acceptable behavior in the church by observing the way worship is led.

A sermon that is delivered in a loud, angry voice and punctuated by a closed fist banging down on the pulpit sanctions, at least by example, such behavior as appropriate to the Christian community. On the other hand, to speak of reconciliation, and to stand before the congregation in an open and vulnerable way, is to embody the beginning of reconciliation. If the center of the Christian world view is a gracious and loving God, then the sermon will be delivered in a gracious and loving way. Grace and love can be expressed in tones that range from the passionate and strong to the quiet and gentle.

The prophetic sermon deserves a special comment. In popular parlance, the classical Hebrew prophets are described as thundering. (In fact, we do not know whether they spoke in tones of thunder or anguish, or both.) But the modern preacher is not Amos. The preacher stands in solidarity and love with the congregation under the Word of the text. If it is a word of judgment, the preacher will speak the word in pain. Ideally, the style of delivery should be consistent with the tone and content of the sermon.

Exegesis and Homiletical Strategy: Philippians 2:5-11

Sermon preparation is centered around two kinds of exegesis: one of the biblical text and the other of the situation of the congregation. Based on the critical theological correlation of these concerns, the preacher develops a homiletical strategy.

The text on which the following sermon is based is Philippians 2:5-11.[40] This text is almost certainly an early

Christian hymn in which Paul addresses a Hellenistic congregation that is troubled and divided.

The religious world view of the Hellenistic mind was centered in the notion of Fate, the belief that life was under the heel of blind and unfeeling forces over which one had no control. Each person was a slave of some principality and power. From this fatalistic determinism, the gospel offered salvation and freedom.

In response to Paul's preaching, the Philippians embraced the gospel; in Paul's absence, the congregation has become ingrown. It appears that "false teachers" have entered the community and have offered the congregation a world view other than that of the Pauline gospel. Selfish ambition, conceit, and preoccupation with their own interests to the exclusion of those of others, complement bad feelings toward one another (2:3-4, 14; 4:2-3) and ethical confusion (4:8-9).

In this milieu, Philippians 2:5-11 pictures the exaltation and self-emptying of Christ as the center of Christian existence and as the paradigm for the life of the church in the world. Christ was humiliated for the world, freeing it from the power of Fate, and thereby making it possible for the Philippians to enjoy true community by giving themselves for one another. This is the common mind (that is, way of looking at the world) that they have been given in Christ Jesus (2:5).

A key exegetical decision concerns the word "servant." The Greek word servant *(doulos)* may also be translated "slave." As mentioned above, the Hellenistic world of the first century believed that people and situations were slaves of cosmic powers. Paul shared in this viewpoint (for example, Rom. 8:35-39; I Cor. 2:6-8; 15:55-56; Gal. 4:3, 9). In this light, for Christ to take the form of a slave was to leave the form of God and to identify with the human situation in such a way that he became slave of the cosmic powers of Fate. When God exalted Jesus, the power of these rulers was broken and they (in heaven, on earth, and under the earth) acknowledge the cosmic sovereignty of Christ. Note that the hymn is ultimately theocentric: "to the glory of God."

The form of the text, as a hymn, is somewhat suggestive. More than simply words set to music, or content added to a tune, a song is a living image. In evocative language, the christological hymn functions as a master image of the Christian view of the world. Easily committed to memory, the hymn can be carried by the congregation from the place of worship into all the places of the world where it has business. It therefore functions as a living lens through which to interpret daily relationships and events.

The sermon was prepared for the installation of a friend as pastor of an American Baptist congregation located just beyond the suburbs of Indianapolis, Indiana. I learned that the congregation is all white, largely middle class, politically conservative, and has few college graduates. The congregation is somewhat evangelical in theology. Although it is small, it has been troubled some by power plays on the part of several members. In the process of being interviewed, called, and beginning his ministry, the pastor has discovered that the congregation is primarily concerned with institutional maintenance, such as raising the budget and adding new members to the rolls.

The congregation lives in the larger cultural milieu of the United States. In this setting, consciousness is increasingly shaped by technology, bureaucracy, and pluralism.[41] The individual is becoming more and more the center of the universe. The chief ends in life are individual expression and success, with decreasing attention to the public good and even less ability to talk about the public good.[42] Arenas in which the drive toward individualism is particularly entrenched are the family, sexuality, and the mobility ethos.[43] Christopher Lasch contends that an apt metaphor to describe our time is narcissism.[44]

Given the similarity between the situations of the text and the modern church, the strategy of the text is appropriate for the sermon. It is usually inappropriate for someone from outside an established community to recommend a specific social program to the community. Like the text, the sermon is intended to offer a living image through which the congregation can understand itself and its situation in the world. The living image of the sermon will be composed of many little images, like the pieces of a puzzle that all lock together to form the big picture.

The Difference

PHILIPPIANS 2:5-11

Can you hear it? (pause)

There it is again.
Did you hear it?

A shout.
A shout from a big crowd.

And can you see them?

The white robed martyrs.
The myriad of angels.

The saints from all the ages.

And more.

Old people with aluminum walkers,
   rising up off broken legs to walk.
Clear-eyed women in their strength,
   standing to oppose the City Council.
Men with faces as tanned as their suits,
   just returning from the treatment centers, born again.
Students with test tubes and floppy disks,
   coming alive to the meaning of it all.
Fresh-scrubbed children bursting out in song
   "Jesus loves the little children . . ." (singing)

And more.

A welfare mother, sweating from the tenements,
   a bounce in her step as she starts school.
Peasants from Nicaragua, sixty years old,
   eyes bright as they learn to read.
Blacks from South Africa, wrists and ankles bleeding from
      the chains,
   staggering to their feet to march again.

And all of them together,
   kneeling down in the dust,
      crying out in one great voice,
         Jesus Christ is Lord.

From the white robed martyrs
  to the black people in chains,
    they know the difference Christ makes in life
    and they join in the great exaltation.

What about you? (pause)

They knew the difference in the days of Paul.
For in those days they believed that the world
  was full of forces and fates
    that controlled human life,
      and bent it
        and broke it.

  The Bible calls these forces by names like
    principalities,
    powers,
    dominions,
    thrones,
    rulers of this age,
    elemental spirits of the universe.

They took human life
  and tied it in a knot
    and pulled it tight—
      and tighter—
        and tighter—
          and tighter—
            until there was nothing left to
            pull.
No wonder the people of that world
  felt closed in,
    like they were living
      in a room with
        no doors,
        no windows,
        no fresh air,
        no lights.
      Trapped.
      No way out.

Que sera sera.
What will be will be.
Murphy's law: if anything can go wrong, it will.
They made this decision down at City Hall.
    Nothing I can do about it.
    "Sorry, ma'am. Not qualified."

An outburst at a Board Meeting.
    People standing up,
    shouting,
    pointing their fingers at one another like guns.
And afterward out on the parking lot,
    somebody says,
    "Well, when you work with people,
    you've just got to expect that."
Expect that?
Expect pain and brokenness to be normal?

And yet that's the way it was.
A world resigned to its Fate.

That was the way the world was
    when Christ Jesus was in the form of God.

And the form of God is the form of love.

What was it that God said to Israel?
    "I have loved you with an everlasting love" (Jer. 31:3).
    And the psalmist knew that God's steadfast love endures
                                            forever.

You know how it is when you love someone.
    When they have joy,
        it becomes your joy
            and you do all you can
                to multiply it.

When they have pain,
    it becomes your pain
        and you do all you can
            to ease it.

When I was a child,
    maybe four or five years old,

I had pneumonia.
They brought the hot plate into the bedroom,
   and filled the big old Revere Ware pot
      with water and Vicks,
         and turned it up high.
But when my fever went up
   my mother got a damp wash cloth
      and sat up
         all through the night,
           wiping
              my forehead.

Hour after hour,
   all through the night,
      until morning came.

To touch the fevered world
   Christ Jesus emptied himself,
He "did not count equality with God
   a thing to be grasped,"
      but took on the biting chains of slavery,
         "and became obedient unto death,
           even death on a cross."

Therefore, God has highly exalted him,
   and given him the name
      which is above every name.

And what happened to Christ Jesus
   is our clue to God,
      and to life
         and to the principalities and powers
         that bind and strangle.

For when God exalted Christ Jesus,
   God said, "No!" to the principalities and powers.
Not a big red-letter
   neon-flashing
      horn-tooting
         baton-waving
           "No!"
But a "No!" written by the blood of the cross.

The principalities and powers
  are brutal and strong,
    but they do not determine the meaning of life.
    They do not give out the blueprints of existence
    to those who are in Christ Jesus.
    Theirs are not the last options
      to be considered
        before making a decision.

For God has given Christ Jesus
  the Name that is above every name

To those who are in him,
  the name of Jesus
    is greater than any name
      given by the principalities and powers:
        Divorced
        Single parent
        Old hag
        Alcoholic
        Nigger
        Subversive
        Communist

Because God has given Christ Jesus
  "the name that is above every name,"
    those who confess him
      are not ruled by the names
        given to them by the principalities and powers
          but are freed
            to live to God.

And it makes all the difference in the world.

The woman wakes up in the morning,
  her life as shattered as the bottle
    she threw against the wall
      before she passed out.
But the name of Jesus
  is above the name alcoholic
    and those who are in him
      know that booze does not have the final word.

Those old people with their walkers,
   they get up off their broken legs
      and walk.
         And when they cannot walk anymore,
            they lie down to die.
               And they call it sleep,
                  because Christ Jesus
                     is stronger than death.

The black people in South Africa
   chafe in their chains;
      some of them are taken off the streets
         and left in cages,
            four feet wide,
            four feet high,
            four feet deep,
         left there for months,
            not enough room to stretch out,
            not enough room to stand up.
      But still they stagger out
         in the face of the principalities and powers.

Sri Lanka is an island in revolution.
Constant conflict between the Tamils,
   a minority population,
      and the majority group
         who refuse to share
            money,
            jobs,
            land,
            hospitals,
            schools,
            power.

A Tamil student came to our school
   because his life had been threatened
      too many times.
As the year came to a close,
   and he packed his bag to go back,
      someone asked him,
         "Why?"

"Why are you going back to that danger?"
"I have seen the Lord of glory," he said.
"What can those two-bit caesars do to me?"

When we confess him,
   his victory is our victory
      and no matter what our circumstances
         it makes all the difference in the world.

And your calling, Wyatt,
   is to make that clear:
      Jesus is Lord.

         Lord over cocaine.
         Lord over IBM.
         Lord over Ronald Reagan.
         Lord over the church.

   It is also your calling
      to make clear
         how the church lives
            in the light of the sovereignty of Christ.

You have help,
   and from a reputable source.
The Apostle Paul quotes an ancient Christian hymn.

   "Have this mind *among yourselves,*
      which *is* [*already*] yours in Christ Jesus,
         who, though he was in the form of God,
            did not count equality with God
               a thing to be grasped,
                  but emptied himself,
                     taking the form of a
                        [slave]."

   Do you get the picture?

The mind of Christ Jesus
   is the mind of self-emptying.
The mind of Christ Jesus
   is the mind that asks,
      "What can our church give
         for the life of the world?" (pause)

This, of course, is just contrary
    to the way we usually think.
        In a world of uncertainty and anxiety,
            a world in which we live
                in the shadow
                    of the mushroom cloud,

in this world our natural inclination
    is to gather security to ourselves,
        to hang on
            to what we've got,
                and to ask,
                    "What's in it for me?"

But in the church,
    this way of thinking
        neglects just one thing:
            God has already exalted Christ Jesus,
                and given him the Name
                    which is above every name.

Even when we are emptied,
    we are in the hands
        of the One
            who is the power of life itself.

        And it makes all the difference
            in the way we think and act
                in the church.

        What can those two-bit caesars do to you now?

First thing in the morning
    the parents of two twelve-year-olds
        stop by the office.

        "We're *concerned*," they say.
        "We're concerned about that boy Jimmy
            going on the church retreat this weekend.
        You know he was held back a year in school,
            so he should really be in the tenth
                grade.
        He comes from a broken home

and he's by himself a lot
and he roams the streets at night.
He uses some words
I have never even heard
and I was in the Navy.
We're just concerned
that he is going to be at the retreat
with *our children*."

And as they spoke those words, "Our children,"
you could almost smell
the sweet flowers of innocence and
purity.

But the issue is not,
how can we protect our kids from Jimmy?
is it?
The issue is:
how can we take the form of a servant
for him
and for these fearful parents?

That afternoon on a pastoral call,
a couple announces
that they will cancel their pledge
if the piece of lint
underneath the southwest corner
of the refrigerator
has not been removed
before Sunday.

Well, I am not in favor of lint.
But isn't it better
to put to the pastor
a question like this:
How can we empty our refrigerator
to feed hungry people
to the glory of God?

At the board meeting that night
the first item of business
was the new speed bump

on the parking lot.
Should it be painted
fluorescent green
or fluorescent yellow?

What do you think?
Under the high-beams on a dark night,
which better reflects the vision
of the exalted Christ,
fluorescent green
or fluorescent yellow?

Suppose you heard
that Gleaners Food Bank
was running out of food?
What would you do?
What would your vote be
if a family moved out
from the near east side
and came forward
on the invitational hymn
to join this church,
and they were black?

How would you respond
if someone stepped forward
to teach Sunday school,
and he or she had AIDS?

Surely by now it is clear.

When Jesus is Lord,
every vote of the board
is a vote of self-emptying.
When Jesus is Lord
every decision of the congregation
is a decision for servanthood.
Every knock on every door
is a knock of confession.
Every sermon, Wyatt,
is given on bended knee.

And it makes all the difference in the world.

Reflection

The goal of the sermon is to give the congregation the opportunity to realize afresh the freedom and security that has been given to it in the emptying and the exaltation of Christ Jesus and to encourage the congregation to think again about its response to that soteriological event. The sermon does not make specific social recommendations but sets forth a perspective which, when applied to specific situations in the life of the congregation and the world, can lead to specific attitudes, decisions, and programs.

The sermon is structured in two large parts that are related to each other like an hour glass with two unequally sized sections.

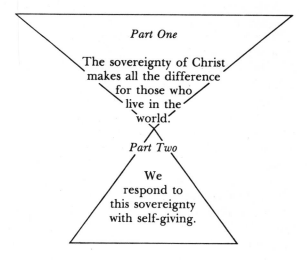

Part One

The sovereignty of Christ makes all the difference for those who live in the world.

Part Two

We respond to this sovereignty with self-giving.

The first part moves to a climax ("Jesus is Lord . . . Lord over cocaine, over IBM, over Ronald Reagan, over the church") and is the basis for the second part. The second part presents a single idea through a clear statement that is made concrete by a series of images.

This structure was chosen for three reasons. First, as

indicated in the essay above, the inductive structure is well suited to sermons that ask the congregation to look at life from a perspective different from its usual one. The text and the sermon ultimately challenge the self-centered ethos of our culture and the similar tendencies in the congregation.

Second, the assuring images of the exaltation and sovereignty of Christ intentionally appear in the sermon before the possibility of congregational self-emptying because the latter is possible only on the basis of the former. The listener experiences the power and strength of God and thereby is given the strength to respond to God. Under ordinary circumstances we change only to the degree that we feel secure. When we are assured of our ultimate security in God, then we are freed to entertain new and different possibilities. In a world in which the dominant pattern is to gather security for oneself, even at the expense of others, the church is *given* the final security.

Third, the structure of the sermon demonstrates the theological priority of grace. Self-giving is an appropriate response to the sovereignty of God expressed for the church through Christ.

The images of people and situations in the sermon are intended both to reflect the constituency of the congregation and to give them a vision of the sovereignty of Christ that transcends both time and space. The congregation thus realizes the significance of the exaltation of Christ for its own life and for lives and situations far removed from the cornfields west of Indianapolis.

Several aspects of the sermon intentionally echo the hymnic form of the text. Obviously the intent of the sermon is close to the intent of the text: to create a living image that can be carried from the sanctuary as a source of power for living and as a lens through which to interpret the world. Indeed, the text becomes a norm by which all structures of authority are measured. Do they embody the world view (epitomized in Phil. 2:6-8) that gives glory to God? Further, the sermon, like the hymn, employs extensive parallelism and repetition and also has a rhythm (which is easier to speak and hear than to read). These are characteristic of oral speech patterns and aid the congregation in both remembering and internalizing the sermon.

Throughout, contemporary themes, images, and allusions are used to establish similarity between the Philippian situation and the modern situation. This accomplishes several things. For one, it makes the situation of the Philippians interesting to the modern listener. For another, it allows the perspective of the text to become plausible as a perspective for the modern congregation. For still another, it leads the community to look for other contemporary situations to which the text might speak. The hymnic patterns of parallelism, repetition, and rhythm reinforce this aim as they help the hymn and the sermon get under the skin of the congregation.

When a series of images or vignettes is used, they always move from the most familiar to the least familiar, from the least threatening to the most threatening. For example, at the end of the sermon, the snapshots from the life of the congregation go from the two parents, with whom the congregation can readily identify, to the questions about the acceptability of a Sunday school teacher who has AIDS. Such a progression allows the hearers first to establish a sympathetic identification with the line of thought and then to have that identification sensitively enlarged. The congregation is more likely to stay with the preacher and to give the latter images a fair hearing than it would if it is shocked and stunned at the beginning.

The second part of the sermon begins with the approach that Fred Craddock calls "overhearing."[45] Rather than being addressed directly, the congregation "listens in" as I say a few words to the pastor. Although the words are spoken to him, they are heard by the worshipers. The preacher speaks directly to the local pastor with the congregation present and listening in. Gradually the congregation is addressed directly.

The sermon suggests that our view of the world and all our relationships take their cue from the vision of Philippians 2:5-11. Words spoken on special occasions can have special power. I hope that the sermon gives the pastor and the congregation something to which they can return again and again.

Notes

1. What I am calling the "world view" is called by other names. Peter Berger and Thomas Luckmann, for instance, refer to it as the "symbolic universe," *The Social Construction of Reality* (New York: Doubleday, 1966), especially 85 ff. Kenneth Boulding speaks of this as "the image," "what I believe to be true," *The Image* (Ann Arbor: University of Michigan Press, 1956), 6. Essential to the discussion from a sociological perspective is the work on "the life world" by Schutz. See Alfred Schutz and Thomas Luckmann, *The Structures of the Life World*, trans. R. M. Zaner and H. T. Englehardt, Jr. (Evanston: Northwestern University Press, 1973), especially 247-51; Schutz, *Life Forms and Meaning Structures*, trans. R. Wagner (London: Routledge & Kegan Paul, 1982) and Schutz, *Collected Papers*, vol. 1 (The Hague: Nijhoff, 1973), 5. See further, Peter Berger, *The Sacred Canopy* (New York: Doubleday, 1967), note 1, 13. Among theologians who use a very similar notion of the "world" from the discipline of literary criticism are Amos Wilder, for example, "Story and Story World," *Interpretation*, 37, 1983, 353-64, and John Dominic Crossan, for example, *The Dark Interval* (Niles: Argus, 1975). To say that the Christian community designs and furnishes its own world is not to deny the existence of God. But the Christian (as well as others, for example, Jewish and Moslem) claim that the world is created, redeemed, and sustained by a gracious and loving God is an *interpretation*. A problem for the Christian community, especially for the Christian preacher, is the implausibility of this interpretation in the eyes of many people today. Therefore, an important vocation for the pulpit is the justification of the Christian world view. *Why* can we believe today?

2. Berger and Luckmann, *Social Construction*, 91, 116. On the motif of terror, see Mircea Eliade, *The Myth of the Eternal Return or Cosmos and History*, trans. W. R. Trask (Princeton: Princeton University Press, 1954), 139 ff.

3. Berger and Luckmann, *Social Construction*, 92. On the question of religious identity, see Hans J. Mol, *Identity and the Sacred* (New York: Free Press, 1976).

4. Schutz, *The Structures of the Life World*, 2, 3-19. Berger points out that every social role has a world view dangling from its end, *Invitation to Sociology* (New York: Doubleday, 1963), 120. For other functions of world view, see Berger and Luckmann, *Social Construction*, 89-96.

5. On the importance of myth, in addition to the essay by Thomas H. Troeger in this volume, see also Susanne K. Langer, *Philosophy in a New Key* (Cambridge: Harvard University Press, 1942), 171-73; Ernst Cassirer, *Language and Myth*, trans. S. K. Langer (New York: Harper & Brothers, 1956); Cassirer, *The Philosophy of Symbolic Forms*, trans. R. Mannheim, vol. 2 (New Haven: Yale University Press, 1955). Ian Barbour has argued that we no longer live as much by myth as by models. But the effect upon human community is much the same in either case, *Myths, Models and Paradigms* (New York: Harper & Row, 1974).

6. On the social power of a community of memory and hope, see Robert N. Bellah et al., *Habits of the Heart: Individualism and Commitment in American Life* (Berkeley: University of California Press, 1985), 152-55. See also James Gustafson, *Treasure in Earthen Vessels* (New York: Harper & Row, 1961), 71-98.

7. Berger, *The Sacred Canopy*, 20.

8. Boulding, *The Image*, 6.

9. George Lakoff and Mark Johnson, *Metaphors We Live By (Chicago: University of Chicago Press, 1980). See also George H. Mead, Mind, Self, and Society* (Chicago: University of Chicago Press, 1934), 337-53; Philip Wheelwright, *Metaphor and Reality* (Bloomington: University of Indiana Press, 1962); Northrop Frye, *The Educated Imagination* (Bloomington: University of Indiana Press, 1954), 1-33; Paul Ricoeur, *The Rule of Metaphor*, trans. R. Czerny (Toronto: University of Toronto Press, 1977); J. D. Sapier and J. C. Crocker, eds., *The Social Use of Metaphor: Essays on the Anthropology of Rhetoric* (Philadelphia: University of Pennsylvania Press, 1977); and Max Black, *Models and Metaphors* (Ithaca, N.Y.: Cornell University Press, 1962), 153-69.

10. Gibson Winter, *Liberating Creation: Foundations of Religious Social Ethics* (New York: Crossroad Publishing Co., 1981), 6. Similar themes are developed by Joe Holland, "Linking Social Analyses and Theological Reflection: The Place of Root Metaphors in Social and Religious Experience," *Tracing the Spirit*, ed. J. E. Hug, S.J. (New York: Paulist Press, 1983), 170-96.

11. Winter, *Liberating Creation,* 1.

12. Ibid., 21. The church, as a community, is organized by its own root metaphors. These deserve our most careful attention. For help, see Susan B. Thistlewaithe, *Metaphors for the Contemporary Church* (New York: Pilgrim Press, 1983); Avery Dulles, *Models of the Church* (New York: Doubleday, 1974); and Paul Minear, *Images of the Church in the New Testament* (Philadelphia: Westminster Press, 1960).

13. The metaphor for God that is most difficult to assess for its contemporary usefulness is "father." For representative critiques and critical appropriation see Mary Daly, *Beyond God the Father* (Boston: Beacon Press, 1973); Sallie McFague, *Metaphorical Theology* (Philadelphia: Fortress Press, 1982), especially 145-92; Diane Tennis, *Is God the Only Reliable Father?* (Philadelphia: Westminster Press, 1985).

14. In some quarters today the words "sermon" and "preaching" have remarkably negative connotations, for example, "Don't preach to me!"

15. James Cone finds that in traditional theological discourse, issues relative to race have received remarkably little attention, *God of the Oppressed* (New York: Seabury Press, 1975), 62-83.

16. For example, see Rosentenne B. Purnell, "Teaching Them to Curse: Racial Bias in Language, Pedagogy and Practice," *Phylon*, 43, 1982, 231-82.

17. Ossie Davis, "The English Language Is My Enemy," *Negro History Bulletin*, 30, April 1967, 18.

18. A foundational study is still Robin Lakhoff, *Language and Woman's Place* (New York: Harper & Row, 1975), 4, 19-21.

19. Cassey Miller and Kate Swift, *Words and Women* (New York: Doubleday, 1976), 59.

20. Alma Graham, "The Making of a Non-Sexist Dictionary," *Language and Sex*, eds. B. Thorne and N. Henley (Rowley, Mass.: Newbury Press, 1975), 58.

21. Joseph M. Scheidler, *Closed: 99 Ways to Stop Abortion* (Westchester, Ill.: Good News Publishers, 1985).

22. For a series of fascinating studies of this phenomenon, see *Language and the Nuclear Arms Debate*, ed. Paul Chilton (Dover, N.H.: Pinter Press, 1985).

23. Dwight Bolinger, *Language: The Loaded Weapon* (New York: Longmans, 1980).

24. By itself, a single sermon will usually be insufficient to effect a shift in congregational world view. But the sermon is the most consistent and public statement of the Christian vision and thus plays a crucial role in the social life of the community. When the Christian world view consistently informs each sermon, and when the whole of its life is shaped by the Christian world view, then the congregation will be likely to live out of that view.

25. Rudolph Bultmann, "Is Exegesis Without Presuppositions Possible?" *Existence and Faith,* trans. Schubert Ogden (New York: World Books, 1960), 289-96.

26. One of the values of the various liberation movements is the clarity with which they see the vested interests of traditional modes of interpretation and of interpreters who are a part of the power-base of the First-World establishment.

27. See Allene Stuart Phy, ed., *The Place of the Bible in Popular Culture* (Philadelphia: Westminster Press, 1985).

28. This example was called to my attention by my former colleague, Professor Preman Niles. Professor Niles indicated that it was based on research by Meinhert Grumm.

29. On the hermeneutic of suspicion, see especially the many writings of Paul Ricoeur.

30. For a method of making such an assessment, see Ronald J. Allen, *Contemporary Biblical Interpretation for Preaching* (Valley Forge: Judson Press, 1984), 83-94, 141-42.

31. Schutz, for example, *Collected Papers,* vol. 1, 74-77; vol. 2, 31.

32. For critical presentations of approaches to this correlation, see David M. Tracy, *The Analogical Imagination: Christian Theology and the Culture of Pluralism* (New York: Crossroad Publishing Co., 1981); see also his *Blessed Rage for Order* (New York: Seabury Press, 1975); James A. Sanders, "Hermeneutics," *Interpreter's Dictionary of the Bible: Supplement,* ed. Keith A. Crim (Nashville: Abingdon Press, 1975), 406; and Neill Q. Hamilton, *Jesus for a No God World* (Philadelphia: Westminster Press, 1969), 176 ff.

33. For explorations in this regard, see Walter Brueggemann, " 'Vine and Fig Tree': A Case Study," *Catholic Biblical Quarterly,* 43, 1981, 188-204, and "Theological Education: Healing the Blind Beggar," *Christian Century,* 103, 1986, 114-16.

34. The preeminent study is still Fred B. Craddock, *As One Without Authority,* 3rd ed. (Nashville: Abingdon Press, 1979).

35. Lakoff and Johnson, *Metaphors We Live By,* 144-45.

36. Bolinger, *Language: The Loaded Weapon,* 72-88.

37. Ibid., 86.

38. Ibid., 84.

39. Joyce O. Hertzler, *A Sociology of Language* (New York: Random House, 1965), 267-68. The work of Walter J. Ong has renewed interest in characteristics of oral culture. See especially his *The Presence of the Word* (New Haven: Yale University Press, 1967); and Ong, *Orality and Literacy* (New York: Methuen Press, 1982); see also Werner H. Kelber, *The Oral and the Written Gospel* (Philadelphia: Fortress Press, 1982).

40. The literature on this passage is vast. The most exhaustive study is Ralph P. Martin, *Carmen Christi* (Grand Rapids: Wm. B. Eerdmans Publishing Co., 1983, originally published in 1967). See also his *Philippians,* New Century Bible (Wm. B. Eerdmans, 1980). Gerald F. Hawthorne provides a comprehensive survey of the discussion on each disputed point in *Philippians,* Word Biblical Commentary (Waco, Tex.: Word Books, 1983).

Other worthwhile studies include J. F. Collange, *The Epistle of Saint Paul to the Philippians*, trans. A. W. Heathcoate (London: Epworth Press, 1979); Fred B. Craddock, *Philippians*, Interpretation (Atlanta: John Knox Press, 1985), written especially for the preacher; L. E. Keck, "The Letter of Paul to the Philippians," *The Interpreter's One Volume Commentary on the Bible*, ed. Charles M. Laymon (Nashville: Abingdon Press, 1971). Deserving of consideration is Karl Barth's theological commentary, *The Epistle to the Philippians*, trans. J. W. Leitch (Atlanta: John Knox Press, 1962). Jack T. Sanders, *The New Testament Christological Hymns* (Cambridge: Cambridge University Press, 1971) offers a valuable discussion of the hymn in the context of other hymns of the canonical literature of the early church.

41. See Peter Berger, Brigette Berger, Hansfried Kellner, *The Homeless Mind* (New York: Random House, 1973).

42. The indispensable study is Bellah et al., *Habits of the Heart*. See also Daniel Yankelovich, *New Rules: Searching for Self-Fulfillment in a World Turned Upside Down* (New York: Bantam Books, 1981).

43. Still illuminating is Thomas Luckmann, *The Invisible Religion* (New York: Macmillan, 1967), 107-14.

44. Christopher Lasch, *The Culture of Narcissism: American Life in an Age of Diminishing Expectations* (New York: W. W. Norton, 1978).

45. Fred B. Craddock, *Overhearing the Gospel* (Nashville: Abingdon Press, 1978).

6

The Social Power of Myth as a Key to Preaching on Social Issues

Landscapes of the Heart:
Challenging the Reigning Metaphors

Thomas H. Troeger. Politics begins in poetry, in the metaphors, myths, and symbols that command our loyalties and organize our social consciousness. Tyrants know this; consider Hitler. The first territory he set out to conquer was the landscape of the heart. Before he started annexing land he stormed the cultural consciousness of the German people:

> The Germans were the best-educated nation in the world. To conquer their minds was very difficult. Their hearts, their sensibilities were easier targets. Hitler's strength was that he shared with so many other Germans the devotion to national images new and old: misty forests breeding blond titans; smiling peasant villages under the shadow of ancestral castles; garden cities emerging from ghetto-like slums; riding Valkyries, burning Valhallas, new births and dawns in which shining, millennian structures would rise from the ashes of the past and stand for centuries.[1]

I begin with this observation about Hitler because it presents in glaring light the potency of mythological images and stories to engage a group's energies for corporate action. By "mythological images and stories" I mean those metaphors, symbols, and narratives from which a group draws its reason for being, sustains its current life, and envisions and realizes its future. These mythic-poetic realities constitute the "landscape of the heart," the nexus of meanings that filters our interpretation of the world and shapes our patterns of response and creativity.

The landscape of the heart may be mined for good as well as for evil. Consider Martin Luther King, Jr.:

> By pleading the Negro case with such majestic themes as Christianity, non-violence, and universal brotherhood, and by linking these concepts with the great American traditions of liberty and justice for all, King has been able to demonstrate to the white man of conscience, the hypocrisy of his practice of democracy.[2]

King's appeal to the landscape of the heart awakened moral rage so that people's energies were engaged to bring reality closer to the ideals of their mythological world. King's preaching was effective because he envisioned for his listeners what might come to be if they lived out the best yearnings and hopes of their hearts. He realized that

> most of our models for action are conventional; we simply do things as we have become accustomed to do them. But if we modify the typical patterns of our actions, we do so by imagining and choosing among alternative possibilities for action. Our choices may range from the automatic to the deliberately self-conscious, but in every case a pattern of relationships of a *model* for action is operative. Without such models, our actions would be random and purposeless.[3]

King helped people "modify the typical patterns of [their] actions" by holding up a model—a dream—that was congruent with the landscape of their hearts and that could therefore sustain a movement for moral and legislative change.

Anyone, then, who is going to preach on social issues needs to understand the power of myth and its poetic language of image and symbol, their grip upon the landscape of the heart, and the enormous energies that they may release for good or evil.

Our current mythological world is largely supplied by the mass media:

Far from being merely a neutral communication medium, television in America has become an integrated symbolic world filling the socially functional role demanded of it both by its viewers and its advertisers. . . .

William Fore, the Assistant Secretary for Communication in the National Council of Churches of Christ, suggests that there are several other dominant myths in television programming that are of direct relevance for religious broadcasters. These myths are:

- The fittest survive
- Happiness consists of limitless material acquisition
- Consumption is inherently good
- Property, wealth, and power are more important than people
- Progress is an inherent good

Fore asserts that "the whole weight of Christian history, thought and teaching stands diametrically opposed to the media world and its values."[4]

If this last statement seems extreme, consider a single representative example from a kind of programming that is supposedly informational and educational, news broadcasting. During the "Iranian hostage crisis" (note that even the headline is like a television series, drawing on emotionally charged words) there were nightly special broadcasts, each of them bearing the portentous title "Day One, Day Two . . . Day Fifty-Seven," as if we were marking the passage of one of the most significant events in history. But after all those broadcasts to keep us "informed,"

would it be an exaggeration to say that not one American in a hundred knows what language the Iranians speak? Or what the word "Ayatollah" means or implies? Or knows any details of the tenets of Iranian religious beliefs? Or the main outlines of their political history? Or knows who the Shah was, and where he came from?[5]

Instead, the meaning of the event was shaped by a daily ritual broadcast of the images of chanting Iranians and burning American flags. The gospel values of trying to understand our enemies and the source of their alienation from us were superseded by the values of national pride as the media took control of the landscape of the heart, providing a melodramatic plot of good and evil. This, I believe, is a case in point of what William Fore means when he says, "The whole weight of Christian history, thought and teaching stands diametrically opposed to the media world and its values."

It is also an example of what Sam Keen calls "the hostile imagination," the way our consciousness is shaped to depersonalize the enemies so that we can feel justified in our hatred and destruction of them. "In the beginning we create the enemy. Before the weapon comes the image. We *think* others to death and then invent the battle-axe or the ballistic missiles with which to actually kill them. Propaganda precedes technology."[6] Propaganda is the manipulation of the mythic-poetic world of the heart for the purposes of those with political and social power. We are apt to recognize propaganda in its most glaring forms, such as the nationalistic posters of earlier wars that illustrate Keen's book, but its impact is absorbed without notice when it flows through the river of images that pours out of the television set. For as Neil Postman points out, we have lost the sense of critical distance that we had when television first arrived; now "the world as given to us through television seems natural, not bizarre."[7]

A purely rational appeal from the pulpit cannot counter the deleterious effect of the media's mythic world upon the life of faith and grace. Information and well-reasoned analysis belong in sermons, but they are ineffectual as long as the preacher has not entered the landscape of the heart and challenged the reigning metaphors of secularist national culture with the images and narratives of faith.

The first step in preparing for this task is to sharpen our consciousness of those assumptive metaphors that shape and rule our own hearts:

> Whether consciously or unconsciously, all people live by metaphors. . . . To become aware of the metaphors that govern basic perspectives is, among other things, a political act, for the possibility of change both at the personal and public levels depends upon consciousness of hidden metaphors. . . . Once we become aware that we *are* interpreters and interpretation means seeing one thing in terms of

> something else, in other words, using one thing as a
> perspective on something else, then we have forever lost what
> we thought we had—the innocent eye.[8]

One of the chief tasks of homiletics is to make the innocent
eye the alerted eye, the eye that probes and detects the
shadowed depths of our mythological worlds and is aware of
its own distortions and blind spots.

The alerted eye sees that the assimilation of the gospel to
media methods and images results in burying the gospel's
demands. This is evident in the distortions of religious
"broadcasters [who] now conduct regular market research to
detect which aspects of the Christian message will evoke
greater response from their audiences, even to the point of
evaluating the acceptability of a particular host's prayers."[9] In
effect, "the Christian faith, which stresses such things as
self-discipline, sacrifice, and service," is reshaped "by a
medium which stresses instant personal gratification."[10]

The distortions that the alerted eye identifies in religious
broadcasting are not limited, however, to the gospel as
presented on television. The mythological world and values
of the electronic media often pervade and find reinforcement in the local church and the surrounding culture of
popular literature and iconography. Thus, Allene Stuart Phy
concludes her survey of best-selling religious novels by
observing that they

> display only the vaguest understanding of the classical
> Christian definition of the nature of Jesus. There is, in fact, an
> antitheological bias implied in most of these books. The
> reader is presented a Jesus of American culture, stripped of
> "theological accretions.". . . In this manner traditional Chris-
> tianity has been sacrificed to a bland and colorless American
> religious pluralism.[11]

In a similar way, Ljubica D. Popovich summarizes her survey
of popular American biblical imagery by concluding:

> This art does not strive to expand experience but rather to
> reflect a piety that already exists in the viewer. The
> monotonous reiteration of established patterns and conven-
> tions, which may be likened to the familiar refrains of popular

music, soothes and reassures but rarely poses intellectual
challenges or expands and explores visual possibilities.[12]

We may be tempted to dismiss these observations as
immaterial to so weighty a topic as the social dimensions of
the gospel, but they are central to any attempt to mobilize the
energies of the church on behalf of justice and peace. For
unless we enter the landscape of the heart where these images
are stored, no ecclesiastical pronouncement or pulpit
proclamation—however well reasoned and argued—will
budge people from the dominant mythological world that
provides them with the spiritual essentials of meaning,
purpose, security, and a sense of the sacred.

This observation is supported by my work with a colleague,
Carol Doran, on revitalizing the hymnody of the church.
After a recent presentation to an editorial committee for a
new hymnal, the head of the project told us how startled
many of the denominational executives were at the outpour-
ing of response to proposed changes in the language and
selection of hymns. It exceeded the reaction to any of the
denomination's social pronouncements. Rather than brush
this aside as an example of the irrelevance of the church, it
deserves to be examined as a revealing example of what I
mean by the social power of myth. For hymns are one of the
single most important ways that the landscape of the
believing heart is shaped and revealed: "If you know what
hymns a person loves most, or what hymns a congregation is
most addicted to, you will be able to infer what, in
Christianity, means most to that person or that church. And
that inference won't be speculative: it will be perfectly
sound."[13]

The hymnal committee had touched the power center of
faith: the religious imagination, the hunger for beauty and
poetry, the mythological world that sustains and energizes
the believing community. The surprise, and sometimes
disdain, that such a reaction awakens in people who are eager
to see the church take a stand for justice, reveals an ignorance
of the peculiar nature of the church's political power. Such
power derives primarily not from defining Christian positions on specific problems of civil governance, but rather

from the mythological world that is inscribed in the heart by the community's corporate ritual. Thus the most radical action of the early church was the way it transfigured the dominant consciousness of the surrounding culture:

> Those odd little groups [of Christians] in a dozen or so cities of the Roman East were engaged, though they would not have put it quite this way, in constructing a new world. In time, more time than they thought was left, their ideas, their images of God, their ways of organizing life, their rituals, would become part of a massive transformation, in ways they could not have foreseen, of the culture of the Mediterranean basin and of Europe.[14]

The transforming power of the church declines whenever it loses its religious imagination, by which I mean its ability to envision and communicate images of an alternative reality that can break the rim of normative consciousness. It is the loss of such imagination that makes ineffectual so much of the social preaching that I hear.

I think of a particular preacher who has a passion for setting things right in our society, most of whose sermons are a call to action. Even though the congregation is in sympathy with these concerns, the listeners' energies are not mobilized by the pulpit. An examination of the sermons reveals that the preacher's vocabulary and style are indistinguishable from that of the media which form the congregation's information network and world view. The preacher often uses the Scriptures in ways that show sound scholarship, but that does not make much difference because, in the final analysis, most of the sermons sound like nothing more than another editorial, worthy perhaps of a responsible citizen's reflection but never sending lightning and thunder over the landscape of the heart.

A more effective strategy for the preacher would be to realize it is not "enough to propose 'Christian solutions' to the problems of our society, because it is the whole framework in which these 'problems' are perceived which has to be called in question."[15] That current framework "can no longer satisfy us," and we therefore face the task of envisioning reality in a way that "will meet our sense of being at a dead end and open new horizons of meaning."[16] It is this "sense of being at a dead end" that cuts the nerve of action in this preacher's listeners.

Such a feeling arises whenever a closed system of meaning has exhausted its repertoire of interpretations and solutions to the puzzles of human existence. Newbigin identifies this situation as the central issue for the Western church as it approaches the twenty-first century. His analysis in the theological realm receives confirmation in the literary reflections of Czeslaw Milosz, who believes that the vitality of the poet's voice requires

> some basic confidence . . . a sense of open space ahead of the individual and the human species. . . . As a youth I felt the complete absurdity of everything occurring on our planet, a nightmare that could not end well—and in fact it found its perfect expression in the barbed wire around the concentration camps and gas chambers. . . . Today I think that, while the list of dreaded apocalyptic events may change, what is constant is a certain state of mind. This state precedes the perception of specific reasons for despair, which come later.[17]

There is a striking similarity of language between Newbigin and Milosz. The theologian speaks of a "dead end" and the need to "open new horizons of meaning." The poet describes a "future laden with catastrophe" and the requirement for a "sense of open space ahead of the individual and the human species." This similarity is no accident.

As Geoffrey Wainwright exclaims: "If the Western world is experiencing a crisis in lyric poetry, liturgy, and theology, the simultaneity of these critical manifestations should not be surprising."[18] The crisis in all three areas springs from a commonly shared sense of being at a "dead end," a situation in which socially responsible preaching involves far more than addressing particular issues.

The preacher I have already mentioned who is unable to move people to take action for the cause of justice and peace is communicating clearly enough. But the preacher never acknowledges the listener's primary state of mind that precedes their "specific reasons for despair" and that leaves them with no "sense of open space ahead of the individual and the human species."

Our analysis reveals why the distinction that is commonly made between prophetic and pastoral preaching is inaccurate. The terms are often used to distinguish sermons of social action from those that address more personal issues of meaning and faith. Newbigin and Milosz help us see that people do not move into action when the landscape of the heart is lost in a deep shadow and they perceive the world as a closed reality whose possibilities of transformation are spent. In the face of such a profound spiritual crisis the task of homiletics is to revitalize the religious imagination so that it creates a sense of open space in front of people, thereby giving them enough hope to work for social change. This requires the ability to witness to God with a language that grips the landscape of the heart.

Speaking a Communal Poetic Idiom to an Individualistic Technical Culture

Because of the individualistic character of our culture, the language that engages the heart often tends to be solitary rather than communal. Thus the authors of *Habits of the Heart,* an analysis of individualism and commitment in American life, discovered that most of their interviewees: "are limited to a language of radical individual autonomy . . . [so] they cannot think about themselves or others except as arbitrary centers of volition. They cannot express the fullness of being that is actually theirs."[19] Revitalizing the religious imagination will not transform this situation if we assume that the imagination belongs solely to the individual and is thus limited to the "language of radical individual autonomy." Tragically, this has been the assumption of most Western people who have lived after the romantic rebellion against the Enlightenment, when poetry, the primary language of myth, retreated more and more into " '[the] paltry ego, [humanity's] often empty and always cramped ego . . .' [until] it withdrew from the domain common to all people into the closed circle of subjectivism."[20] The result has been a severe alienation between the poet and the larger human family so that the most imaginative users of language—the poets—no longer supply a vitalizing pulse to the myths of the larger culture. Thus Helen Vendler in her introduction to a recent collection of *Contemporary American Poetry,* explains:

> The poets included here write—as the earlier modernists did not—from a Freudian culture, one in which a vaguely Freudian model of the soul has replaced an older Christian- ized Hellenic model. . . . Finally, all of these poets write within a culture in which physical science has replaced metaphysics as the model of the knowable. The epistemological shift toward scientific models of verification has caused the usual throes of fundamentalist reaction in American culture, as elsewhere; but there is no significant poet whose work does not mirror, both formally and in its preoccupations, the absence of the transcendent.[21]

In no way do I desire to fuel the "fundamentalist reaction in American culture." But I want to stress what Vendler's observation means for a medium as dependent on words as preaching is. The imaginative use of poetic language to reach the landscape of the heart has now become isolated from its original theological and corporate roots and has become increasingly the constricted domain of a specialized literati. The separation between the language of the heart and the "Word from whom all words have sprung,"[22] means there is no longer a dialectic between the generative power of the poets and the pulpit. This is as crucial a separation for theology as for literature since "to lose the *vis poetica* is at the same time to lose the *vis religiosa.*"[23]

In my experience of leading homiletics workshops with experienced preachers I have found many pastors who grasp this problem at an intuitive level. They give sermons that are technically accomplished—biblically sound, lucidly organ- ized, well spoken. Yet they sense their language sounds "tired" or "worn" or "like the same old thing." I admire these preachers for their refusal to settle for the religious cliché. But living in a world where the connection of poetry and theology has been ruptured, most of their attempts to vitalize their sermons have been limited to employing the culture's dominant language in the pulpit. Such a strategy makes sense because whatever area of thought a society invests with the power of discovering truth is the area from which it takes much of its leading language. This is reasonable: we want our words "to tell the truth" and the persistent hope is that if certain words tell the truth in one place, they'll continue to tell it in another. For the past few hundred years in Western society, and especially the past one hundred, science has been seen as the place where truth is found and told.[24]

Notice the complexities this analysis poses for telling the truth from the pulpit. On the one hand, to communicate with authority requires using the "language" of our listeners. But on the other hand, the truth we have to communicate is one that calls into question the stranglehold of that language upon the way we perceive things:

In a structure of thought dominated, as secular humanism's is, by the strict opposition of "human intelligence" to "divine guidance" and by the insistence that any reference to a transcendent reality is meaningless, obviously most traditional religious terms are going to be missing from respectable discourse (or mentioned only to be demeaned). . . . So in the list of words deliberately missing from expressions of the currently dominant ideology we'll find, for example, *absolutes, humility, transcendence, truth, wisdom, wonder, soul, sin, grace, gratitude,* and *God.*[25]

In other words the language of the culture shows the same theological bankruptcy as the language of the poets. Drawing on the analysis of *Habits of the Heart* and Peggy Rosenthal's *Words and Values,* we discover that popular speech possesses two main qualities: it is technical in dealing with the objective world of things and personalistic in dealing with the world of meaning. Such language supports the myths that science can control nature and that the meaning of life is limited to what is personally true for the individual.

How, then, do preachers find a *poetic* and *communal* idiom that will speak with authority to a society whose verbal medium is *technical* and *individualistic?*

We begin by creating some degree of critical distance between ourselves and the language that lies immediately at hand in the culture, by realizing the historically conditioned nature of language and its attendant values. The language of our culture does not necessarily present things the way they really are. Peggy Rosenthal has traced how the areas of thought invested with power have changed over the years, and subsequently so has the language that was considered to express the truth. Language that modern society disdains was once held in esteem, and language that used to have negative connotations has accrued positive value. These verbal transformations represent more than the quirks of popular usage. They reflect shifts in the substrata of society's structure of meaning, in the mythological worlds that occupy the landscape of the heart.

Preachers who lack a historical consciousness of how their speech is shaped by these shifts in language and values can easily bury the gospel in attempting to make it relevant. I remember a few years ago when T. A.—Transactional Analysis—was the rage in popular psychological culture. I lost count of the number of sermons I heard that equated Christ's acceptance of us with the psychological claim, "I'm okay. You're okay." I was finally able to break through this puerile excuse for a theology of grace with the help of a cartoon that showed Christ upon the cross asking, "If I'm okay, and you're okay, what am I doing here?" It took the crudeness of that humor to snap the spell that had descended on one particular class of preachers.

The story reveals both the desire for a keener language in the pulpit and the weakness of the materials that are often uncritically accepted in that quest. Peggy Rosenthal concludes from her study of the interrelationship of words and values that we cannot

> simply switch to some ideal set of terms or train of thought and expect that if we ride it religiously, we'll reach the good life automatically at the end of the line. . . . Neither are we simply trapped in those other (currently dominant) terms, simply stuck on the main train of thought of our time. As individuals with free will, we do have the power to get off the going lines at any point.[26]

This, however, is only an initial step since effective preaching can never remain long at a "position of detachment."[27] Having established some degree of critical distance from the assumed language and values of the culture, how do we develop a poetic and corporate language that can break the rim of normative consciousness and revitalize the religious imagination as a source of energy for social change? There is help in answering this poetic-theological question in both the history of Western poetry and the history of interpreting God's Word.

T. S. Eliot, in making his distinction between "classical" and "romantic" poets, suggests that classical poets, meaning all of the major poets of Western literary tradition prior to the rise of romanticism,

> arrive at poetry through eloquence; . . . wisdom has the primacy over inspiration; and [they] are more concerned with the world about them than with their own joys and sorrows, concerned with their own feelings in their likeness to those of other [people] rather than in their particularity.[28]

What a radically different understanding of the poetic voice this is from the contemporary understanding that "the price paid for individuality of voice—the quality, after all, for which we remember poets—is absolute social singularity. Each poet is a species to himself [or herself], a mutant in the human herd, speaking an idiolect he [or she] shares with no one."[29] The shift from a concern for commonality of feeling to social singularity in the poet's voice parallels the development of the "language of radical individual autonomy" that dominates the general culture. One way of conceptualizing the task of homiletics is to think of preachers as classical poets who draw on the language of metaphor and myth in order to illumine how our feelings draw us together in community rather than isolate us in "absolute social singularity." Such a conception of the task of preaching leads us to recover the corporate, social dimensions of the imagination:

> We are so habituated to conceiving of the imagination as a private act of the human spirit that we now find it almost impossible to conceive of a common act of *imagining with.* But what happens in despair is that the private imagination, of which we are so enamored, reaches the point of the end of inward resource and must put on the imagination of another if it is to find a way out.[30]

To reclaim the concept and discipline of a communal imagination is to do nothing more than what the Old Testament prophets did when they gathered in schools; or the psalmists did when they used the first person singular in a way that was expressive of the whole congregation's experience; or what the Gospel writer John did when he related "all things in his own name, aided by the *revision* of all"[31]; or what John Calvin did when he gathered the preachers of Geneva to study the Scriptures together so that their interpretations would not fall into idiosyncratic distortions[32]; or what the early English separatists did when they practiced communal biblical interpretation in their prayer meetings; or what the base communities of Third-World countries do when they reflect on their corporate experience in light of God's liberating Word. In every case the imaginative act of discerning the Word involves more than the individual preacher; it draws on the larger circle of the community so that a wider web of meanings and insights is available to the preacher's imagination.

This does not mean that preachers abdicate their calling to proclaim the gospel or that they do not bring their peculiar insights to the pulpit. These gifts are as necessary as ever, but now the minister reconstrues the role of preacher to be

> the catalyst and guide for this common imagination. He or she opens up new avenues of imagination by helping the community envision what cannot yet be seen: creative ways of solving racial conflict, a world without weapons and war, possibilities for sharing the earth's resources. The minister suggests to a community that the boundaries of the possible are wider than they seem.
>
> Where does the minister obtain such hopeful assurance? In the treasure house of the community's traditions. It is the role of the minister to bring these traditions to life again so that they can call the community to conversion and comfort.[33]

That phrase, "the treasure house of the community's traditions," is significant not only because it resonates with Jesus' observation: "Therefore every scribe who has been trained for the kingdom of heaven is like a householder who brings out of his treasure what is new and what is old" (Matt. 13:52), but because it is richer than simply "the Bible."

Scripture is central to preaching; I will not debate the point. But to speak about "the treasure house of tradition" is to honor the revelations and gifts that the Spirit has made that fall outside the canon, particularly through the work of those creative artists who have not retreated to "absolute social singularity," but who have possessed the faith and grace to bend their talent to the sovereign source of all art and to express what lies in the community's heart.

Any homiletics that is going to engage the religious imagination for the cause of social change must enter this treasure house of tradition and rediscover there the connection to the transcendent and corporate dimensions of imagination that have been lost since the rise of romanticism and the technological society.

In a sense, the historical process of alienation between the religious imagination and the dominant Western consciousness is similar to what happens when late adolescents attend college and are swept up in the tide of novel ideas. At first, they dismiss what they have been taught to value, what has shaped and nurtured them. Their delight and their delirium is in what is new, in all that seems to liberate them from their old constraints. But if they are healthy persons, over a period of time they will begin to look critically at what they formerly granted facile acceptance. They will not merely return to their past—that is neither possible nor desirable—but they will draw on what was best in their upbringing and meld it with what they have learned and experienced beyond the boundaries of their initial environment. We say of such people: they have matured, they have grown up, they are adults now.

So it is with Western consciousness. It has been in a period of extended adolesence since the Enlightenment, discovering wonderful new ideas through science, technology, psychology, and art. But it has also distorted its health by forgetting its earlier upbringing, by discounting what century after century knew to be true: that there is a depth to our existence that is the source of all life and that claims the first loyalty of our hearts. And this reality is none other than God, who has so patterned the motions of the molecules of the human cranium that they give rise to a subjectivity never satisfied by anything less than being in harmony with the Creator.

The peculiar calling of preachers in this age is to help Western consciousness move beyond adolescence, to integrate the ancient wisdom with contemporary knowledge so that the religious imagination may be reengaged in the cause of personal and social transformation. Such integration needs to take place not only through content and concept but also through the character of the language that marks the pulpit. I believe the great stress on story in homiletics during recent years represents in part the eruption of this need: that is, the non-discursive and poetic qualities of narrative have appealed to preachers as a way of breaking beyond the constraints of an overly argumentative rhetoric. However, a transition to purely narrative and poetic forms of language would be no healthier in the pulpit than the former domination of cognitive, rational speech.

Interweaving Depth and Steno Languages: From Rhapsody to Reason

Preaching effectively for social change requires fluency in two languages: that which is evocative, narrative, and metaphorical, and that which is denotative, logical, and discursive. Philip Wheelwright identifies these different modes of speech as "depth" and "steno" language.[34] I shall use these terms as a convenient shorthand without implying that I fully accept Wheelwright's theory of language.

The spectrum of possibilities for our language is a witness to the fullness of the divine Word. Our capacity to draw on such a range of speech may be rooted in the way our brains are created and the physiological processes of thought.[35] Being made in the image of God means in part that we have been endowed with an ability to articulate reality through a richness of language that extends from rhapsody to reason. Nevertheless, there is in most people a tendency to favor one language over the other, to use predominantly either steno or depth speech. But the public role of preachers requires that they do not restrict their pulpit speech to their own natural tendencies. Confining themselves either to steno or depth language is more than a stylistic limitation: it is a theological distortion because

> the fullest possible understanding of Christian faith (which is necessarily an understanding of the "witness" of scriptures and our common human experience) is inherently dialogical and "dipolar." It does not employ a single mode of thought but, rather, moves back and forth between . . . poetry and theology. As it does so, it not only uses concepts to interpret metaphors but also uses metaphors to interpret concepts, both the metaphoric and the conceptual entering into and interpreting the common ground of life experience, action, and commitment that gives rise to all understanding whatsoever.[36]

Burch Brown names this dialectical process "transfiguration," evoking the Gospel accounts which reveal the nature of Jesus and connecting the term as well to the transforming power of art.

Transfiguration has not been the dominant characteristic of homiletics. Instead of maintaining the dialogical process between theology and poetry, between steno and depth language, the church from the second century on tended to favor a more discursive approach in its proclamation: the "history of preaching, for all its complexity and diversity, bears one remarkable constant: the reflective shape of the sermon."[37]

The general bias of homiletics described in these broad historical terms has had a profound impact on individual preachers as they have stood in the pulpit. It has been one of those forces that has shaped their voice even when they were not aware of it.

David Grayson gives us a sense of how the imbalance of steno language influenced a minister from his childhood in ways that muffled the preacher's authentic witness:

> Somewhere, I said, he had a spark within him. I think he never knew it: or if he knew it, he regarded it as a wayward impulse that might lead him from his God. It was a spark of poetry: strange flower in such a husk. In times of emotion it bloomed, but in daily life it emitted no fragrance.[38]

This effort to repress the poetic for fear that it is "a wayward impulse that might lead him from his God" represents something more than the preacher's personal preference. It is the breaking to the surface in an individual preacher of the historical bias of homiletics toward "the reflective shape of the sermon" whose mental processes of ratiocination inevitably favor steno language.

And yet if the pulpit does not engage the landscape of the heart with the appropriate use of depth language, then preachers of other gospels will step in to conjure up their own visions, and the poetically attractive invocation of satanic powers will lead to brutal historical consequences. At the opening of this chapter we have already seen how this happened with Hitler. He bypassed the people's steno language and appealed to them through depth language. The pulpit can only counter this kind of tyranny by maintaining the full spectrum of speech, using the depth language of Scripture to challenge the idolatrous images of nationalism and using the fire of that language to re-ignite rational faculties in the service of challenging and changing the state. Preachers who think they are being prophetic by delivering sermons that are purely rational are politically naïve and ineffective. The pulpit that fails to regenerate the vitality of the church's primal images through the use of the poetic is helpless against the quasi-religious appeal of secular leaders. Despite the fact that we live after Copernicus, the universe we carry in our hearts and minds is still poetic and mythological:

> Ideologies and superstitions, concentration-camp utopias and interplanetary folklore occupy the void left by the withdrawal of the Christian soul and scientific humanism, by the ebbing of Christian intellect and the élitist encystation of men [and women] of science in their special languages, waterproof compartments.[39]

When the pulpit ceases to be poetic, it creates a vacuum that sucks in the pathological images of a spiritually bankrupt and often demonic culture.

Augustine knew this. It was the basis of his argument for eloquent sermons as a counter-force to the malevolent uses of rhetoric: "While the faculty of eloquence, which is of great value in urging either evil or justice, is in itself indifferent, why should it not be obtained for the uses of the good in the service of truth if the evil usurp it for the winning of the perverse and vain causes in defense in iniquity and error?"[40]

The most radical voice for social change in the pulpit is not the one that sounds like the editorial page of the evening paper or a television commentator. Instead, it is the voice whose analytical speech draws fire from the visionary energies of depth language and (like the biblical prophets) shakes the foundations of the state with poetic thunder. This process also works in reverse: sometimes images and stories that on their own would seem merely decorative and anecdotal, bristle with life because they have been preceded by the clear rational speech of a carefully developed argument.

The process of transfiguration lies, then, at the heart of the fullness of the gospel and the ability of preaching to engage all of us for all of God. This does not mean that every sermon will be a perfect balance of depth and steno languages. There are biblical texts and pastoral circumstances when one language is more appropriate than the other. What concerns us here is that ministers examine their preaching over time, asking, Am I employing the full range of language that gives witness to the wholeness of God's Word, from rhapsody to reason? Preachers who can answer yes to this are participating in a process of transfiguration that reaches beyond their own personal development into the renewing cycles of poetry and philosophy that can sustain the energies needed for social change.

The Sermon: Preparation, Preaching, and Reflection

An ecumenical service celebrating the three-hundredth anniversary of the birth of Johann Sebastian Bach is the occasion for this sermon. The liturgy is patterned after the Leipzig service of Bach's own time and features the performance of the Easter cantata "Christ Lag in Todesbanden" as an integral part of the proclamation of the Word. I realize this is a special occasion and one that might even seem strange for a sermon on social change. But I have chosen it because it throws in bold relief the issue of how social change is facilitated by the poetic. Far too often, people contrast the aesthetic side of faith with the gritty business of changing society. But this dichotomy, as I have tried to indicate in my essay, is a modern phenomenon occasioned by the loss of the corporate and theological dimensions of the poet's voice.

The combination of Bach's genius and the Gospel text that was appointed for the day, Mark 16:1-8, telling of the women's discovery of the empty tomb, provides in my view an opportunity to break the rim of normative consciousness and revitalize the religious imagination. Many of the listeners are leaders in their own congregations, people already hard at work on the church's mission, many of them sometimes wondering if it really is possible to bring about social change.

I live with the text for several days, using standard reference works. I am struck with the observation that perhaps the reason Mark ended his Gospel on this strange note of fear was "to emphasize human inadequacy, lack of understanding, and weakness in the presence of supreme divine action and its meaning."[41] For these are the very realities that break through our normal ways of perceiving the world, and they are also the qualities of Bach's music.

I spend two hours with the pastoral musician, Carol Doran, who will conduct the choir and instrumentalists. I take notes as she explains the background and nature of the music. Like good exegetical notes, all of them will not get in the sermon but they make me secure about what I will preach, and they lead me to a deeper appreciation of Bach's interpretation.

My colleague lends me a recording of the work and I listen again and again, as intently as I have studied the biblical passage. Bach is helping me understand the Spirit, the depths of the text, the wonder of it all. The weeping strings in E minor have led me to the landscape of the heart, and I wait there in wordless prayer, perceiving truth that is like mist rising from a lake; it is neither water circumscribed by the curve of shore nor cloud silhouetted against the blue of sky, but effluvium from the source rising toward an articulation of form that cannot be predicted or controlled. Wonder, image, concept, clarity—a sermon is condensing into a discernible shape.

A Primal Fearsome Wonder

And they went out and fled from the tomb; for trembling and astonishment had come upon them; and they said nothing to any one, for they were afraid.
(MARK 16:8)

What a strange ending for a book that opens,
"Here begins the Good News of Jesus Christ."
How does Mark get from Good News
to trembling and astonishment
and they said not a word to anyone for they were
afraid?
His ending has bothered Christians
almost from the moment he wrote it down.
Over the years, readers have come up with all kinds of
theories about why the book concludes this way:
Some people speculate Mark got sick and did not finish.
Some say he intended to finish but never did.
And others think he had another ending
but
it was the last page of the manuscript
and somehow it got torn off and lost.
It's understandable how people came up with these theories.
They must have wondered:
where is the high rhapsodic note of Easter joy?
If we want to find that, we will have to turn to Matthew.
Or Luke.
Or John.
I like Matthew for power.
Matthew knows how to end on a strong note.
The risen Lord gets the last words:

"All authority in heaven and on earth has been given to me.
Go therefore and make disciples of all nations, baptizing them in
the name of the Father and of the Son and of the Holy Spirit,
teaching them to observe all that I have commanded you; and
lo, I am with you always, to the close of the age." (Matt.
28:18-20)

So if we want that high, thrilling vision of Easter,
   the one that lifts us up and makes us sing,
      we will have to turn to another Gospel than Mark's.
   For Mark seems intent instead on giving us
      the primal fearsome wonder of the resurrection.
And even
   if we were ever to find some long-lost original ending,
      there still is no way to hide Mark's bluntness:
"trembling and astonishment had come upon them;
   and they said nothing to any one, for they were afraid."

Now the greatness of Bach
   is that he is not like some preachers
      who might look at this text and think:
   "Oh, my, it doesn't seem suitable.
      We better fix this up
         and write the sermon in a major key."
   Bach has too much integrity for that.
      Instead he writes the cantata in E minor.
      Remember that opening sinfonia,
         the strings playing rich minor chords.
Or think of the chorus singing
   "the death," "the death," "the death"
      again and again and again
      so we feel the inescapability of death.
Or later on we hear the strings weeping over the Paschal
Lamb.
   Bach leads us into the heart of Mark's words:
   "Trembling and astonishment had come upon them;
      and they said nothing to any one,
         for they were afraid."

How could it be otherwise?
   Think about it for a moment.
      How could the first reaction be anything other
      than trembling and astonishment?
Trudging through the dawn of that first Easter morning
   those women carried with them a single comfort.
      Just one:
         they knew it was all over.

The task now was to grieve,
   to come to terms with their loss.
      That is not much comfort.
      But it is some comfort.
I think of all the dear people who have died whom I have loved.
   I have known comfort in the finality of death.
      Have you not known it?
You realize all is over.
   You have no choice but to accept it.
And so the women made their way to the tomb.
   They knew what the future held for them.
      Tears.
         And more tears.
         Then fewer tears.
   Then getting used to the hollow place in the heart
      that would never again fill up.
On the way to the tomb
   maybe they dreamed of the empty days to come
      and what they would say to one another:
         "Oh, we had such high hopes,
            but I know now it was all an illusion."
      "Goodness glimmers for a moment.
         Love lasts a little while—
            then evil wipes it out."
      "Yes,
         let's be realists.
            Let's be honest about the world.
               It's rotten. And the bad win."
   Maybe they were thinking like this
      until,
         as Mark says,
            "Looking up, they saw . . ."
               Wait.
                  What did they see?
When they were here Friday, their pain and grief were so sharp
   they did not take in many details.
      "But the stone?
         Wasn't it right there?"
            "I don't understand.
               Things are not the way I remember."

And entering the tomb, they saw a young man sitting on the right
side, dressed in a white robe; and they were amazed. And he
said to them, "Do not be amazed; you seek Jesus of Nazareth,
who was crucified. He has risen, he is not here; see the place
where they laid him. But go, tell his disciples and Peter that he is
going before you to Galilee; there you will see him, as he told
you." (Mark 16:4-7)

Wait.
Do you mean that the world is not the way we thought it was?
You mean we cannot be content to nurse our grief and hurt?
You mean our hard-earned realism
is called into question now?

If death,
if the one absolute certainty,
if the one ineradicable truth of our lives,
is not fixed and closed,
then what about all the other certainties?
If death has been overcome, what about this certainty?
I will never forgive him.
If death has been overcome, what about this certainty?
I will never find it in my heart to love that person.
If death has been overcome, what about this certainty?
It is impossible for us to negotiate a meaningful arms
reduction with the Soviets.
If death has been overcome, what about this certainty?
We can have no impact on apartheid in South Africa.
If death has been overcome, what about this certainty?
Women cannot do that!
If death has been overcome, what about this certainty?
You can't expect to overcome centuries of prejudice.
If death has been overcome, what about this certainty?
There is no way I will ever get rid of my addiction.
"Trembling and astonishment had come upon them;
and they said nothing to any one, for they were afraid."
Of course they were afraid.
More than a stone had been moved.
The whole world had shifted.
They needed time to absorb that truth.

Time. Time—
Yet I can imagine over the next few days,
as they saw others who knew the risen Lord,
the truth began to grow in them.
They began to remember those stories
that on Good Friday
had seemed merely the vain efforts
of some dreamy-headed idealist.
I can hear them recalling various incidents in Christ's life:
"Do you remember when we were in the synagogue
and there was that man in the back?
He was possessed and the demon cried out,
'Jesus of Nazareth!'
And Christ healed him."
"You know what I will never forget
is the time there was that big crowd
in front of the door.
And four brazen men
got up on the house
and dug a hole through the roof
and lowered down their paralyzed friend."
"When I was making bread the other day,
I thought of those five thousand people
out on the hillside.
And all the food we could find
was what some child's mother had packed him for lunch."
So the stories began to flood back,
only now,
instead of thinking of them as glimmers of grace,
they were seen for what they really were:
signs of God transforming the world
and breaking their assumptions
that this is the way things have to be—
cruel, bitter, unjust.
God was showing them other possibilities
for life: the lame walking,
the hungry fed, the blind seeing.
And I can picture Mark,
having listened to all these stories,
getting ready to write them down

before they slipped away from memory
        or get changed anymore than they already had been.
He has to come up with the hardest sentence of all:
        the first sentence.
He thinks about the trembling and astonishment of the
resurrection
        and the light that Easter throws upon the exorcisms
                and the feedings
                        and the healings
                                and the cross.
While he thinks, the Spirit moves within him.
        He writes: "Here begins the Good News of Jesus Christ."
And the sentence rings true for Mark.
        It does not sound facile
                or cheaply happy
because Mark,
        like Bach who followed him,
                has looked at the trembling and the astonishment
                        of the resurrection,
at the primal fearsome wonder of what God had done.
        In some way in your own life you have been touched by that
trembling and astonishment.
        Otherwise you would not be here.
                And that is why I am here also
                        worshiping with you.
        Because if I go back behind every reason for my being here,
                I get to this final one:
                        Jesus Christ is risen.
How have you known that in your life?
        Was it at the bedside of someone who was dying?
                Was it when you walked from a grave and thought,
        "I'll never get through this?"
                But you did.
                        Or was it when you took a stand for justice
                                and you could have sworn
                        there was someone who steadied your trembling legs?
And afterward,
        You walked away saying,
                "Jesus Christ, you are my all.
                        I love you.

Not nearly as perfectly as you love me.
But I will follow you.
I will serve you.
I will stand bravely for what is right."
And then the fear and the trembling gave way
and there was Good News.
Our prayer is that this day,
through the ministry of Johann Sebastian Bach
and these musicians, you may know again
the fear and the trembling,
the primal fearsome wonder
of the resurrection of Jesus Christ
so that when you walk out of here,
your life will declare to other lives:
"Here begins the Good News of Jesus Christ."

Reflection

First a word about the form of the sermon. I originally preached it, as I do most of my sermons, with no notes. Then I made a transcript from a tape. I have polished some of the language for publication and left out a few comments that were germane only to that particular congregation, but the sermon is basically as I *spoke* it. I stress this because sermons are above all a spoken, not a written communication. The pace, inflection, pitch, and color of speech are among the most important aspects of preaching, and they are vital to the process of engaging listeners for social change. I am convinced that one of the reasons Martin Luther King, Jr., was able to facilitate change is that his delivery was so credible. Listen to his voice. You can hear the weeping of his people in it at the same time that it is fired with a passion for justice. The cadence, the pacing, the accents—all reveal someone who is in touch with the music of language, that music that is the very spring of myth and poetry.

Robert Frost identifies the speaking voice as "the voice of the imagination."[42] And that is why it is vital, even if we do write out our sermons, that we write them with our ears and not our eyes. To make this our standard practice would be a way of disciplining ourselves to reclaim the religious imagination and to speak more effectively to the landscape of the heart.

The sermon also draws on the listeners' experience of hearing the cantata immediately beforehand. This is a deliberate strategy to integrate Bach's sonic manifestation of ultimate meaning with the structures of thought and feeling that constitute the organization of the sermon. I call on the music to help engage the imaginative capacities of the listeners so that they have more spiritual energy to respond to the issues of social change that are presented in the form of a litany: "If death has been overcome, what about this certainty?" and so on. Notice that the litany uses a primary logical pattern, "If . . . then . . . ," thus blending the rational with the poetic and providing a balance of steno and depth languages.

I have deliberately connected the resurrection of Christ to the task of social transformation. I want it to be clear that there is a theological reason, and not merely my personal bias, for the church's involvement in society. Easter addresses the ultimate fear of human existence—the threat of not being—and thereby frees us to look skeptically at all those other limitations in life that we unjustifiably excuse as "the way the world is." By drawing on the reality of Christ's resurrection I simultaneously address the existential anxiety of the individual while challenging the church to claim the full meaning of what it believes.

Easter points us beyond "our sense of being at a dead end" that Newbigin has identified as the root of our passivity (see pages 212-13) and opens what he calls "new horizons of meaning." We facilitate social change, not by promulgating a particular program but by entering the landscape of the heart and revitalizing—through music, poetry and reason— the listeners' belief in the source of all just and lasting change: the risen Christ

> [Whose] high rhapsodic vision
> Of truth and love and peace
> Has loosened dreams and yearnings
> That will not fade or cease.
> We fear no earthly power
> For we are claimed as friends
> By that all-gracious ruler
> Whose kingdom never ends.   THOMAS H. TROEGER

Notes

1. Paul Johnson, *Modern Times: The World from the Twenties to the Eighties* (New York: Harper & Row, 1983), 130-31.

2. D. H. Smith, *Martin Luther King, Jr.: Rhetorician of Revolt* (Ann Arbor: University Microfilms, 1969), 245.

3. Roger Lundin, Anthony C. Thiselton, Clarence Walhout, *The Responsibility of Hermeneutics* (Grand Rapids: Wm. B. Eerdmans Publishing Co., 1985), 59.

4. Peter G. Horsfield, *Religious Television: The American Experience* (New York: Longman, 1984), 47-48. The quotation that is cited is from William F. Fore, "Mass Media's Mythic World: At Odds with Christian Values," *Christian Century,* January 19, 1977, 34-35.

5. Neil Postman, *Amusing Ourselves to Death: Public Discourse in the Age of Show Business* (New York: Viking/Penguin, 1985), 107.

6. Sam Keen, *Faces of the Enemy: Reflections of the Hostile Imagination, the Psychology of Enmity* (New York: Harper & Row, 1986), 10.

7. Postman, *Amusing Ourselves,* 79.

8. Sallie McFague, *Metaphorical Theology: Models of God in Religious Language* (Philadelphia: Fortress Press, 1982), 55-56. The quotation cited by McFague is from Kenneth Burke, *A Grammar of Motives* (Berkeley: University of California Press, 1969), 503.

9. Horsfield, *Religious Television,* 42.

10. Ibid., 45.

11. Allene Stuart Phy, "Retelling the Greatest Story Ever Told: Jesus in Popular Fiction," *The Bible and Popular Culture in America,* ed. Allene Stuart Phy (Philadelphia: Fortress Press, 1985), 76.

12. Ljubica D. Popovich, "Popular American Biblical Imagery: Sources and Manifestations," in Phy, *The Bible and Popular Culture,* 209.

13. Erik Routley, *Christian Hymns Observed: When in Our Music God Is Glorified* (Princeton: Prestige Publications, 1982), 3.

14. Wayne A. Meeks, *The First Urban Christians: The Social World of the Apostle Paul* (New Haven: Yale University Press, 1983), 192.

15. Lesslie Newbigin, *The Other Side of 1984: Questions for the Churches* (Geneva: World Council of Churches, 1983), 55.

16. Ibid., 16.

17. Czeslaw Milosz, *The Witness of Poetry* (Cambridge, Mass.: Harvard University Press, 1983), 14.

18. Geofffrey Wainwright, "Theological Table-talk: Liturgy and Poetry," *Theology Today,* 41, 1975, 453.

19. Robert N. Bellah et al., *Habits of the Heart: Individualism and Commitment in American Life* (Berkeley: University of California Press, 1985), 81.

20. Milosz, *The Witness of Poetry,* 26. Milosz draws heavily here on the writing of his uncle, Oscar Milosz.

21. Helen Vendler, *The Harvard Book of Contemporary American Poetry* (Cambridge, Mass.: Harvard University Press, 1985), 10-11.

22. Carol Doran and Thomas H. Troeger, *New Hymns for the Lectionary: To Glorify the Maker's Name* (New York: Oxford University Press, 1986), 55.

23. Wilbur Marshall Urban as quoted by Nathan A. Scott, Jr., *The Poetics of Belief* (Chapel Hill: University of North Carolina Press, 1985), 47.

24. Peggy Rosenthal, *Words and Values: Some Leading Words and Where They Lead Us* (New York: Oxford University Press, 1984), 53.

25. Ibid., 255-56.

26. Ibid., 257.

27. Ibid., 258.

28. T. S. Eliot, "An Essay on Rudyard Kipling," in *A Choice of Kipling's Verse* (New York: Charles Scribner's Sons, 1943), 26.

29. Helen Vendler in a review of William H. Prichard, *Frost: A Literary Life Reconsidered, The New York Times Book Review,* 14, October 1984, 41.

30. William Lynch, *Images of Hope,* as quoted in Kathleen R. Fischer, *The Inner Rainbow: Imagination in Christian Life* (Ramsey, N.J.: Paulist Press, 1983), 156.

31. Raymond E. Brown, quoting the Muratorian Fragment in *The Gospel According to John (i-xii),* vol. 29, Anchor Bible Series (New York: Doubleday, 1966), xcix.

32. I am indebted to my colleague Professor Charles Nielsen for this example.

33. Fischer, *The Inner Rainbow,* 156-57.

34. Frank Burch Brown, *Transfiguration: Poetic Metaphor and the Languages of Religious Belief* (Chapel Hill: University of North Carolina Press, 1983), 15. I am indebted to Burch Brown's discussion and development of Wheelwright's theory throughout this section.

35. For a thorough treatment of the possible connections between theology and brain research see James B. Ashbrook, *The Human Mind and the Mind of God* (Lanham, Md.: University Press of America, 1984).

36. Brown, *Transfiguration,* 175.

37. Don M. Wardlaw, *Preaching Biblically: Creating Sermons in the Shape of Scripture* (Philadelphia: Westminster Press, 1983), 12.

38. David Grayson, *Adventures in Contentment* (New York: Grosset & Dunlap, 1907), 125.

39. Petru Dumitriu, *To the Unknown God,* trans. James Kirkup (New York: Seabury Press, 1982), 113.

40. Augustine, *On Christian Doctrine,* trans. and ed. D. W. Robertson, Jr. (New York: Liberal Arts Press, 1958), 118-19.

41. D. E. Nineham, *Saint Mark* (Harmondsworth, England: Penguin Books, 1981), 447, quoting R. H. Lightfoot, *The Gospel Message of St. Mark* (Oxford: Oxford University Press, 1952), 92.

42. Lawrance Thompson and R. H. Winnick, *Robert Frost* (New York: Holt, Rinehart & Winston, 1981), 172.

Afterword:
Selected Lines
on an Extended Canvas

Arthur Van Seters. As noted in the introduction, this final chapter moves in two directions. It is an Afterword that interweaves material from the previous chapters—an analysis on analysis. It has been organized around five broad themes: theology, context, interpretation, language, and so-called "prophetic preaching." In drawing from the contributors of these chapters, I have indicated what comes from whom. Generally I have summarized, but even where I have used excerpts, I have usually omitted quotation marks.

But I also use the term Afterword in a future sense. It is what comes next, what is still to be explored. Using this meaning, I have taken each of the five themes and pushed them further, introducing additional sources. For this reason the narrative endnotes have been more fully developed than is usual. Preaching draws on so many resources and utilizes so many disciplines that even such an array should, on reflection, not be surprising. In extending the discussion in this way I am also indicating the open-endedness of our study. Our canvas has become a scroll that keeps on being unrolled.

1. Theology—Shaping Perception and Reality

"It is only a real spiritual revolution that can save us." Those are the words of an economist who works with the

World Bank. They were uttered after a review of the growing economic gap between rich and poor nations and of the escalation of military defensiveness in the world.[1] The priority of "the spiritual," and of theology, is a paramount thrust in the analysis and description of preaching in the preceding chapters. It is also pervasively evident in the accompanying sermons.

God's *free* presence is not just the footnote but the theological key in the temple-dedication account of I Kings 8. In this free presence the world is viewed differently. God is not cifference for those who live in the world (Allen). This is the theological starting point of preaching's content, but it also shapes the structure of the sermon.

There are times when the evening newspaper unloads such an unrelenting litany of tragedy, escalating tension, and leadership failure that I feel despair. Others, I know, feel it too. Preachers, at such moments, cannot withdraw into some private realm or focus primarily on the hereafter. Eschatology as the consummation of God's rule gives us an alternative vision of that rule and sends us back to the empowerment of the Spirit of Pentecost[2] (Wardlaw). As Constance Fitzgerald has put it, "Contemplation, and ultimately liberation, demand the handing over of one's powerlessness and 'outsider-ness' to the inspiration and power of God's Spirit."[3]

Another theological theme concerns the Bible and its interpretation in preaching. The authority of the sermon rests with Scripture (the Gonzálezes) and this primacy of the Word of God is an explosive power (Wardlaw). But the normativeness of Scripture should still take seriously the reality of a spectrum of other views among listeners, ranging from the Bible as an imprimatur on the preached word to the biblical text as having little inherent authority (Allen). This spectrum may reflect a misunderstanding of the formation of the Bible as both an act of faith (and therefore normative) and an act of vested interests (and therefore humanly conditioned).[4] But this double character of the formation of the text, as well as its interpretation and reception, is a dialectic in which the act of faith persists and evidences from start to finish the guidance of God's Spirit of truth (Brueggemann).

The community that receives this Word of God is a human community, but it is also a community where God is at work and this leads to its understanding of inclusiveness. This is a strange perspective, from a human point of view, because God can say to the Jews that the enemy Ninevites are included—not because they have cultural or military superiority, but because of the massive presence of children and cattle. This is a sacramental community that sees its human connectedness through its sacramental connectedness (the Gonzálezes).

Those who lead such a community are those who have stood on holy ground, for whom the spiritual is the integrating, synthesizing element of life. They have been called to preach and have experienced "burning, burning, burning, burning" because God has "plucked" them to be passion-filled messengers (Hunter).

The foregoing theological positions affect or ought to affect our world view. A commitment to God, to the Word of God and to the calling of God can enable us to see with the eyes of faith. The radicalness of this approach to perception is sharpened by Rosemary Haughton's skepticism about our acceptance of a biblical view of what the world ought to be:

> A church of friends, a world of compassion without domination or privilege, winners or losers—we dismiss that as impossible because our imaginations, conditioned by un-examined political and economic assumptions, cannot grasp it as a practical possibility.[5]

There is a clash between our perception of reality shaped by our theology and that shaped by our culture and traditions. A couple of chapters have called attention to ways in which our world views (our "landscapes of the heart") are influenced by our socialization, especially through the medium of television (Allen and Troeger). It is not only our perception of the world that is influenced by television, but also our way of perceiving. As Colin Morris points out, television blurs the distinction between messages that are true and those that are false. What is important is the credible and the fascinating. The "visual statements" of advertisers dispense conventional wisdom with a power to evoke a positive response. Programming is so shaped that the communication of serious ideas becomes unlikely and the linkage between knowing and acting is severed. "Information bits" are presented with such rapidity and oversimplification that the viewer can only, it seems, suspend judgment or "believe tentatively and with elasticity."[6] The result is also apathy, the inability to feel passion that would enable action toward others in need.[7]

This media force, along with other cultural and social influences, shapes the disposition as well as the substance of theology associated with our view of the world. This affects what is believed as well as attitudes toward believing. In chapter two "Faith Church" struggles to discover the world views of its members by making use of categories (comic, romantic, tragic, and ironic) laid out by Carroll and Hopewell.[8] Members are asked how they believe God is at work in life, and the responses enable the pastor to communicate the gospel more specifically to the congregation (Wardlaw). In a somewhat broader way, Troeger explores the "rim of normative consciousness" and, following Newbigin, calls for the creation of a whole new framework within which to understand the gospel. We cannot work within the present general outlook to offer solutions to problems in life. Theology must furnish an alternative view of reality.

Throughout the previous pages (and preceding chapters) we have been speaking about the priority of theology and its critical role. But this, it seems to me, is not enough. What particular theology we hold makes a significant difference to how we view the world. Or we could say that how we view the world influences the theology we hold. A primary motivation in developing the substance and approach of this book came out of a desire to point to the relationship between declared theology and de facto theology. To what extent is the theology that is implicit in our behavior and attitudes toward society different from the theology we articulate?

An appropriate example is our theology of the church's mission and religious identity. Francis Schüssler Fiorenza identifies six interpretations. (1) On the dichotomous model, transcendence and immanence, religion and politics are totally separated. The natural and the supernatural are distinct orders; and the first belongs to the state, the second to the church. (2) A substitutive view holds that the church enters the realm of service in society only when the latter's institutions are inadequate to meet imperative needs. (3) A third position holds that social mission is voluntary, unofficial. Officially the church is not directly involved but it can inspire and motivate Christians to organize in the service of the world. (4) Partial mission is a fourth view. Here social mission is only one legitimate function of the church. To some it may be more central, to others less so. (5) On an overtly political model, the proclamation of the Rule of God has implications that function as a negative criticism of society. (6) Finally, in a liberation perspective, salvation history and world history are so linked that theology critiques the present but also strives to anticipate eschatological reality within history.[9]

Preaching is one aspect of the church and its mission. In the present volume the various contributors have demonstrated that preaching in all of its aspects is social. From beginning to end it is theologically motivated. But what sort of theology has which social effects is beyond the scope of this book's design. Such correlations are certainly important and will require careful historical analysis and interdisciplinary study. In an ambitious project of precisely this nature, William Everett and T. J. Bachmeyer work out an elaborate paradigm in which they interrelate three theological approaches— cultic (Catholic), prophetic (Protestant), and ecstatic (Anabaptist)—with three sociological traditions—functionalism (unitary view of society), dualism (conflictual), and pluralism (balance of powers)—with three psychological viewpoints— conflictual, fulfillment, and equilibrium.[10] This highly provocative study is criticized by Gregory Baum as overly schematic and as favoring a liberal reformist (vs. prophetic) position.[11] While there are strong connections between our

views of theology, personality, and society, similar commitments to social compassion may arise from different
theological perspectives and we ought not to prejudge
people's social commitment when we are only exposed to
their theology or their views of personality.[12]

2. Context—Church and World

The context of preaching is a community with a memory
and a present reality (Brueggemann). To state it this way is to
view context in terms of time: the influence of the past on the
present and of contemporary society on our way of hearing
and interpreting. Preaching is "the interface of two social
worlds," the world of the Bible and our world. The horizons
of perception in these two worlds are joined in the act of
preaching. This assumes that attention has been paid by the
present Christian community both to its own social reality
and to the social, and not just to a narrow perception of the
historical nature of the biblical communities (Wardlaw). With
David Tracy, proclamation is more than a distillate of
social/historical study; it is a dynamic word of address calling
for faith because there has been a "disclosure of a reality we
cannot but name truth."[13] The intensity of this encounter is
comparable to the abandonment with which people fully
enter into a game.[14]

Another way of viewing the context in temporal terms is to
see the congregation as sacramentally connected in the
communion of saints in all ages. Cutting across the borders of
time, Christians are linked with both the past and an
eschatological future. At the same time this sacramental
connection is geographically global; it is spatial. The
congregation is open to the world, and preaching should
address as well the community of faith throughout the world.
This inevitably includes aspects such as gender, race, and
status (the Gonzálezes).

Looking at "Faith Church" in the context of the city of
Metro City, the structural aspect of this spatial dimension is
stressed. The people listen to preaching both out of and
toward their engagement in community organizations.
Those organizations also touch matters that are national and

international. This structural dimension is far harder to deal with in preaching. Often it is complex, diffuse, in flux, and even controversial. This is why the preaching moment is "a confluence of people, times and contexts" and therefore requires the engagement of the congregation not only as careful, critical listeners, but as participants in preparation and follow-up (Wardlaw). Increasingly our globe is a web of interconnections. We not only know what is happening on the other side of the earth, but in a myriad of ways our decisions and actions affect other countries, and their actions affect ours. Therefore, the Word of God, in a world of gross inequalities, cannot avoid addressing these linkages. In the words of Walter Johnson, written twenty years ago, "To refuse to pursue the question of the radical change effected in our situation by the hearing of this word is to be ethically irresponsible."[15]

The preceding chapters clearly urge that preaching be open to the world. This surely includes seeing it with Third- (and Fourth-) World eyes. For example, Justo González's collection of sermons, *Proclaiming the Acceptable Year*,[16] are the words of those who see with eyes of Asia, Africa, Latin America, and minority groups in North America. In one of these, the words of Jesus to people in an authoritarian society, to "make up your minds not to prepare your defence beforehand" (Luke 21:14, NEB), make eminent sense. As C. S. Song explains regarding Taiwan, "Christians brought to trial because of their allegiance to Jesus have changed a military court into a court of testimony!"[17] This contextualization can help us reflect on the judicial system in North America, for it allows us to penetrate the politicization of the rule of law when judgments are handed down that favor order over justice.[18] This is but one example of how the marginalized of the world have much to teach the Western world about social compassion.[19]

Although Canada, like the United States, is a part of the First World and has much to learn from the Third World, there are substantial differences between the two countries. As a Canadian editing a book written by United States citizens for a U. S. publisher, I am conscious that readers on my side of the border have to read with Canadian eyes in order to make an appropriate translation of this work for their own context. Canada, from its British roots, has a stronger non-conformist church tradition and in its treatment of immigrants from other countries has tended more toward a cultural mosaic than an assimilating melting pot. Further, the use of the term "American" as a synonym for the United States in some of the preceding chapters feels presumptuous to me in my Canadian setting and therefore even more so for people who belong to the other Americas. Attitudes toward the state, cultural assumptions, and self-designations all bear on how we do theology and should raise sensitivity in the area of preaching.

Two points have been made in the preceding paragraphs that can now be related to specific sociological studies of preaching. Contexts are interconnected and, when viewed together, they manifest considerable diversity. As part of an exhaustive study (examining forty thousand speeches) of religious pronouncements relating to cultural change in Finland, Tapio Lampinen discusses open and closed communications systems. An open system is adaptable to its environment; it grows under external pressure and adjusts to rapid, external change. A closed system fits better with a stable environment, is slow to adapt, and strives to change in its context. It becomes more differentiated from its environment in times of change and emphasizes its own traditions and distinctive language. This means that in a primarily closed system, the sermon content is determined by church tradition and, to a lesser degree, by the personal life of the preacher. In an open system there is substantial input from the environment and dialogue between the church and a changing society. As a result of this feedback, church doctrine is revised.[20]

One is reminded of Weber's church/sect typology in which the "church type" is more open, pluralistic, and inclusive whereas the "sect type" is a closed, exclusive community with more rigid doctrinal requirements.[21] Of course, these distinctions need to be put on a continuum since "pure" types do not exist as such. Nevertheless, preaching does tend to move toward transformation *or* equilibrium (Brueggemann) even though theologically these two tendencies are dialectically related in the judgment and grace dimensions of the gospel.

In an earlier study of preaching in the Federal Republic of Germany, Osmund Schreuder examines listeners in terms of a six-point continuum from heteronomous, group-oriented, duty-bound people, to those who are more autonomous and cosmopolitan. He finds that the vast majority of members are in between these extremes and that their appreciation of sermons is strongly determined by their subjective, religious, and church attitudes and by their feelings of solidarity with the preacher. He also finds that "listeners are more attentive and remember more, if the sermon is more closely linked to the world as they know it," and if it is not transcendent. But overall, few listeners remember very much of the sermon (though this does not affect their appreciation of it!) and there is "a fairly undifferentiated reaction." The latter causes him to conclude that there is a "crisis" in preaching; it is the crisis of a mass of listeners "whose feelings of solidarity are characterized by unarticulated totality." This, he adds, "prevents the Churches from functioning in a differentiated way for their members." This is " 'blind' solidarity, which is insensitive to differentiation."[22] Over against a superficial "unity" stands a catholicity of the church that enriches its life with a variety of perspectives and keeps it open to the diversity of human beings in our world (the Gonzálezes). The preacher will want this to be reflected in the way people are included and pictured in the sermon (Allen).

3. Interpretation—Subjective and Corporate

Schreuder's contention, that a close association between preacher and people exists in preaching, points toward the subjective and corporate dimensions of interpretation. The distinctive background, upbringing, and experiences (spiritual and social) of preachers shape the kind of preaching they offer. This socialization may be deeply rooted in the community of faith which is subsequently involved in validating the call to preach (Hunter). Some may also be formed in major ways outside the church. Karl Gaspar's experience of political repression is but one obvious example. The socialization models are often varied. Shils singles out three institutions that are, in his view, the primary transmitters of tradition: family, school, and church.[23] Role models are drawn primarily from these, but there are also others, for example, public figures and media personalities. When it comes to preaching models, they have been predominantly male figures whose interpretive approaches have tended, until recently, to be more limited and subjective than we have cared to admit.[24]

It is not too much to speak of interpretation as "an act of vested interest" (Brueggemann). This does not mean that we should not try to listen with openness to the text and its interpretive tradition nor that the congregation should listen to preaching with only their own interests in view. It is simply the acknowledgment that neutrality and objectivity are elusive and that admitting our biases can help us interpret more responsibly. As interpreters we are both socially and theologically subjective (Allen). Sociology is one of those disciplines that can assist us to see "through" and "beyond" our primary socialization and to become more aware of our vested interests.[25]

In the biographies of J. Alfred Smith and David Bartlett, we find both spiritual formation and the development of social consciousness (Hunter), which may be termed conversion and consciousness-raising experiences. Some people might distinguish between them more sharply than others, but both processes involve a major movement affecting our subjective limitations and, therefore, they deeply influence our interpretation of Scripture and tradition. They are, of course, highly subjective experiences. They involve adopting a new system of meaning that reorders the various elements that make up our own biographies. We feel a satisfying newness rooted in a sense of order and purpose. Our meaning-system has changed and our perspectives have refocused. In some cases these have narrowed and in others expanded. With them we also change our social relationships, drawing closer to the interpreting community or becoming part of a new one.[26]

In view of the subjective nature of interpretation, attention ought to be given to a shift from a linear model of communication to a dynamic and corporate one. The linear model is simple, fixed, two dimensional and moves a message from preacher (sender) to congregation (receiver). This is a reified understanding of both the message and the congregation; an object placed into containers, so to speak. Yet this linear model thus stated helps us see that, in general, preachers have been socialized to be loners and congregations to be passive recipients. But what is really needed is "a dynamic, multidimensional model" that sees the preached Word as a living event and the preacher and congregation *both* as participants. The biblical tradition is then an active partner and the congregation becomes a community alive to the world in which that tradition will be heard afresh (Wardlaw). The text is not "a contextless absolute," but a bold, responsive, assertive, imaginative act that stands as a proposal of reality to the community (Brueggemann). The exposition of a text is mediated through world views of preacher and people, and the preacher needs to be aware of the congregation's view both of the world and of the Bible (Allen). But the more that preacher and people handle the text together, the more they are influenced by it and influence one another (Wardlaw and Brueggemann). People who have tried this model of "Faith Church" have found it effective. At the very least the preacher can follow a long interpretive tradition of some form of communal study and present the sermon as a "common act of imagining with" so that a wider web of meanings and insights is available to the preacher's imagination (Troeger).[27]

Implied in the above is the element of involvement. A linear deductive approach to life (and hence to preaching) can become "an infinite regress, always receding into finer and finer analysis." This could postpone "the action that might reveal life anew to us." Rather than think our way into a new kind of living, we need to live our way into a new kind of thinking.[28] Preaching, in a dynamic model, arises from our choices of how we live and act. It is rooted in where we take our stands.

4. Language—Creative and Critical

"Language," says Claude Levi-Strauss, "is a social phenomenon" and it "lives and develops only as a collective construct."[29] Because language is a primary medium of communication, its very structure is affected by social organization and culture. In oral culture, for example, language is sound; it is what is heard. Through it people are generationally (temporally) connected in the retelling of stories, myths, and traditions. Language is communal, it functions within the cultural group. With the introduction of script, later intensified by print, the visual (space) aspect of language becomes more important than the sound (time) aspect. So in Hebraic culture, understanding is primarily a kind of hearing while in Greek culture it is primarily a matter of seeing. Language as speech is dynamic, fleeting, irreversible, but print breaks the strictures of time and leads to permanence. With the introduction of audio and audiovisual communication, sound can be played back and print can be sent across vast distances almost instantaneously.[30]

Against this backdrop we can expect to be influenced by reigning metaphors (Troeger), to be shaped by language in the way we think and act (Allen). Even at the most basic level of everyday speech, as George Lakoff and Mark Johnson point out, we are subliminally conditioned by our culture. So it is more normal to say "up and down" than "down and up" or "good and bad" than "bad and good."[31] On a grand scale, whole cultures have lived by "root metaphors," to use Gibson Winter's language. In the premodern world the dominant metaphor was organicistic. With the development of the modern world the organicistic metaphor was replaced by the mechanistic. Since this too has run its course, Winter seeks a new metaphor in the artistic process[32] (Allen). This suggests that language is not only influenced by culture but also has the potential to be an influence on culture. Sexist or racist language reflects social reality, but inclusive language can create an awareness of these realities and can provide us with a social world in which they are no longer dominant (Allen).

To proclaim the gospel of the Rule of God in our age calls for an interweaving of "depth" and "steno" languages. Scripture itself is both metaphorical and discursive. As human beings we have two sides to our brains that respond respectively to the denotative (left side) and the evocative (right side) (Troeger). We need the creative, poetic, and

narrative in our preaching and also the analytical, explana-
tory, and hortatory. One expands our imaginations, the
other penetrates our closed categories; together they enable
us to become more holistic.

Rationality in preaching is not enough to counter reigning
metaphors. What is needed are the images and narratives of
faith, and the awareness that the use of metaphors can be a
political act (Troeger drawing from Sallie McFague). While
this is true, Winter reminds us that radical change does not
come about just by altering metaphoric interpretation. Acts
of oppression are caused by political and economic institutions. Symbol systems expose the structures of oppression[33]
and therefore serve the political process, but the institutions
themselves also need to be changed.

Although in the history of preaching since the second
century the church has favored a discursive rather than a
poetic approach (Troeger), there has been a long tradition of
metaphor and analogy in theology. These are two kinds of
tensive language reflecting different theological streams and
functioning with different emphases. Protestants have
tended to use metaphor because it connects dissimilar ideas
and realities and therefore suits a Protestant preference for
seeing the world in terms of contrast and dialectic. This
negative dialectic destroys illusions and pretensions in
society. Theologically, a metaphorical approach contrasts
God's transcendence with human finitude and sinfulness.
Analogical thinking and language emphasize similarities and
have been more characteristic of Catholic theology. God is
seen in terms of harmony with creation. According to Tracy,
the analogical needs the negative dialectic of the metaphorical. McFague argues that images (whether symbolic/analogi-
cal or parabolic/metaphorical) need interpretation through
concepts and theories, but interpretation never exhausts the
meaning of images.[34]

So far, except for the brief discussion of the difference
between oral and written cultures, we have concentrated on
language as such. A comment needs to be added about
speech as distinct from text. This is crucial for preaching
though it also has implications for liturgy.[35] Sound produces
a closing of meaning. Text has polysemy; it is open to

multiple meanings that increase the farther their distance is
from the author. As soon as words are audibly pronounced,
some interpretation happens, some color is added that both
reflects the new context in which the text is exposed and the
particular meaning decided on by the speaker. This is a
further creative and critical act and preachers sound like
"print" when they are reluctant to risk this particularity.
When *they* speak, the sound forms in the listener a mental
image of structure like lines of printed text. When, however,
the text is internalized and its meaning and descriptions
understood and sensed (by the various senses), there is
closure. This is but the most recent stage in the tradition of
opening and closing the meaning of the original utterance.
Meaning, then, cannot be fixed absolutely; it is always
contextual.[36]

In connection with our earlier discussion of steno and
depth language and the present distinction between open
and closed communication, two tendencies need to be
avoided in preaching. One is a false kind of objectivity that
views the world, language, and interpretation as fixed
(Brueggemann). Religious orthodoxy, concerned about
certitude, may deny the dynamic nature of metaphor. This
objectivist position seeks a consistent view of the world, clear
expectations, and no conflicts, but this is not what reality is
like.[37] The other tendency is a subjectivity that assumes we
can conjure up private meanings without public accountability (Brueggemann). This denies (perhaps not intentionally)
the structural nature of language, the importance of context,
and the possibility of adequate representation of meaning
through language.[38] The Bible itself, says McFague, "is a
metaphor of the word or ways of God." As such, she adds, it
"is a crucial issue for a metaphorical theology" against
conservatives "who absolutize Scripture, refusing to admit its
metaphorical quality," and against "liberation theologies,
especially radical feminist theologies" which "relativize
Scripture to the point of undercutting the relevance of its
basic images."[39]

Earlier, in the section on context, I drew attention to
Schreuder's observation about German congregations ap-
preciating the sermon out of their sense of solidarity with the

preacher. Lampinen calls this the "phatic function" of language. By this he means "a reinforcement of the feeling of togetherness."[40] When familiar and expected words or expressions are repeated in certain settings, form and substance recede in importance. The main function of this form of communication is neither one of conveying information nor of creating feelings, but of establishing social cohesion. What is remembered is not what was said or how it was expressed, but the sense of being together.[41] This may be acceptable in certain social settings (a cocktail party, a casual greeting on the street), but it is certainly inadequate in preaching. Yet, for some, such banality is all they expect in a sermon, with the result that such preaching becomes a totally inward experience unconcerned with the issues of life outside the four walls of the sanctuary. The gospel, on the contrary, calls for language that is both critical in its exposures and creative in its vitalizing commitment.

5. Reexamining "Prophetic" Preaching

"Every church is in permanent danger of the rise of *prophets*."[42] As a general statement about religion, there would be many who would disagree. But prophets are generally regarded as a danger to the church to the extent that this designation, in the case of a preacher, conjures up a radical, condemning voice standing over and above the congregation thundering against the evils of society. W. W. Finlator points to the naïveté in this view when he asks rhetorically, "Did my seminary realize that its 'prophets' would not last six months if they tried to teach the true words of prophecy to their congregations?"[43] A number of studies show that the "prophetic" preachers of the sixties were often in deep difficulty with their congregations. All too frequently they became lone and lonely activists.[44] There is, to be sure, a need for public critics and iconoclastic individuals in both society and church. But in the pulpit? Not as a rule, and that for several reasons.

First, the prophet (as iconoclast) is incongruous in what Weber (and, with modifications, Troeltsch after him)[45] called the "church" type of faith community. Because this type is

open to society as a whole, it is best led by a "priest" who cares
for the needs and encourages the growth of an ongoing
community. In Weber's typology, a prophet is an agent of
radical social change, a charismatic figure claiming a
personal, divine call to act and sometimes attracting
followers. If, in the latter case, these followers begin to
become a more traditional congregation, then there is a
"routinization" and the prophet becomes more like a priest or
gives way to a priest.[46] To the extent that Weber's paradigm
clarifies the experience of mainline churches, it points to an
incongruity that should not be lightly dismissed.

Second, there is a particular time and situation when
prophets are needed. Otto Maduro, writing in the context of
Venezuela,[47] lists a number of factors. Prophets emerge, he
claims, when other avenues of reform are blocked and other
movements for change are in formation. In addition, the laity
who have been subordinated by the state must make religious
demands on the church regarding their human situation.
Finally, the church itself has to be the seat of new theological
developments favorable to the demands of the people.

At this point a prophetic movement requires a charismatic
leader, an innovator who can mobilize a following. By
introducing innovations this charismatic leader or prophet
tends to subvert the established religious order and is
rejected. But by excluding the prophet, the church already
begins to shift because it can only partially disqualify the
innovation. The church must also partially incorporate the
innovation in order to control the spread of the movement
and reclaim its followers by meeting some of their demands.
True and effective prophetic movements are those that are
faithful to the roots of the ecclesiastical tradition as a new but
recognizable interpretation of the church's foundational
message.

The "lone ranger" in the pulpit who will set the
congregation and the world straight is a muddled caricature
of the prophet. No wonder David Bartlett says, "I don't see
myself as prophetic." But with candor he admits to *feeling* like
a prophet, "Only on the days I feel despised and rejected"
(Hunter). Prophets are not self-made; nor are they called just
when *they* think they are called. Prophets arise at certain

historical, social moments and are invariably part of movements.[48]

A third reason why we should be careful to avoid speaking of preachers as prophets is that the more far-reaching and creative need in both the church and society in North America is for prophetic *churches*. Western society, says Lesslie Newbigin, is waiting for the church to present it with a new vision of reality. Our decaying culture and our broken world need radical renewal. This renewal requires a commitment to fundamental values within a framework of belief—in this case Christian faith—that is in dialogue with other frameworks.[49] From a similar perspective, Robin Gill sees the primary function of the church in society as that of generating "key values which alter the fundamental moral, social, and political vision."[50]

This emphasis on frameworks and values moves away from activism as the sole focus of prophetic ministry. It recognizes the complexity of society as a fabric made from many interwoven threads—economic and political, social and cultural, philosophical and spiritual. In their connectedness, the spiritual can have "social effects." Gill stresses this in his understanding of the church's prophetic ministry. He finds more problematic the working out of concrete and public "social implications." Prophetic ministry, he says, should articulate *general* values for society as a whole, but *specific* moral, social, and political implications are for individual church members only.[51] This is a kind of "trickle-down theory" of social transformation that seems both too theoretical and too politically naïve.

The need for prophetic churches arises not only because of the structural connectedness of the church to society implied in the fabric image, but also because little will happen to transform society if attention is not given to specific issues, problems, and examples. These can be talked about best when, as in the case of the "Faith Church" community, the process of preaching is a corporate act and its prophetic dimension is in the life of the church (Wardlaw). Awareness and gospel insight come with concreteness and seldom without it. We have to see the church as a sacramental community, but this seeing is much more profound when we elaborate it in terms of social status, inclusiveness, attitudes toward change and false spiritualities (the Gonzálezes). The Canadian and U. S. Catholic Bishops' Pastorals on the economy were corporate productions. They would not have become prophetic if they had stayed with general values. It is because they were specific that people in and outside of the Catholic Church saw what their values really were and how they stood over against the dominant economic thinking in North America.[52] But it is precisely this specificity that calls for the corporate engagement of people in a prophetic movement rather than one person speaking alone.

"Prophetic," as I am now using the term, is not to be understood in the negative sense with which I began this section. Nor is it a predicting of the future. Rather, prophetic is connected with God's creating and redeeming work. It is an affirmation of life in faithfulness to God's purposes and therefore against the forces of death and destruction. It affirms life concretely on the level both of persons and of the wider world, but is also ready and daring in naming the powers that dehumanize and mar God's creation. In the light of this, how can the church be nurtured through preaching to become a prophetic community[53] rather than a "sacred canopy?"[54] A number of factors have already been stated explicitly or by implication in the preceding chapters.

1. The preacher is the pastor who is not primarily bringing God to the people but helping the people discover the presence of God (Wardlaw). The distinction between pastoral and prophetic is inaccurate (Troeger). Preaching is "struggling with" not "over against" because grace is transforming and guilt is debilitating. Bonnie Benda's examination of "social justice preachers" who are effective in their congregations confirms Hunter's description and analysis of J. Alfred Smith and David Bartlett. According to Benda's research, their charisma is not everything. They know Scripture and they know the facts in relation to the issues on which they speak. They are credible and trust-worthy. Their integrity, openness, fairness to the position of others, confession of limitations, and personal warmth are transparent. Finally, they start *with* the congregation, *not against* it.[55]

2. A prophetic community is nurtured when the interpretation of Scripture is seen as both transformative and nurturing (Brueggemann), when its sagas renew identity, its parables explode prevailing views, and its apocalyptic passages offer hope amid crisis (Allen). Through the faithful interpretation of Scripture, according to David Bartlett, the congregation is inevitably led to get "involved in social and political concerns" (Hunter). For those in a lectionary-based tradition, the collection of essays in *Social Themes of the Christian Year* demonstrates a way of thinking theologically about the liturgical seasons in order to discern their prophetic dimensions.[56] But Justo and Catherine González express a caution "that lectionaries are a selection which reflects the prevailing tradition of the church, and that therefore they must be seen with the necessary 'ideological suspicion,' and corrected accordingly."[57]

3. The language of the sermon can awaken new vision and deepen fresh insight. The language of myth and metaphor draws us into community so that preaching is "imagining with" (Troeger). Exhortation and poetry, imperative and indicative moods combine to ground the demands of the gospel in the narrative of grace (Allen). Imagination in all its vividness, newness, and concreteness, *and* analysis that is clear, specific, and well-researched are both needed. Jürgen Moltmann's unassuming title, "The Disarming Child" (for his sermon on Isa. 9:2-7), is full of insight. There, in a simple metaphor, a profound connection is made between the birth of a child and the answer to war.[58] In a different way Ron Sider's *Rich Christians in an Age of Hunger*[59] bombards the reader with statistics and factual comparisons to arouse a deep awareness of wealth and poverty. Although each of these approaches is effective in its own way, yet "images without concepts are blind; concepts without images are sterile."[60]

4. The sermon that fosters prophetic living in the church is one that connects preaching, liturgy—especially the celebration of sacraments—and the corporate life of the church. This is what Stanley Hauerwas and William Willimon describe in a recent account of an inner-city church. It was a church that did not think of itself as socially radical. But it did

act prophetically as it gradually demonstrated its determination to stay in its "declining" neighborhood and extend its eucharistic celebration to a weekly lunch for the people of the community. One element in this process was the theological interpretation by the preacher of these common activities that were constituting the congregation's new life.[61]

5. Finally, a prophetic expectation is created when the sermon is viewed dynamically as an event of proclamation (Brueggemann and Wardlaw). Then it is more than human words, passionate communication, and open, dialogical listening. It is an activity of the Spirit, enlivening, enabling, and encouraging.

The prophetic church that gathers to hear the Word of God on Sunday is also a people scattered on Monday and the days thereafter. As scattered people they are still the church, still seeking to be prophetic. Their common life will include open sharing of daily life and work and theological reflection on this sharing so that they can feel supported and can become discerning as Christians in the world. This will help them face the inevitable contradictions and institutionalized disharmonies that mark their ordinary experiences, but they will make their contribution amid the ambiguities and pluralisms that are everywhere evident.[62]

The scattered church is also open to participation through groups and movements struggling to respond concretely and systematically to particular socio-economic realities of injustice. Some of these are interchurch, Christian movements; some are interfaith; and still others are regional or national organizations outside the church. Often such specialized communities can mobilize expertise and engender the commitment and visibility necessary for constructive action.[63]

That action may be social, but within that, in our society it is also political. The care of the poor and the needy, an obligation so central to the church that from earliest times it was associated with the Eucharist, used to be the church's direct responsibility. But when the state, in structured societies, took over much of this responsibility, the church's ministry became more and more political. In our highly complex Western society "social help becomes increasingly a matter of political-social legislation."[64] The church's prophetic role has to be appropriate both to its vision of creation and redemption and to the particular way in which its society is structured.

It may seem that there are so many issues and dimensions to living prophetically that congregations could feel quite overwhelmed and immobilized. But this is more likely if people see themselves as an aggregate rather than a community and if the preacher addresses them individualistically. However, the more they form networks and share their part in the whole, the more prophetic they can become.

A Closing Comment

Some years ago William Stringfellow gave a series of lectures in Montreal. Each lecture was followed by extensive and lively discussion. But not immediately. He always seemed to stop lecturing before he was finished. Each time there was an awkward silence. Suddenly the very incompleteness we sensed sent us back through the lecture and impelled us forward into all kinds of unexplored avenues. But more, this incompleteness reminded us of our humanity and our need to journey on in faith.

This book is unfinished. I was reminded of this as I was preparing to write this Afterword. I had a fascinating conversation with Max Stackhouse of Andover-Newton Seminary who felt that one of our greatest needs in the subject area of this book was for an examination of the history of preaching on certain texts as the "Rich Young Ruler" to see how sermons related to different contexts. I also recall Doris Lessing's words in her 1985 Massey Lectures about the importance of reading history to see the larger recurring patterns of human behavior and to be more modest about our own "discoveries."[65] This is only one of many ways in which the theme of preaching as a social act can be continued. Continue I hope it will, in new directions and from diverse perspectives.[66]

Notes

1. Quoted by Tilden Edwards, Jr., in his introduction to *Living with Apocalypse: Spiritual Resources for Social Compassion,* ed. Tilden H. Edwards (San Francisco: Harper & Row, 1984), 1.

2. Cf. "The magnitude of the problems needing to be addressed in our time should incline us to acknowledge that the Church could scarcely aspire to have significant impact without a fresh empowerment of the Spirit. Biblical understanding assures us that Pentecost was an event that needed to be repeated." James A. Forbes, Jr., "Social Transformation," in *Living with Apocalypse,* 59.

3. Constance Fitzgerald, "Impasse and Dark Night," in *Living with Apocalypse,* 112.

4. Faith and vested interests, as noted below, is a dialectical relationship in which normativeness may also be associated with the latter as in the case, for example, of the vested interests of the poor.

5. Rosemary Haughton, "Liberating the Divine Energy," in *Living with Apocalypse,* 89.

6. Colin Morris, *God-in-a-Box: Christian Strategy in a Television Age* (London: Hodder & Stoughton, 1984), 28-29, 40-46, 49, 147, 165-67. Robert Jewett and John S. Lawrence have made an analysis and theological critique of television's superhero whose redemptive acts destroy stereotyped evil and impart "the relaxed feeling that society can actually be redeemed by anti-democratic means." In addition, reality is thought to be what is presented on the evening news. *The American Monomyth* (Garden City, N.Y.: Anchor Press/Doubleday, 1977), xx, 210-16. But there are also counter-culture series such as "M.A.S.H." and exposés such as "60 Minutes" in the U. S. and "W5" in Canada.

7. For an important theological critique of apathy, see Dorothy Soelle, *Suffering* (Philadelphia: Fortress Press, 1975), 36-49.

8. Actually they were borrowed from Northrop Frye, *The Anatomy of Criticism,* 131-239, as is noted by the authors, *Handbook for Congregational Studies,* ed. Jackson W. Carroll, Carl S. Dudley, and William McKinney (Nashville: Abingdon Press, 1986), 32-33. The treatment of these categories by Carroll and Hopewell lacks theological and social critique as though all four perspectives have equal validity.

9. Francis Schüssler Fiorenza, "The Church's Religious Identity and Its Social and Political Mission," *Theological Studies,* 43, 1982, 197-204. The scheme developed in this article requires, I believe, more stress on the fact that religious and cultural symbols inevitably have a political meaning. For different views of belief in relation to the world see the introduction, note 23.

10. William W. Everett and T. J. Bachmeyer, *Disciplines in Transformation: A Guide to Theology and the Behavioral Sciences* (Washington: University Press of America, 1979). "We have assumed that considerations about Christianity, personality, and society have many points in common. From the Christian side in particular, there exists a drive for linkage with personality and social concerns. . . . At the same time we believe that personality and society matters both relate to one another and have definite associations with religion as well" (111).

11. Gregory Baum, "Ecumenical Theology: A New Approach," *Ecumenist,* 19, 1981, 65-78.

12. A sociologist turned spiritual director, Parker J. Palmer, sums up the point of this section when he says that there are three ways of approaching reality: through data and logic, through emotion and instinct, or through faithful relationships and community. A spiritual approach, he says, is relational, in community with God and through God with the whole created order. "The Spiritual Life: Apocalypse Now," *Living with Apocalypse,* 35. This reference to the created order is a reminder that nature is also an important

concern of preaching. Douglas John Hall speaks of "three dimensions of human being-with," namely, God, neighbor and the "unsilent" creation, all of which, he says, are connected, *Imaging God: Dominion as Stewardship* (Grand Rapids: Wm. B. Eerdmans Publishing Co., 1986), 123-31.

13. David Tracy, *The Analogical Imagination: Christian Theology and the Culture of Pluralism* (New York: Crossroad Publishing Co., 1981), 108, 269-75. "Without a sense of the religious event-character of proclamation, the New Testament itself ceases to be a religious classic open to properly theological interpretation and lives on in memory, if at all, as literature" (275).

14. Tracy, *Analogical Imagination*, 120. The four steps in interpreting a "classic" are: (1) recognition of pre-understanding (the interpreter is always a social, communal subject); (2) a claim calling the interpreter to attention; (3) a back-and-forth dialogue between text and interpreter (the game); and (4) the larger conversation of the entire community of inquirers (118-21). On the intensity of dialogue with the biblical text (and the biblical world) see also William A. Beardslee, *Literary Criticism of the New Testament* (Philadelphia: Fortress Press, 1970), 10.

15. W. Walter Johnson, "The Ethics of Preaching," *Interpretation*, 20, 1966, 429. For a carefully reasoned presentation of the global responsibility of the church, including its task of proclamation, see Vincent Cosmao, *Changing the World: An Agenda for the Churches,* trans. John Drury (Maryknoll, N.Y.: Orbis Books, 1984).

16. Justo L. González, ed., *Proclaiming the Acceptable Year: Sermons from the Perspective of Liberation Theology* (Valley Forge: Judson Press, 1982).

17. Choan-Seng Song, "Truth-Power and Love-Power in a Court of Testimony," *Proclaiming the Acceptable Year,* 34.

18. One thinks, for example, of the trial of church leaders involved in the Sanctuary Movement in recent times.

19. While this is abundantly obvious, it still needs to be restated. See Tilden Edwards, "A Conversation with Henri J. M. Nouwen," *Living with Apocalypse,* 15-22, and Robert McAfee Brown, *Unexpected News: Reading the Bible with Third World Eyes* (Philadelphia: Westminster Press, 1984).

20. Tapio Lampinen, "The Content of the Parochial Sermons in the Evangelical Lutheran Church of Finland as Indicators of the Openness and Closedness of the Church as System," *Social Compass* 27, 1980, especially 422, 426, 428-29.

21. For a discussion of Weber's typology with reference to the church and preaching, see Robin Gill, *Prophecy and Praxis: The Social Function of the Churches* (London: Marshall Morgan & Scott, 1981), 21-30. Edward Shils has been critical of Weber's insufficient attention to the role of tradition in both church and sect types, *Tradition* (Chicago: University of Chicago Press, 1981), 175-79.

22. Osmund Schreuder, "The Silent Majority," *Communication in the Church,* eds. Gregory Baum and Andrew Greeley (New York: Seabury Press, 1978), especially 14-19. Another sociological study, from a symbolic interactionist perspective, examines Roman Catholic preachers in a number of U. S. Catholic parishes. In this view the preacher creates social order through preaching, and, therefore, the understanding of social order in a parish is the preacher's view of this order. Because of this natural inclination in the preaching process, both the preacher and the congregation need to develop a counter-balancing critical view of preaching. Thomas J. Mickey, "Social Order and Preaching," *Social Compass,* 27, 1980, 347-62.

23. Shils, *Tradition*, 168-85.

24. Some years ago in Montreal I heard James Cone speak about his "white" education in a similar vein. This subjectivity in interpretation of Scripture was bluntly stated in Walter Wink's highly polemical monograph, *The Bible in Human Transformation: Toward a New Paradigm for Biblical Study* (Philadelphia: Fortress Press, 1973), 1-15.

25. See Peter L. Berger, *Invitation to Sociology: A Humanistic Perspective* (New York: Doubleday, 1963), 23-38, and C. Wright Mills, *The Sociological Imagination* (New York: Oxford University Press, 1954), 5-8.

26. See Berger, *Invitation to Sociology*, 51-64, and Berger and Thomas Luckmann, *The Social Construction of Reality: A Treatise in the Sociology of Knowledge* (New York: Doubleday, 1967), 156-63.

27. Cf. what Henri Nouwen says about the preacher needing to have a capacity for dialogue and to be personally available, *Creative Ministry* (New York: Doubleday, 1971), 33-39. See also Tracy's description of the dynamic character of both the interpretation and formation of a "classic," *Analogical Imagination*, 115-30.

28. Palmer, "The Spiritual Life," 31. Especially important in this connection is Parker J. Palmer's *The Company of Strangers: Christians and the Renewal of America's Public Life* (New York: Crossroad Publishing Co., 1981).

29. Claude Levi-Strauss, *Structural Anthropology* (New York: Basic Books, 1963), 56-57. Levi-Strauss later explores "the fact that both language and culture are products of activities which are basically similar" (71). On the social nature of language, see also Berger and Luckmann, *The Social Construction of Reality*, 34-46.

30. Morris, *God-in-a-Box*, 181, and Walter Ong, *The Presence of the Word* (New Haven: Yale University Press, 1967), 3, 17-23, 32-35, 50-54, and 87-91. Ong draws attention to the fact that the introduction of typography in many ways helped produce the modern age (8-9) and contributed to the Protestant Reformation's view of Scripture (265-74).

31. George Lakoff and Mark Johnson, *Metaphors We Live By* (Chicago: University of Chicago Press, 1980), 132.

32. Allen is drawing on Gibson Winter, *Liberating Creation: Foundations of Religious Social Ethics* (New York: Crossroad Publishing Co., 1981). Compared with organicistic and mechanistic metaphors, the root metaphor of artistic process is difficult to understand. Root metaphors furnish clues for understanding institutional struggles and the clash of symbols in our world. They are constellations of metaphors called forth by each other. Artistic process is not reducible to metaphor but uses metaphor; art is itself a metaphoric activity. It penetrates hidden things and finds bonds between them. In an age of transforming power in nature and history, art is both transformative (like the mechanistic) and bonding (like the organicistic). In particular it binds humanity and nature when these have been wrenched apart by technology and mechanistic thinking. Artistic process, in effect, integrates organicistic and mechanistic processes in "creative dwelling" (5, 9, 11, 12).

33. Winter, *Liberating Creation*, 5. See also Fitzgerald, "Impasse and Dark Night," 110.

34. David Tracy in Tracy and John B. Cobb, Jr., *Talking About God: Doing Theology in the Context of Modern Pluralism* (New York: Seabury Press, 1983), 17-28 and 29-38, and McFague, *Metaphorical Theology*, 13-18, 26, 60-63. On the "shocking" use of metaphor in the New Testament, see Beardslee, *Literary Criticism*, 11.

35. Naturally this will vary with the kind of liturgical tradition. Those who use pew Bibles and/or prayer books or other written documents distributed to all worshipers may be less attuned to the *sound* of liturgy than those without a written text. This is a conclusion from my own experience and a deduction from the discussion below. Others may have a different experience where the presence of a text enhances an awareness of the particularity of sound.

36. See J. Severino Croatto, "Biblical Hermeneutics in the Theologies of Liberation," *Irruption of the Third World: Challenge to Theology*, eds. Virginia Fabella and Sergio Torres (Maryknoll, N.Y.: Orbis Books, 1983), 140-68. This in no way contradicts Troeger's distinction between steno and depth languages but simply adds a further dimension to both. On the attempt in the eighteenth century to establish written control over the spoken word through the publication of dictionaries and grammars, see Ong, *The Presence of the Word*, 50-79, and more recently, *Orality and Literacy: The Technologizing of the Word* (London: Methuen, 1982).

37. See Lakoff and Johnson, *Metaphors We Live By*, 210-11, 220-21, and also 186-88.

38. Ibid., 223-24, 188-89.

39. McFague, *Metaphorical Theology*, 54.

40. Lampinen, "The Content of Parochial Sermons," 430-31.

41. S. I. Hayakawa, *Language in Thought and Action*, 3rd ed. (New York: Harcourt Brace Jovanovich, 1972), 77-84. Hayakawa calls this presymbolic language and finds it in sermons and political speeches. People, he says, "often come away from church services without any clear memory of the sermon." This makes no sense from the viewpoint of symbolic language, but fits with the social function of presymbolic language which is social cohesion, (84).

42. Otto Maduro, *Religion and Social Conflicts* (Maryknoll, N.Y.: Orbis Books, 1982), 106. Maduro acknowledges that this statement goes back to Max Weber whose whole approach to the sociology of religion indicates that religion is world-shaking.

43. W. W. Finlator, "Preaching in America: An Impossible Task?" *Christian Ministry*, 16/5, September 1985, 25.

44. See Gill, *Prophecy and Praxis*, chapter 4 and especially the bibliography in the endnotes (71-72); and Hart M. Nelson, "Why Do Pastors Preach on Social Issues?" *Theology Today*, 32, 1975, 56-73.

45. Max Weber, *The Protestant Ethic and the Spirit of Capitalism*, trans. Talcott Parsons (New York: Charles Scribner's Sons, 1958), 254-55, n. 175. In the following discussion, the definition of "prophet" may seem too restrictive. Nevertheless I think Weber's typology, as a heuristic device, elucidates the social development of institutions.

46. Gill, *Prophecy and Praxis*, 24-39, and Shils, *Tradition*, 228-31. There is an irony in Weber's church/sect, prophet/priest typology. The prophet is more likely to be associated with a sect that is a closed community, even though prophets were often concerned with social reform. Gill's assertion that social reform was only a means to an end, namely salvation (25), does not eliminate this anomaly. Within the church, some clergy have felt constrained by their denomination. They were, in the official view of the church, ordained to expound the doctrine and maintain the traditions of the church. To claim direct communication from God as the basis for prophetic utterance against these traditions could mean being at least threatened, perhaps silenced, or even excommunicated. Morris West, *The Clowns of God*,

quoted by Louise Kumandjek Tappa, "God in Man's Image," *New Eyes for Reading: Biblical and Theological Reflections by Women of the Third World*, eds. John B. Pobee and Bärbel Von Wartenberg-Potter (Geneva: World Council of Churches, 1986), 106.

47. Maduro, *Religion and Social Conflicts*, chapters 25, 33-35. Maduro's views closely follow those of Max Weber and also Antonio Gramsci. In North America there have been effective "prophets" who have spoken largely outside of the organized church, people such as Will Campbell, Clarence Jordan, and William Stringfellow.

48. On the corporate dimension of prophecy in ancient Israel, see John S. Kselman, "The Social World of the Israelite Prophets—A Review Article," *Religious Studies Review* 11/2, April 1985, 120-29. Two prophetic figures of the twentieth century, Mahatma Gandhi and Martin Luther King, Jr., were both involved in massive movements and were both highly innovative, charismatic leaders. Neither, of course, fits into Weber's typology.

49. Lesslie Newbigin, *The Other Side of 1984: Questions for the Churches* (Geneva: World Council of Churches, 1983), 27-29. Newbigin clearly wants to avoid the "Constantinian" model of the church aligned with supreme political power, 30-37. The notion of "church" in this and the following paragraphs is different from either church or sect in Weber's typology. It would be useful, however, to explore these differences and also any similarities.

50. Gill, *Prophecy and Praxis*, 129.

51. Ibid., 95, 130-31.

52. See Gregory Baum, "Call for Social Justice: A Comparison," *Ecumenist*, 23/3, 1985, 43-45, and "The Theology of the American Pastoral," *Ecumenist*, 24/2, 1986, 17-22. The same point can be made about the nuclear arms industry. See, for example, Steven Schroeder's review of A. G. Mojtabai, *Blessed Assurance: At Home with the Bomb in Amarillo, Texas*, in *Christian Century*, 103, 1986, 651-53.

53. This assumes some general agreement with H. Richard Niebuhr that Christ is "the *transformer* of culture," *Christ and Culture* (New York: Harper & Brothers, 1951), 190-229. See also, Walter Brueggemann, *The Prophetic Imagination* (Philadelphia: Fortress Press, 1978), 110-11.

54. This is Peter Berger's phrase and reflects a view of the church that is a "buffer" protecting people from the negative effects of technological, bureaucratic culture. For a critique of Berger's sociology, see Gregory Baum, "Peter Berger's Unfinished Symphony," *Sociology and Human Destiny: Essays on Sociology, Religion and Society*, ed. Gregory Baum (New York: Seabury Press, 1980), 110-29. There are, however, situations like Native American communities where the notion of sacred canopy is appropriate.

55. Bonnie Benda, "Preaching on Social Justice Issues," 9 pages, a paper presented to the Academy of Homiletics, 1982. There are, of course, times when the preacher does stand against some of the positions of those in the pew, but always with the pain of a disappointed pastor before God.

56. Dieter T. Hessel, ed., *Social Themes of the Christian Year: A Commentary on the Lectionary* (Philadelphia: Geneva Press, 1983).

57. Justo L. González and Catherine G. González, *Liberation Preaching: The Pulpit and the Oppressed* (Nashville: Abingdon Press, 1980), 40, see the whole section 38-44. See also Lloyd Bailey, "The Lectionary in Critical Perspective," *Interpretation*, 31, 1977, 139-53. J. Irwin Trotter pays particular attention to the way the lectionary functions corporately in non-lectionary-based traditions to subvert the individualism of North American culture, "Are We

Preaching a 'Subversive' Lectionary?" *School of Theology at Claremont Bulletin*, 28/2, December 1985, 1-7.

58. Jürgen Moltmann, *The Power of the Powerless*, trans. Margaret Kohl (London: SCM Press, 1983), 28-37.

59. Ronald J. Sider, *Rich Christians in an Age of Hunger* (New York: Paulist Press, 1978).

60. McFague, *Metaphorical Theology*, 26. McFague also characterizes "symbolic, sacramental thinking as priestly and metaphorical thinking as prophetic" (17).

61. Stanley Hauerwas and William H. Willimon, "Embarrassed by the Church: Congregations and the Seminary," *Christian Century*, 103, 1986, 117-20.

62. See M. L. Brownsberger, "From the Other Side of the Pulpit," *Christian Century*, 103, 1986, 746-48.

63. Examples of such communities springing up across Canada (and I am sure there are similar ones in the U. S.) are outlined by Tony Clarke, "Communities for Justice," *Ecumenist*, 19/2, 1981, 17-25.

64. Francis Schüssler Fiorenza, "The Church's Religious Identity," 224. See the whole section, 222-25.

65. Doris Lessing, *Prisons We Choose to Live Inside*, CBC Massey Lectures (Montreal: CBC Enterprises, 1986).

66. Since completing this last chapter I have read three works that advance the discussion of the preceding pages, especially the section on prophetic preaching. Andrew Kirk, from an "evangelical" perspective, challenges the separation that often exists between evangelism and social responsibility in *The Good News of the Kingdom Coming, The Marriage of Evangelism and Social Responsibility* (Downers Grove, Ill.: Inter Varsity Press, 1983). Charles Elliott in *Prayering the Kingdom, Towards a Political Spirituality* (New York: Paulist Press, 1985) also links the gospel with the coming of the Kingdom and argues for an approach to the social needs of the world that emphasizes grace rather than guilt and powerlessness. Finally, Gregory Baum agrees that guilt is an inappropriate response to the radical social message of the churches. Mourning and lamentation are the appropriate biblical reactions, followed by responsible action ("Resistance to Prophetic Preaching," *Arc*, 14/2, 1987, 47-53).

Appendix:
Questions to Sharpen
Social Awareness

Arthur Van Seters. In order to assist the pastor, teacher, or student to become more conscious of the social nature and responsibility of preaching, I have formulated five sets of questions. These generally follow the order of the preceding chapters and, in the main, are drawn from their contents.[1] This order is roughly similar to Fred Craddock's approach in his book, *Preaching*,[2] where reflection on life comes before the interpretation of a text and is followed by the formation and language of the sermon. The process of "shaping the message into a sermon" that Craddock outlines so lucidly can be a practical companion piece to the questions listed below. In view of what has been said over and over again in this present work about the corporate nature of the preaching process, questions are primarily in the "we" form and can be shared with the parish or congregation.[3] In developing these questions I am also making a few assumptions:

- that preaching is a dynamic event in which we seek to discern the grace and will of God for us, for our church, and for God's world.

- that the process of developing a sermon extends over enough time to allow for careful study of the text(s), theological reflection beyond the text(s), and direct influence from the life of the world and from the life of the congregation.[4]

• that sermons are partial and limited statements, primarily selections for the moment, and that they benefit from some form of reflection and feedback.

As noted in the introduction, I am also making another, different kind of assumption that readers will make use of these questions in whatever way seems most helpful. Taken all together, this list could be rather overwhelming. Some people may want to focus on one section of questions at a time; others may select one or more question(s) from each section. In all likelihood, some questions will be more stimulating than others for any given person or group at any particular time.

The Wider Context

1. What is happening in the world as this sermon is being prepared?
2. Which news reports are we talking about most?
3. Which issues or events are we avoiding?
4. How do we as a congregation/parish view the world and what are our attitudes toward change?
5. On which views of what is going on around us do we find a consensus and which are controversial?
6. What is the general mood of life in our community as this sermon is being preached?
7. What forces of evil in the world do we specifically identify as needing to be addressed by preaching?

Congregational Context

1. How diverse is the congregation/parish and how are minorities viewed and treated?
2. How is this congregation/parish organized, who gives leadership (officially and unofficially) and who is left out of decision-making processes?

3. What are our present preoccupations as a faith community and where is this sermon coming in the movement of our corporate life?
4. What spectrum of theological viewpoints is represented among us, how are they respected, and what sense of mission do we, together, hold?
5. How do we as a congregation/parish view preaching and how do we see it related to our lives?
6. Who do I, as preacher, tend to think of in the congregation as I prepare my sermon and why?

Personal Socialization of the Preacher

1. What in my own life journey is influencing me in the preparation and delivery of this sermon?
2. How have my "peak experiences" of faith shaped my theology and the expression of my faith?
3. What negative life experiences, circumstances, or influences have a bearing on my preaching and how?
4. How has my socialization influenced the way I involve (or am reluctant to involve) the congregation/parish in the preaching process?
5. How has my socialization shaped my views about preaching on social or political issues?

Biblical Interpretation

1. Why has this text (these texts) been chosen for this sermon?
2. How has this Scripture been shaped by and for its social setting?
3. How is the theological thrust and social strategy of the text(s) related?
4. How does the text affirm and/or confront us in our present social setting?
5. What vested interests of ours prevent us from hearing what this text is saying?
6. With whom or what in this text do we identify and how does this reflect our socialization?

7. What genre, language, symbols, or metaphors have shaped the text and how do they affect the fabric of the sermon?

Language

1. What is the language of the congregation/parish? How has it been influenced by the media and how does it reflect our view of social relationships (race, gender, class)?
2. When do we find helpful language that explains and clarifies, and when do we prefer imaginative language that is open to multiple meanings?
3. When and how do poetic and narrative elements in preaching create a new openness to God and to the world?
4. How does the sermon combine exhortation, information, and illustration to enable the hearing of the gospel in its societal scope?
5. How does the use of adjectives and adverbs, as well as the voice modulation of the speaker, affect a social hearing of the Word of God?

A Final Question

How is God calling us to respond—quite concretely in our situation—to our hearing this sermon today and are we willing to pay the cost?

Notes

1. I have also been impressed by the excellent sets of questions focusing social aspects of biblical preaching listed by Forbes, "Social Transformation," 51, and Ronald J. Allen, "Sociological Exegesis: Text and Social Reality," *Contemporary Biblical Interpretation for Preaching* (Valley Forge: Judson Press, 1984), 91-93.

2. Fred B. Craddock, *Preaching* (Nashville: Abingdon Press, 1985).

3. Ideally, this social reflection on preaching is part of a larger congregational process using such resources as Holland and Henriot, *Social Ministry*, especially 95-112; Hessel, *Social Ministry*, especially 121-23; Carroll, Dudley and McKinney, *Handbook for Congregational Studies,* especially chapter 6, "Methods for Congregational Studies," 153-78. See further, Jackson W. Carroll, William McKinney, and Wade Clark Roof, "From the

Outside In and the Inside Out," *Building Effective Ministry, Theory and Practice in the Local Church,* ed. Carl S. Dudley (New York: Harper & Row, 1983), 84-111.

4. Long-range planning for preaching can be assisted by formulating an annual grid listing the months of the year along one side and three sets of factors along the other: (1) human factors (personal and public) relating to the seasons of the year beginning with spring; (2) congregational factors relating to the church life cycle usually beginning in September; (3) theological factors relating to the Christian Year, to lectionary selections or *lectio continua,* and to spiritual and theological themes needed by the church in its life and mission beginning with Advent. A second grid of five years can focus on the larger movement of the church. Sermons are then seen as the expression of an integration of theology, church life and mission, and human life in its various dimensions.